The grace of godliness

Wow! I really like this book. Matthew Barrett has given us history, theology, ministerial counsel and impetus to true piety in this treatment of the Synod and Canons of Dort. The brief but vibrant historical accounts are informative, his guidance in some thick theological discussion is expert, and his focus on piety leads us to the true purpose of all theology—the production of a sincere and pure devotion to Christ. Dr. Barrett's continual insistence on the necessity of monergism for a truly biblical grasp of the character of salvation from beginning to end is a much needed emphasis for contemporary evangelicalism. The appendices provide valuable source material. This is an excellent account of a vitally important subject.

Tom J. Nettles
Professor of Historical Theology, The Southern Baptist Theological Seminary, Louisville, Kentucky

---

Matthew Barrett offers a wonderfully simple and direct exposition of one of the more misunderstood confessions of faith. The Canons of Dort are often vilified, but under closer examination Barrett demonstrates that they are biblical and pastoral and a potent tonic for a flagging faith. *Tolle et lege*, take up and read!

J.V. Fesko
Academic Dean, Professor of Systematic and Historical Theology, Westminster Seminary California

---

By breathing new life into historic events, documents and people, Matthew makes them speak to our culture, our churches and our hearts.

David P. Murray
Professor of Old Testament and Practical Theology, Puritan Reformed Theological Seminary, Grand Rapids, Michigan

---

By reducing the discussion of Calvinism and the doctrines of grace to the simplified acrostic T-U-L-I-P, I'm afraid we have generated far more heat than light. A book that looks deeply within, behind and around the five points of Calvinism is long overdue. Whether you find yourself saying "Yea" or "Nay" to the five points, we all need to say thank you to Dr. Barrett for his delightful, informative and light-generating book.

Stephen J. Nichols
Research Professor of Christianity and Culture, Lancaster Bible College, Lancaster, Pennsylvania

---

Matthew Barrett has given us a thoroughly enjoyable introduction to and review of the history and the source documents of the Calvinist-Arminian debate. And with that he has given us a vivid reminder that a right understanding of these doctrines—in themselves considered and in the minds of the framers of the Canons of Dort—is indispensable to Christian worship and devotion. Highly recommended.

Fred G. Zaspel
Pastor, Reformed Baptist Church; Professor of Systematic Theology, Calvary Baptist Seminary, Lansdale, Pennsylvania

---

Christians speak freely and often about the Canons of Dort and the international synod of 1618–1619 which produced them without really knowing much about either. Matthew Barnett's *The Grace of Godliness* will do much to remedy this lamentable situation. In a very accessible manner, referring to a number of important background documents, Barrett provides the historical context of the Synod of Dort. He also makes a solid case that the Canons themselves are filled with careful biblical reflection, wise pastoral application and exhortations to a warm and genuine Christian piety. Dort's stalwart defense of divine monergism in the salvation of sinners does not produce a fear of God, lack of assurance of one's salvation or indifference to good works—as critics often charge. When read and understood, the Canons of Dort present the so-called doctrines of grace as the foundation for a believer's confidence in God's mercy and, as the consequence, the basis for a life of gratitude.

Kim Riddlebarger
Senior Pastor, Christ Reformed Church (URCNA), Anaheim, California; co-host of the White Horse Inn radio broadcast

---

Matthew Barrett has produced an excellent and much-needed treatment of the intimate connection between the Canons of Dort and vibrant Christian piety. Whatever the readers' attitude toward those canons, this book will reward them with greater understanding and appreciation of the spiritual richness and practical value of Reformed theology. I highly recommend it.

Steven B. Cowan
Associate Professor of Christian Studies, Louisiana College, Pineville, Louisiana

---

The GRACE of GODLINESS

An introduction to doctrine and piety in the Canons of Dort

Matthew Barrett

p r e s s
www.joshuapress.com

Published by
Joshua Press Inc., Kitchener, Ontario, Canada
Distributed by
Sola Scriptura Ministries International
www.sola-scriptura.ca

First published 2013

Cover and book design by Janice Van Eck.
Typeset in Schwager (Luciano Vergara) and Whitman.

The publication of this book was made possible by the generous support of The Ross-Shire Foundation

Library and Archives Canada Cataloguing in Publication

Barrett, Matthew, 1982-
      The grace of godliness : an introduction to doctrine and piety in the Canons of Dort / Matthew Barrett.

Includes bibliographical references.
ISBN 978-1-894400-52-7

      1. Synod of Dort (1618-1619). Canones Synodi Dordrechtanae. 2. Reformed Church—Doctrines. 3. Piety. I. Title.

BX9478.B37 2013   262.9'842   C2013-901722-4

For Cassandra and Georgia—
may the Lord open their hearts.

Contents

Foreword

In this new study of the doctrine and piety of the Synod of Dort, Matthew Barrett fills a great lacuna—it is really amazing that hitherto there has been really no monograph on the piety of the declarations of this significant synod—and also clears away a lot of the misunderstanding about the synod and its theological pronouncements. In the theology of the synod we see, not a cramped departure from the soteriological core of the Reformed tradition as found, for instance, in the writings of a Martin Bucer, a John Calvin or a Thomas Cranmer, but a proper fulfilment of the interests and ideas of such Reformed authors as these. In other words, the common argument that there is a sad declension in the epigones of the Reformation is just far too simplistic. New issues had arisen, namely those broached by the teaching of Jacob Arminius, that needed addressing, and the synod members drew upon the rich doctrine and piety of their Reformed heritage to frame a response that was not only a powerful rebuttal of Arminianism, as it came to be called, but also one that contained a theology and spirituality that was in essential harmony with the theological vision of the first Reformers. Barrett's study also abundantly reveals that the framers of the Canons of Dort were first and foremost *pastoral* theologians, concerned for the nurture of souls and their growth in grace. Sad it is when advocates of their theology overlook the soil in which this theology best flourishes!

I find it interesting that such a book as this has been written by a committed Baptist. For, of late, some Baptist circles have labeled the theology of Dort as being anti-mission and essentially uninterested in evangelism. But a close reading of the Synod's theological pronouncements reveals an evangelical passion that belies such a label. Article 5 of the Second Main Point of Doctrine urges the indiscriminate preaching of the gospel "together with the command to repent and believe… to all nations and people." Here the evangelical impulse of the Reformation that saw Reformed preachers in France and Switzerland, Holland and England warmly offering the gospel to all and sundry finds concise expression.

It was a privilege to have had Matthew as a student and now it is my privilege to commend his studies to a wider public.

Michael A.G. Haykin

Professor of Church History and Biblical Spirituality, The Southern Baptist Theological Seminary, Louisville, Kentucky; Director of The Andrew Fuller Center for Baptist Studies; Research Professor of Irish Baptist College, Belfast, Northern Ireland

Preface

One would think that with the impact Calvinism has had on genera-
tions of Christians since the seventeenth century there would be a
multitude of both academic and popular publications on the Synod of
Dort. After all, the canons that the synod produced became the hallmark for what we today label the doctrines of grace. However, perhaps
to the surprise of many, even a cursory attempt to locate readily available books on the Canons of Dort proves disappointing. While the
number of volumes on John Calvin, the Heidelberg Catechism or the
Westminster Confession, are legion, the same cannot be said concerning the Synod of Dort. Such was my experience as I began research on
the canons. My disappointment at the lack of literature available only
increased when I sought to narrow my research to the topic of "piety"
in the Canons of Dort. As far as I know, no book exists in English on

Dort's emphasis on piety. And yet, the topic of piety and godliness is one that saturates the canons.

When one thinks of the controversy at Dort between the Calvinists and the Arminians, the words "piety," "godliness" and "holiness" are not usually mentioned. It does not help that those unsympathetic to the theology of Dort typically characterize the doctrines of grace as a theology of the head and not of the heart and, worse yet, as a theology harmful to Christian godliness. But again, even a cursory reading of the Canons of Dort reveals that such a popular assumption is not the case. To the contrary, the canons are filled with constant references to Christian progress in godliness. Furthermore, the Calvinists at Dort saw the doctrines of grace as the very *foundation* of godliness, piety and progress in holiness. The canons, as I discovered, are not only a bastion for the doctrines of grace against the attacks of Arminianism, but a fountain from which gushes forth the river of biblical piety. Dort is not merely concerned with unconditional election but also with how unconditional election is the origin from which we have assurance, humility and holiness. Dort is not merely concerned with limited atonement but also with how limited atonement is the source of corporate and personal thanksgiving and worship. Dort is not merely concerned with total depravity and effectual grace but with how these doctrines produce humility and destroy pride. Dort is not merely concerned with the perseverance and preservation of the saints but also with how these doctrines are an incentive to holy living. This book seeks to expose the vivid connection Dort makes between the doctrines of grace and godliness, a connection few scholars seem to have recognized.

This book has not been without the help and encouragement of others. First, I would like to thank Michael A.G. Haykin. It was in a seminar with Dr. Haykin on Puritan spirituality that the topic of this book first sprouted. Dr. Haykin's teaching and writing has been inspirational to me, and his quality of scholarship is impeccable. His knowledge of church history is nothing short of impressive, and he possesses the uncommon talent of making historical figures come alive. Second, I would like to thank my wife, Elizabeth. Her combination of encouragement and close analysis were exactly what was needed. She is my best companion in life, a gift from the Lord.

A word about translations

For the Canons of Dort, I have chosen the English translation provided by Jaroslav Pelikan and Valerie Hotchkiss in *Creeds & Confessions of Faith in the Christian Tradition*.[1] Pelikan and Hotchkiss draw their translation from *Ecumenical Creeds and Reformed Confessions*, a translation that is from the Latin and authorized in 1986 by the Synod of the Christian Reformed Church and also adopted by the Reformed Church in America. For the original text of the Canons of Dort see: *Acta Synodi Nationalis, In nomine Domini nostril Iesu Christi, Autoritate Illustr. Et Præpotentum DD. Ordinum Generalium Foederati Belgii Provinciarum, Dordrechti, Habitæ Anno MDCXVIII & MDCXIX. Accedunt Plenisima, de Quinque Articulis, Theologorum Judicia* (Dordrechti: *Typis Isaaci Elzeviri, Academiæ Typographi, Societatis Dordrechtanæ Sumptibus*, 1620). I have included the Canons of Dort as an appendix for the reader's benefit and consultation.

Regretfully, Pelikan and Hotchkiss do not provide many other documents besides the Canons of Dort surrounding the Remonstrant controversy. Therefore, I have chosen to follow Peter Y. De Jong when quoting from the following: The Remonstrance of 1610, The Counter Remonstrance of 1611 and The Opinion of the Remonstrants.[2] These documents have also been included as appendices.

---

1 *Creeds and Confessions of the Reformation Era*, vol. 2 of *Creeds and Confessions of Faith in the Christian Tradition*, ed. Jaroslav Pelikan and Valerie Hotchkiss (New Haven: Yale University Press, 2003), 2:569–600.

2 *Crisis in the Reformed Churches: Essays in commemoration of the great Synod of Dort, 1618–1619*, ed. Peter Y. De Jong (Grand Rapids: Reformed Fellowship, 1968), 207–213, 221–229.

Timeline
1559–1619

1584–1586 Arminius studies at Geneva
  1584 William of Orange assassinated by Balthazar Gerard
  1586 Synod of The Hague
  1588 Arminius begins preaching in Amsterdam
  1591 Johannes Uytenbogaert made pastor at The Hague of
        Walloon congregation
  1591 Controversy begins over Arminius's preaching on
        Romans 7
  1594 Franciscus Gomarus appointed professor at Leiden
  1601 Plague strikes Holland
  1603 Arminius receives Doctor of Theology
  1603 Arminius appointed professor at Leiden University
  1604 Arminius presents theses on predestination and
        Gomarus responds
  1607 Gouda Catechism published
  1608 October 30, Arminius presents *Declaration of Sentiments*
        before States of Holland in The Hague
  1609 July 25, Final public disputation at Leiden University
  1609 August 13–21, Final conference with Gomarus in
        The Hague
  1609 October 19, death of Arminius in Leiden
  1610 January 14, the Remonstrance (*Articuli Arminiani sive
        Remonstrantia*) is drafted by over forty Arminians in the
        city of Gouda under the leadership of Uytenbogaert
  1610 Uytenbogaert publishes treatise arguing that the political
        authorities have the right to determine doctrine for the
        Reformed churches
  1611 Conference at The Hague, six Arminians led by
        Uytenbogaert meet with six Calvinists led by
        Petrus Plancius
  1611 Counter-Remonstrance is drafted
  1613 Conference at Delft
  1614 Hugo Grotius writes his "Resolution for Peace in the
        Churches"
  1617 Johan van Oldenbarnevelt has his "Sharp Resolution"
        passed by the States-General
  1617 Prince Maurice of Orange sides with the Reformed

1618 November 13, National Synod of Dordrecht convened

1618 In December the Remonstrants first appear on the floor of the synod, led by Simon Episcopius

1618 December 13 and 17, at the 31st and 34th sessions the Remonstrants presented their *Sententiae* or The Opinions of the Remonstrants

1619 January 1, the States-General approves the synod to act as an ecclesiastical court

1619 January 14, the Arminians are dismissed from synod for failure to cooperate

1619 April 23, synod adopts the Canons of Dort

1619 March 22, all the written opinions of the delegates had been reviewed by the synod

1619 May 29, closing session of the synod

The distinguishing feature of the Canons...is that the Canons deal solely with the deepest truths revealed in the Scriptures.... The subject matter of the Canons does not commend itself to "babes in the faith." The positions set forth have been rejected and even scorned by many sincere Christians. One who undertakes the study of these higher points must do so humbly, lest his lack of spiritual capacity coupled with pride cause him to reject that which he merely cannot fathom. ...all those who have grown in the stature of Christ, whose sanctification has progressed to the point at which they are prepared to digest the "strong meat" of the Word, and all those whose sanctified intelligence reaches out for an understanding of deeper things, will turn to this tremendous document and the Scriptural truths which it sets forth. In the theological superficiality of the twentieth century it is tragic indeed that many who consider themselves to be truly Reformed in their religious thinking often have only the vaguest conception of those pivotal points upon which Reformed theology turns. To be Reformed is not, first of all, to be affiliated with a certain church, nor to be identified with certain social or racial mores. To be Reformed is to hold within one's heart a deep conviction concerning the most basic truths set forth in the Word of God. Nowhere will one find them set forth more succinctly nor more magnificently than in the Canons of the Synod of Dort.**—GORDON GIROD**

1

Introduction

The 'uninformed pastor"

Edwin H. Palmer was unmistakably accurate when he said that for the "uninformed pastor, the 'Five Points of Calvinism' seem harsh, cold and spiritually deadening."[1]

> The terms *Calvinism, total depravity, election, reprobation, limited atonement and irresistible grace* give him the shivers. As he views it, the God of Calvinism is arbitrary and his decree of reprobation is "horrible." Such "fatalistic" teachings, he believes, make men

---

1 Edwin H. Palmer, "The Significance of the Canons for Pastoral Work," in *Crisis in the Reformed Churches: Essays in Commemoration of the Great Synod of Dort, 1618–1619*, ed. Peter Y. De Jong (Grand Rapids: Reformed Fellowship, 1968), 137.

morally lazy, give a false sense of security, hinder missions and deaden human responsibility. Therefore, instead of utilizing these teachings in his pastoral work, he may oppose them or at least ignore them.[2]

Palmer's observation is proven entirely correct when we read the same complaint from the pen of Jacob Arminius himself. Unconditional election, he writes, prevents

> saving and godly sorrow for sins, …it removes all pious solicitude about being converted, …it restrains…all zeal and studious regard for good works, …it extinguishes the zeal for prayer, …it takes away all that most salutary fear and trembling with which we are commanded to work out our own salvation, …[and] it produces within men a despair both of performing that which their duty requires and of obtaining that towards which their desires are directed.[3]

Arminius's complaint is alive and well today. The word "Calvinism," as Steve Cowan observes, "conjures up the image of a cruel God who determines the fate of each human in an arbitrary and capricious manner, or perhaps the image of a cold, dead Church, unconcerned with discipleship or spiritual purity."[4] And again, "Perhaps the worst accusation leveled at Calvinism is that its doctrines of predestination and unconditional grace provide license to sin. This is the dangerous heresy of antinomianism, which even many of the NT writers had to confront."[5] Or, if it is not antinomianism that Calvinism fosters, it is a lack of assurance of one's own salvation. Cornelis Venema explains the popular complaint,

---

2   Palmer, "The Significance of the Canons for Pastoral Work," 137.

3   James Arminius, *The Works of James Arminius, D. D.* (Grand Rapids: Baker, 1956), 1:230–231.

4   Steven B. Cowan, "Common Misconceptions of Evangelicals Regarding Calvinism," *Journal of the Evangelical Theological Society* 33, no. 2 (June 1990): 189.

5   Cowan, "Common Misconceptions of Evangelicals Regarding Calvinism," 192.

A common prejudice against the biblical and Reformed teaching concerning election claims that it undermines the assurance of salvation. If the salvation of believers depends ultimately upon God's sovereign choice to save some of the fallen race of Adam and not others, a kind of fatalism is introduced into the order of salvation. Who, after all, can withstand the will of God (cf. Rom. 9:19)?[6]

Venema elaborates,

It is alleged that the specter of uncertainty begins to overshadow what we can know of God's grace and favor toward us in Jesus Christ. Since no creature is privy to the "secret things" of God, including the specifics of his sovereign choice to save some and not others, there is no avenue for believers to be confident of God's good will toward them in Christ. Consequently, the teaching of sovereign and gracious election undermines assurance or certainty of salvation. According to this prejudice, the awesome reality of God's foreordination of the salvation of some and the non-salvation of others reduces everything to arbitrariness and uncertainty.[7]

Are such accusations true? Does Calvinism ruin assurance of salvation and create laxity in sanctification and godliness?

Biblical Calvinism and piety

Thankfully, such accusations against the doctrines of grace are caricatures. Yes, there may be certain persons who label themselves "Calvinist" who justify their immorality by appealing to God's sovereignty. However, as is the tendency with all things good, this is a distortion of the truth, a masquerade for biblical Calvinism. Biblical Calvinism

---

6   See Cornelis P. Venema, "The Election and Salvation of the Children of Believers Who Die in Infancy: A Study of Article I/17 of the Canons of Dort," *Mid-America Journal of Theology* 17 (2006): 57.

7   Venema, "The Election and Salvation of the Children of Believers Who Die in Infancy," 57.

does not cultivate ungodliness but a contagious incentive for holy living. Biblical Calvinism does not provide a license for sin but a fear of God, an unwavering resolve to know Christ and a Spirit-empowered commitment to pious living. Biblical Calvinism does not destroy one's assurance but provides the very foundation for a sure and certain confidence of one's salvation. Biblical Calvinism is not a vehicle for pride and arrogance but for humility and a Christ-like meekness. Biblical Calvinism is not harsh, cold and spiritually deadening but winsome, warm and full of spiritual life.

Consider John Calvin himself. Concerning godliness in sanctification Calvin writes, "We never dream of a faith destitute of good works." Indeed, "you cannot posses Him [Christ] without becoming a partaker of His sanctification."[8] Cowan is correct when he concludes, "Calvinism teaches that when God elects someone to salvation he works progressively in that person's life to make him more and more Christlike. This is a key aspect of Calvinism's fifth point (perseverance of the saints). A person that claims to be converted but never grows in spiritual maturity is not truly born again." Therefore, it is careless to accuse Calvinism of advancing ungodliness. While some Calvinists have descended into the error of antinomianism, John Calvin and the "best of the Reformed theologians" have always rejected it.[9]

The "best of the Reformed theologians" Cowan speaks of must include the famous Synod of Dort (1619),[10] the hallmark of five-point Calvinism. The Canons of Dort are an expansive and rigorous defense of God's sovereign grace against the synergism of the Arminian Remonstrants. And yet, perhaps to the surprise of many, these same canons which expound biblical Calvinism are also the same canons that view the doctrines of grace as the very spring of evangelical piety and spirituality.[11] The Canons do not merely affirm the doctrines of

---

8   John Calvin, *Institutes of the Christian Religion*, 2 vols., ed. John T. McNeill, trans. Ford Lewis Battles (Louisville: Westminster John Knox, 1960), 3.16.1.

9   Cowan, "Common Misconceptions of Evangelicals Regarding Calvinism," 192.

10   Ed. note: Also known as the Synod of Dordt or the Synod of Dordrecht. For the purposes of this book, the author has standardized his usage to the "Synod of Dort."

11   By "piety" I am not referring to the movement called "Pietism" but simply to piety as godliness. See R. Scott Clark, *Recovering the Reformed Confessions: Our Theology, Piety, and Practice* (Phillipsburg: P & R, 2008), 74–75.

grace as we know them today (total depravity, unconditional election, limited atonement, irresistible grace, perseverance of the saints), but also demonstrate that these doctrines are the foundation upon which godliness is built. In short, this book will demonstrate that for Dort such accusations already witnessed above are illegitimate, for the doctrines of grace are not damaging, destructive and counter-productive to true spiritual grace and humility but rather serve as the very basis for humility, gratitude, assurance and holiness. While it is not the intention or purpose of this book to defend the five points of Dort *per se*, the Canons themselves will be examined one by one in order to identify how exactly the doctrines of grace for Dort serve as the origin for true, authentic piety in the believer.[12]

The marriage of knowledge and piety

It is important to return to Edwin Palmer's observation that many view Calvinism as cold, dead doctrine of the head, not of the heart. Calvinism, some argue, is grave and spiritually deadening. In light of Calvinism's faithfulness to Scripture and biblical accuracy, such a nausea to the doctrines of grace is tragic. The doctrines of grace, as taught by Jesus, Paul and many others, never promoted cold, lifeless spirituality but warm, vibrant holiness.

Behind such an accusation is a faulty bifurcation. While it is legitimate to distinguish between "theology" and "piety," "doctrine" and "practice" or "orthodoxy" and "orthopraxy," it is not possible to divorce

---

12 For such a defense, see Michael Horton, *For Calvinism* (Grand Rapids: Zondervan, 2011); Matthew Barrett and Thomas J. Nettles, eds., *Whomever He Wills: A Surprising Display of Sovereign Grace* (Cape Coral: Founders, 2012); David N. Steele, Curtis C. Thomas and S. Lance Quinn, *The Five Points of Calvinism: Defined, Defended, and Documented*, 2nd ed. (Phillipsburg: P & R, 2004); Robert A. Peterson and Michael D. Williams, *Why I Am Not an Arminian* (Downers Grove: InterVarsity, 2004); Edwin H. Palmer, *The Five Points of Calvinism*, 3rd ed. (Grand Rapids: Baker, 2010); Loraine Boettner, *The Reformed Doctrine of Predestination* (Phillipsburg: P & R, 1932); Thomas R. Schreiner and Bruce A. Ware, eds., *Still Sovereign: Contemporary Perspectives on Election, Foreknowledge, and Grace* (Grand Rapids: Baker, 2000). For a contemporary example that puts into practice the real connection between the doctrines of grace and Christian piety, see Greg Forster, *The Joy of Calvinism: Knowing God's Personal, Unconditional, Irresistible, Unbreakable Love* (Wheaton: Crossway, 2012).

the two. Those in the Reformed tradition, both before and after Dort, have always made such a point. Consider Calvin, for example, who states in his preface to King Francis I that the purpose of his *Institutes* is "solely to transmit certain rudiments by which those who are touched with any zeal for religion might be shaped to true godliness [*pietas*]."[13] Therefore, John T. McNeill can appropriately say, Calvin's theology is "his piety described at length."[14] McNeill's point is demonstrated when we consider the subtitle of the first edition of the *Institutes*, which reads, "*Embracing almost the whole sum of piety and whatever is necessary to know of the doctrine of salvation: A work most worthy to be read by all persons zealous for piety.*"[15]

When we approach the Canons of Dort we find this same emphasis on the union between doctrine and piety. Within each canon the authors drew out specific applications for holy living. Cornelis Pronk rightly observes, "You will be surprised how pastoral our fathers dealt with souls who were distressed with questions concerning election and related issues."[16] Like Calvin, who drew the connection between sovereign grace and piety, Dort also saw the correlation between the supremacy of grace and the pursuit of godliness.

While we must distinguish between certain theological doctrines and piety itself, the two must always be kept together, hand in hand. To forfeit one is to discredit the other.[17] Consequently, as B.B. Warfield pointed out, there can be no such thing as an "academic Calvinist."

---

13 Calvin, *Institutes*, 1:9. This point is made by Joel R. Beeke, *Puritan Reformed Spirituality* (Grand Rapids: Reformation Heritage, 2004), 2.

14 Cited in John Hesselink, "The Development and Purpose of Calvin's Institutes," in *Articles on Calvin and Calvinism*, vol. 4, *Influences upon Calvin and Discussion of the 1559 Institutes*, ed. Richard C. Gamble (New York: Garland, 1992), 215–216.

15 John Calvin, *Institutes of the Christian Religion: 1536 Edition*, trans. Ford Lewis Battles, rev. ed. (Grand Rapids: Eerdmans, 1986).

16 Cornelis Pronk, *Expository Sermons on the Canons of Dort* (St. Thomas: Free Reformed Publications, 1999), 11.

17 Al Martin makes a similar point, "You cannot separate what you are from what you do; you cannot separate the effect of truth upon your own relationship to God personally from the effect of truth through you ministerially" [A.N. Martin, "The Practical Implications of True Calvinism: 1," *The Banner of Truth* 120 (1973): 14].

Such a label is a misnomer.[18] Instead, as Ian Hamilton observes, "It [Calvinism] is not first and foremost a theological system; it is more fundamentally a 'religious attitude' [cf. B.B. Warfield], an attitude that gives inevitable birth to a particular, precise, but gloriously God-centred and heart-engaging system of theology."[19] It is this "God-centred and heart-engaging system of theology" that we are after as we now peer into the Canons of Dort. We will begin by first looking at the historical context in which the Canons were formed. In subsequent chapters we will explore each of the five canons in order to understand the implications Dort drew from the doctrines of grace for godliness and piety.

---

18 As quoted in Martin, "The Practical Implications of True Calvinism: 1," *The Banner of Truth* 120 (1973): 15.

19 Ian Hamilton, "Proud Calvinism," *The Banner of Truth* 496 (2005): 17.

In the Canons of Dort the synod sought to maintain and defend the biblical doctrine of the free and sovereign grace of God in man's salvation. The Arminian teachings were viewed as a revival of the Semi-Pelagian heresy and their presence in the Reformed churches was judged intolerable. The Arminian doctrines were found to conflict with scriptural teaching and to threaten the confessional character of the Reformed churches whose faith was expressed in the Belgic Confession and the Heidelberg Catechism.—**FRED H. KLOOSTER**

The Synod of Dort was concerned to defend the doctrine of the sovereign grace of God against the encroachment upon it by the doctrine of the free will of man.... The apostle Paul tells us that there are two and only two kinds of people in this world. There are first those who, because of their fall in Adam, serve and worship the creature rather than the Creator. There are secondly those who, because of their redemption from the fall through Jesus Christ, have learned to serve God their Creator and Christ their Redeemer rather than the creature. Men of the second group are not, of themselves, any better than men of the first group. It is not because of superior wisdom found in themselves that they of the second group have learned to serve and to worship God. It is, rather, because they have been born of the Spirit, born from above, that they would now dedicate themselves and their all to the Father, the Son and the Holy Spirit. This was the intent of Dort, and it can be understood and evaluated only against the centuries-old struggle of the true church for God's truth.—**CORNELIUS VAN TIL**

In the eyes of the Remonstrants, their "Calvinist" opponents were schismatics and evil spirits whose doctrines made God into a tyrant and bred desperation and immorality among ordinary believers.... The Contra-Remonstrants for their part saw the Arminians, with their talk of peace and toleration, as the new Joabs of the Book of Samuel, outwardly professing friendship while hiding swords behind their backs.—**PHILIP BENEDICT**

Of course, Calvinism is more than the "five points of Calvinism." Calvinism is a system of thought that is as broad as life. It is "a world and life view." It is not restricted to the field of theology but includes every sphere of life and the world. But its central thought "is the great thought of God," and its fundamental principle is the sovereignty of God, "the absolute supremacy of God in all things." If there is one doctrine that permeates the Canons it is that of the sovereignty of God. This doctrine has been called "the highest point of Calvinism." A right understanding of this doctrine, and its relation to human responsibility, will help us to understand all the doctrines of the Canons. The Canons maintain that according to Scripture God is sovereign in the salvation of the sinner, and that the Arminian position violates this truth. They echo the words of Romans 11:36, "For of him, and through him, and unto him, are all things."—**HENRY PETERSON**

2

Historical background to the Synod of Dort

Introduction

The Canons have been caricatured as an expression of a rigid, arid Reformed scholastic theology. Anyone who reads the Canons will find quite a different reality. The Canons are profoundly pastoral in character and were deliberately written in popular language for the edification of the church. They are not speculative, but begin with the misery of the human condition and focus on God's gracious and effective provision of salvation in Christ.[1]

---

1 W. Robert Godfrey, "Calvin and Calvinism in the Netherlands," in *John Calvin: His Influence in the Western World*, ed. W. Stanford Reid (Grand Rapids: Zondervan, 1982), 108. Consider Schaff, for example, who writes that the Canons "prepared the

I could not agree with Robert Godfrey's assessment more. The Canons of Dort are characterized not only by a robust defense of the doctrines of grace, but by a warm, pastoral concern for the edification of the church. God's grace and mercy in Christ are front and centre in the Canons of Dort. Dort defends God's sovereignty in salvation not only because it is biblical but because without it the believer has no confidence in life and in death. Therefore, the Remonstrant view was seen as a threat to God's sovereign grace and the believer's assurance in a Saviour who can save and preserve the Father's elect. Before exploring exactly how Dort defends the doctrines of grace, as well as the implications these doctrines have for godliness, it is imperative that we first begin by understanding the historical context of the seventeenth century debate. In particular, we must give our attention to the rise of Arminianism and the threat it posed to Reformed orthodoxy.

Jacob Arminius

Arminianism bears the name of Jacob Arminius (1559–1609),[2] who studied at the University of Leiden until he moved to Geneva to attend the Geneva academy. In Geneva, Arminius learned from some of the best Reformed theologians of the day, including Theodore Beza, Cal-

way for a dry scholasticism which runs into subtle abstractions, and resolves the living soul of divinity into a skeleton of formulas and distinctions" [Philip Schaff, *The History of Creeds*, vol. 1 of *The Creeds of Christendom* (Grand Rapids: Baker, 2007), 515].

Author's note: Some content in this chapter is adapted from see Matthew Barrett, *Salvation by Grace: The Case for Effectual Calling and Regeneration* (Phillipsburg: P & R, 2013). There my treatment is more extensive.

2   On the life and theology of Arminius, see Carl Bangs, *Arminius: A Study in the Dutch Reformation* (Grand Rapids: Zondervan, 1985); Richard A. Muller, *God, Creation, and Providence in the Thought of Jacob Arminius* (Grand Rapids: Baker, 1991); Roger E. Olson, *Arminian Theology: Myths and Realities* (Downers Grove: InterVarsity, 2006); Marius van Leeuwen, Keith D. Stranglin and Marijke Tolsma, eds., *Arminius, Arminianism, and Europe: Jacob Arminius (1559/60–1609)*, Brill's Series in Church History, 39 (Leiden: E. J. Brill, 2010); Keith D. Stanglin and Thomas H. McCall, *Jacob Arminius: Theologian of Grace* (Oxford: Oxford University Press, 2012); William den Boer, *God's Twofold Love: The Theology of Arminius (1559–1609)*, trans. Albert Gootjes, *Reformed Historical Theology*, 14, ed. Herman J. Selderhuis (Göttingen: Vandenhoeck & Ruprecht, 2010). For a more extensive list of works this chapter is relying on, see Bibliography.

vin's epigone and successor. However, it became clear after Arminius left Geneva to pastor in Amsterdam (1588–1603) that he advocated a synergistic view of grace, especially apparent in his sermons on Romans 7–9, whereby he taught that chapter 7 represented Paul as an unbeliever.[3] As Muller explains, "He first directed his attention to Romans 7 and the problem of the will. He moved away from the traditional Augustinian pattern of the Reformers and argued that the inward struggle of Paul was a pre-conversion, not a post-conversion, struggle. Here already are hints of a synergism in which the human will takes the first step toward grace."[4]

Romans 9 would prove equally monumental, as he came to argue that Paul was not teaching the unconditional election of individuals, but the election of classes of persons (as represented by Jacob and Esau), a view that would bring Arminius into debate with Franciscus Junius.[5] Other colleagues like Petrus Plancius also objected, charging Arminius with Pelagianism. To further solidify his views, in 1601 Arminius decided to write a response (published posthumously in 1612) to the Cambridge Calvinist William Perkins (1558–1602), once again making evident his departure from the Calvinists.[6] Arminius's treatise against Perkins was serendipitous as controversy in England already ensued with certain anti-Calvinists. Eventually, efforts would

---

3   Bangs, *Arminius*, 71–80, 141; Jan Rohls, "Calvinism, Arminianism and Socinianism in the Netherlands until the Synod of Dort," in *Socinianism and Arminianism: Antitrinitarians, Calvinists and Cultural Exchange in Seventeenth-Century Europe*, ed. Martin Mulsow and Jan Rohls, Brill's Studies in Intellectual History, 134 (Leiden: Brill, 2005), 9.

4   Richard A. Muller, "Arminius and Arminianism," in *The Dictionary of Historical Theology*, ed. Trevor A. Hart (Grand Rapids: Eerdmans, 2000), 33. See Bangs, *Arminius*, 140–145, 186–192, for details on Arminius's preaching of Romans 7.

5   On Arminius' response to Junius, see Jacob Arminius, "Epistolary Discussion, concerning Predestination, Between James Arminius, D. D. and Francis Junius, D. D." and "Appendix to the Previous Discussion, Containing the Theses of Junius Concerning Predestination, with Annotations by Arminius," in *The Writings of James Arminius*, trans. W.R. Bagnall (Grand Rapids: Baker, 1956), 3:7–278.

6   James Arminius, "Examination of a Treatise Concerning the Order and Mode of Predestination, and the Amplitude of Divine Grace, by William Perkins," in *Writings*, 3:279–526. See also Herbert Boyd McGonigle, *Sufficient Saving Grace: John Wesley's Evangelical Arminianism* (Carlisle: Paternoster, 2001), 28.

be made to protest the move to give the Church of England a more official Calvinistic position by having the Lambeth Articles of 1595 appended to the Thirty-Nine Articles (1563).[7]

In 1603 Arminius accepted a professorate at the University of Leiden, and while he would receive opposition from many Calvinists, perhaps his most aggressive opponent was Franciscus Gomarus (1563–1641), a student of Beza. The debate between these two opponents became so tense that at one point in his writings Arminius concludes that Gomarus's views are "very well adapted for establishing and confirming it [the kingdom of Satan]."[8] Stanglin explains the key difference between Gomarus and Arminius,

> Gomarus went out of his way to stress that God makes unwilling people into willing people.... For Gomarus and Kuchlinus, there is no free choice in matters of salvation prior to regeneration. Although Arminius would equally stress the necessity of divine grace in initiating conversion, he was careful to avoid language implying that humanity is an unwilling participant in conversion.[9]

Gomarus, believing Arminius to be in agreement with Pelagianism, was not alone when he declared that Arminius's theology violated the Belgic Confession (1561) and the Heidelberg Catechism (1563). As Van Leeuwen states, "To his enemies it became ever more obvious that, by diminishing the role of God and pleading for human freedom, Arminius distanced himself from the Reformed confessions: the Confessio Belgica, the Catechism of Heidelberg."[10] Moreover, as Gerrit

---

7 Bangs, *Arminius*, 206–208; Peter White, *Predestination, Policy and Polemic: Conflict and Consensus in the English Church from the Reformation to the Civil War* (Cambridge: Cambridge University Press, 1992), 101–123. See also Bibliography for further resources on the conflict in England.

8 Arminius, "Examination of Gomarus's Theses on Predestination," in *Writings*, 3:658.

9 Keith D. Stanglin, *Arminius on the Assurance of Salvation*, Brill's Series in Church History 27 (Leiden: E. J. Brill, 2007), 79. See also Th. Marius van Leeuwen, "Introduction: Arminius, Arminianism, and Europe," in *Arminius, Arminianism, and Europe*, xiii.

10 Van Leeuwen, "Introduction," xiv. On Gomarus's opposition to Arminius, see Simon Kistemaker, "Leading Figures at the Synod of Dort," in *Crisis in the Reformed*

Jan Hoenderdaal observes, Arminius, along with Johannes Uytenbo-gaert (1557–1644), "joined in wanting the [Belgic] Confession and the [Heidelberg] Catechism to be 'revisable and reformable.'"[11] Despite the claims of some historians that Arminius was part of the Reformed tradition, Richard Muller has successfully demonstrated that Armin-ius was, in the eyes of seventeenth-century Reformers, in obvious violation of the Reformed confessions for "the basic doctrinal position advanced both in the Confession and in the synods was anti-synergistic, namely, monergistic."[12]

One year before Arminius's death, his departure from the Reformed confessions would become even more explicit in his *Declaration of Sentiments* in 1608 (presented before the Calvinistic Estates General of Holland), which included a clear affirmation of synergism as well as a refutation of Calvinism's decretal theology. For Arminius, Calvin-ism (both supra- and infralapsarian[13]) was in conflict with God's love and man's free will, ultimately making God the author of sin. To the contrary, God's election is conditioned upon his foreknowledge of man's faith.[14] Likewise, the Spirit's effort to apply the grace of God is also conditioned upon the sinner who is able to use his free will to resist and reject God's grace. It is only when the sinner cooperates with God that grace is made effective.[15] While it is necessary for God to

---

Churches: Essays in Commemoration of the Great Synod of Dort, 1618–1619, ed. Peter Y. De Jong (Grand Rapids: Reformed Fellowship, 1968), 42–44.

11 Gerrit Jan Hoenderdaal, "The Life and Struggle of Arminius in the Dutch Repub-lic," in *Man's Faith and Freedom: The Theological Influence of Jacobus Arminius*, ed. Gerald O. McCulloh (New York: Abingdon, 1962), 15.

12 Richard A. Muller, "Arminius and the Reformed Tradition," *Westminster Theologi-cal Journal* 70 (2008): 31 (especially see 48). The main historians Muller is opposing are Gerald Brandt and Carl Bangs. See also "Arminius and Arminianism," *WTJ* 70: 34; Muller, *Jacob Arminius,* 42

13 Muller, *Jacob Arminius,* 10, 19; "Arminius and Arminianism," *WTJ* 70: 34; Louis Praamsma, "Background of Arminian Controversy," in *Crisis in the Reformed Churches*, 29–30.

14 See Arminius, "Declaration of Sentiments," in *Writings*, 1:230–231.

15 On synergism, see Arminius, "Certain Articles To Be Diligently Examined and Weighed," *Writings*, 2:492–501; "Declaration of Sentiments," *Writings*, 1:252–253; "Apology Against Thirty-One Theological Articles," *Writings*, 1:252–300, 328, 364–373. See Bangs, *Arminius*, 342, 358; Olson, *Arminian Theology*, 22.

provide a universal, prevenient grace (grounded in a universal atone-ment[16]) that mitigates man's pervasive depravity and enables belief, God's saving act to finally convert the sinner is conditioned upon the free choice of the sinner to accept or reject grace (synergism). As McGonigle explains, "Arminius saw a man's salvation or his damnation resting ultimately on that man's response to God's offer of grace. His response is not predetermined by a fixed decree."[17]

The Arminian Remonstrants[18]

While Arminius died in 1609, his synergism influenced numerous churches in Amsterdam so that by 1610 there were many Arminian pastors. Perhaps two of Arminius's most important successors were Conrad Vorstius (1569–1622), opposed by King James himself, and Simon Episcopius (1583–1643), both of whom succeeded Arminius at the University of Leiden.[19] As unrest continued, forty-six Arminians, led by Uytenbogaert and Episcopius, gathered in Gouda on January 14, 1610, to subscribe to a Remonstrance (also labeled The Five Arminian Articles) against the Calvinists, which expressed their views and was to be presented to the political authorities. The confession is consis-tent with the writings of Arminius, teaching that God's election is conditioned upon foreseen faith, Christ's atonement is universal in scope and grace is resistible. As Rohls explains, "The Remonstrants presupposed free will, which could either accept God's universal offer

---

16 For an extensive treatment of Arminius on the atonement, see Olson, *Arminian Theology*, 221–241; J. Matthew Pinson, "The Nature of Atonement in the Theology of Jacobus Arminius," *Journal of the Evangelical Theological Society* 53, no. 4 (2010): 773–785.

17 McGonigle, *Sufficient Saving Grace*, 32. See also Hoenderdaal, "The Life and Struggle of Arminius in the Dutch Republic," in *Man's Faith and Freedom*, 24.

18 My exposition of the events is brief. For a more extensive history of Dort, see Aza Goudriaan and Fred van Lieburg, eds., *Revisiting the Synod of Dordt (1618–1619)* (Leiden: Brill, 2011). See Bibliography for further sources.

19 On King James's opposition to Vortius and Arminianism, especially in regards to Socinianism, see White, *Predestination, Policy and Polemic*, 159–166, 175–202; Kistemaker, "Leading Figures at the Synod of Dort," 49–50; Robert Godfrey, "Calvin and Calvinism in the Netherlands," 104–105.

of salvation or reject it."[20] Like Arminius, for the Remonstrants grace is not effectual, but only persuasive so that man's free will is ultimately able to determine whether or not God's grace will be cooperated with. Muller explains,

> The third article argues the necessity of grace if fallen man is to choose the good and come to belief. In the fourth article, this insistence upon prevenient grace is drawn into relation with the synergism of the first two articles. Prevenient and subsequent assisting grace may be resisted and rejected: ultimately the work of salvation, in its efficacy and application, rests on human choice.[21]

The Counter-Remonstrants

Prompted by the Calvinist prince, Maurice, Prince of Orange (1567–1625), six representatives of each side met in The Hague on March 10, 1611, to discuss their differences. The Remonstrants were led by Uytenbogaert and the Calvinists by Plancius.[22] Though the conference lasted until May 20, the meeting was of no success. However, out of the conference came the *Counter-Remonstrance*, a document which responded to the Arminians and would foreshadow the much larger document to come in 1619. However, in the years leading up to 1619 tensions were high. As Godfrey observes,

> The strict Calvinists experienced growing frustration over the Arminian controversy. They believed that the Arminians denied basic truths of the gospel, compromising the orthodoxy of their churches, and that the government was preventing church leaders from fulfilling their right and responsibility to discipline the doctrinal offenders.[23]

---

20 Rohls, "Calvinism, Arminianism and Socinianism," 19.

21 Muller, "Arminius and Arminianism," 34–35.

22 However, Uytenbogaert would eventually flee and so Episcopius would become the leader of the delegation at Dort (Israel, *The Dutch Republic*, 461).

23 Godfrey, "Calvin and Calvinism in the Netherlands," 106.

The situation only worsened when frustrations became so high that some Calvinists withdrew from churches where Remonstrants preached from the pulpit and instead formed their own services outside the city. The state of affairs reached its height in 1615 when riots erupted and word spread that secret synods would be held in order to vacate the state-dominated church.[24]

In July 1617, Prince Maurice refused to worship in the Court church at The Hague where Uytenbogaert was preaching. With Maurice's support, a national synod was called for in November. But matters spiraled downward when Holland declared the States General vote of 4–3 invalid, demanding that a unanimous vote was necessary.[25] Consequently, Johan van Oldenbarnevelt threatened civil war, but the situation was resolved when Maurice had him arrested on August 29, 1618.[26] As a result, other Remonstrants fled the country. Now that Maurice had charge, the States General's initial vote was finally applied and the national synod at Dordrecht first convened in November 1618 as the first and only "truly ecumenical synod that the Reformed churches have ever had."[27]

The Counter Remonstrance at Dordrecht were presided over by President Johannes Bogerman (1576–1637). Bogerman is famous for his dismissal of the Arminians. The Remonstrants tried many tactics in order to disrupt the synod. First, they tried to have Bogerman removed as president. Second, they avoided the doctrinal issues the synod sought to bring front and centre. Third, overall they refused to submit to the synod's authority in their examination. These and many other tactics resulted in their dismissal. On January 14, 1619, President Bogerman erupted,

> The foreign delegates are now of the opinion that you are unworthy to appear before the Synod. You have refused to acknowledge her as your lawful judge and have maintained that she is your

24 Godfrey, "Calvin and Calvinism in the Netherlands," 106.
25 Godfrey, "Calvin and Calvinism in the Netherlands," 106.
26 Philip Benedict, *Christ's Churches Purely Reformed: A Social History of Calvinism* (New Haven: Yale University Press, 2002), 310.
27 Godfrey, "Calvin and Calvinism in the Netherlands," 107.

counter-party; you have done everything according to your own whim; you have despised the decisions of the Synod and of the Political Commissioners; you have refused to answer; you have unjustly interpreted the indictments. The Synod has treated you mildly; but you have—as one of the foreign delegates expressed it—"begun and ended with lies." With that eulogy we shall let you go. God shall preserve His Word and shall bless the Synod. In order that she be no longer obstructed, you are sent away! [*Dimittimini, exite!*] You are dismissed, get out![28]

The synod consisted of eighty-four members, fifty-eight of which were Dutchmen, the rest being foreigners from Reformed churches (see Appendix 2). Therefore, while the assembly was a national synod, it had international support. It gathered some of the brightest Reformed theologians of the time, including men like Gisbertius Voetius and William Ames. The synod's aim was not only to correct the Arminian caricatures of the Calvinist position and refute the Remonstrant position, but also to set forth the "biblical" view.[29] In so doing, Dort showed, as Muller notes, that the "Arminian doctrines were clearly beyond the bounds of Reformed confessional orthodoxy." Muller continues,

The Canons of Dort ought to be viewed as a magisterial interpreta-tion of the extant Reformed confessional synthesis: they condemn predestination grounded on prior human choice; they deny a grace that is both resistible and acceptable by man; they affirm the depth of original sin, argue a limited efficiency of Christ's work of satisfaction and stress the perseverance of the elect by grace.... None of these views modifies the earlier Reformed position— indeed, virtually all of these points can be elicited from Ursinus's exposition of the Heidelberg Catechism.[30]

---

28 Quoted in Homer C. Hoeksema, *The Voice of Our Fathers* (Grand Rapids: Reformed Free, 1980), 27.

29 John R. de Witt, "The Arminian Conflict," in *Puritan Papers*, ed. J.I. Packer (Phillipsburg: P & R, 2000), 5:17–18.

30 Muller, "Arminius and Arminianism," 35. See Zacharias Ursinus, *The Commentary*

The focus of Dort is on the major difference between the two parties: conditionality vs. unconditionality in salvation. Dort is clear: no aspect of God's eternal choice is conditioned upon man's free will for its efficacy or success. As John R. de Witt states,

> Arminianism meant synergism: that is, in however evangelical a form in some of its early proponents, it introduced a cooperate element into the effecting of salvation. And each of the doctrines delineated at Dort was directed against the notion of any cooperation, any grounding of God's favor upon something acceptable in the creature, in the extending of grace to sinners.[31]

Before the delegates of Dort pronounced their verdict, they requested that the Remonstrants, led by Episcopius, set forth their views with greater detail than they had done in the *Five Articles* originally presented. The Remonstrants wrote a confession of their beliefs that more fully presented their views, and it came to be called the *Opinions of the Remonstrants* (see Appendix 6). When Dort pronounced its verdict, condemning the Remonstrant views as outside the bounds of the Belgic Confession and Heidelberg Catechism and, most importantly, in conflict with Scripture itself; such a pronouncement was based upon the *Five Articles* and the *Opinions of the Remonstrants*. The Canons of Dort were officially adopted on April 22, 1619, and were read in front of all the delegates in attendance.[32] All the delegates, including the foreign representatives, pledged their subscription to the canons without exception. The canons were then sent to the States General, which approved them, ordaining their publication on May 5, 1619.[33] While the

---

of *Dr. Zacharias Ursinus on the Heidelberg Catechism*, trans. G.W. Williard (Grand Rapids: Eerdmans, 1954).

31 de Witt, "The Arminian Conflict," 20. See also Fred H. Klooster, "Doctrinal Deliverances of Dort," in *Crisis in the Reformed Churches*, 52–57.

32 On the history of the Remonstrants after Dort, see Israel, *The Dutch Republic*, 462–464.

33 The original title to the Canons read, *Judgment of the National Synod of the Reformed Churches of the United Netherlands: held in Dordrecht in the year 1618 and 1619. which was assisted by many excellent theologians of the Reformed Churches of Great Britain, the Electoral Palatinate, Hessia, Switzerland, Wetteraw, Geneva, Bremen, and Emden:*

canons were originally written in Latin, they were translated into French and Dutch as well.

Ecclesiastical conflict

Dort was not a synod that gathered over minor issues. While today the debate between Calvinists and Arminians does not move beyond the theological arena, in the early seventeenth century the Remonstrant doctrine was not only theological but also ecclesiastical and even political. Arminianism was not only a threat to the Reformed confessional subscription of the Dutch churches but an attack on the autonomy or "Christonomy of the churches."[34] The Reformed churches in the Netherlands were not quite a State Church. However, they did have the support of the government, and to an extent their church polity was even controlled by the political authorities.[35] As already seen, matters became complicated when Arminians began to find support from the government, which led to the persecution of the Reformed churches. Persecution, however, did not stand in the way of bringing the Reformation to the Netherlands. Both in doctrine and polity the Reformed churches were "decidedly Calvinistic" and had adopted the Heidelberg Catechism and Belgic Confession long before the Synod of Dort.[36]

The Arminians, however, were a threat to this ecclesiastical and political solidarity. Praamsma identifies three "famous exponents of Arminian theory and practice" leading up to Dort that foster a better understanding the historical context. First, Uytenbogaert, author of *Tract on the Office and Authority of a Higher Christian Government in Ecclesiastical Affairs*, argued in 1610 that "the highest authority in the affairs of the church belonged under God and his Word to the States of every province in the Netherlands."[37] As Praamsma explains, "In accordance with this view the States had authority to call and install

---

Concerning the well-known five heads of doctrine, about which a difference arose in the Reformed Churches of said United Netherlands. Expressed on May 6, 1619.

34 Praamsma, "The Background of the Arminian Controversy (1586–1618)," 31.

35 Hoeksema, *The Voice of Our Fathers*, 4.

36 Hoeksema, *The Voice of Our Fathers*, 4.

37 Praamsma, "The Background of the Arminian Controversy (1586–1618)," 31.

ministers, elders and deacons, to supervise the preaching, to frame an order for the churches, to convene ecclesiastical assemblies as well as to preside over them."[38]

A second figurehead worthy of mention is Hugo Grotius who wrote "Resolution for Peace in the Churches" in 1614. In this work Grotius argued that the States of Holland could forbid preaching on controversial doctrines. Grotius was sympathetic with Puritan persecutor William Laud. Grotius argues, "In England you can see how well the extermination of harmful doctrines has advanced, above all by reason of the fact that the persons who have there taken this holy work upon themselves have not intermingled anything new, anything of themselves, but have focused their gaze on better ages."[39]

A third leader was van Oldenbarnevelt, father of the "Sharp Resolution" of 1617. In the "Sharp Resolution" the States of Holland "decided that no national synod was to be convened, that the States would retain their authority in ecclesiastical matters, and that the cities were authorized to levy soldiers in defense of the Remonstrants."[40] Consequently, as Groen van Prinsterer records, "a systematic oppression of the Reformed Church and its faith was organized."[41] In one case, Gese-

---

38 Praamsma, "The Background of the Arminian Controversy (1586–1618)," 31.

39 Quoted in Praamsma, "The Background of the Arminian Controversy (1586–1618)," 31. Praamsma comments, "These better ages, according to Laud, were to be found in the period of the Constantinian state-church, of which he believed he saw a new embodiment in the Anglican Church before his aristocratic mind finally found its rest in the bosom of the Roman Catholic hierarchy."

40 Praamsma, "The Background of the Arminian Controversy (1586–1618)," 32.

41 Groen van Prinsterer observes, "Oldenbarnevelt and his followers permitted the Arminians to propagate their doctrine in the name of tolerance. They imposed silence on others to suppress discord. But those whom they wanted to silence refused to abandon their duty to the Judge Supreme. For this refusal they were banished from the church as if they were rebelling against legitimate superiors. Excluded from places of worship, they, with their faithful followers, took refuge in private buildings in order to worship. That refuge, however, was also forbidden. The civil authorities, fearing schism, intervened in the name of public order. To maintain this imposed silence, the authorities used violence. Faithful pastors were forbidden to preach; separatist meetings were not tolerated; houses, barns and ships used for assembling were confiscated; various methods of intimidation were applied to laymen who joined the meetings of the faithful. Such were bereft of the right of citizenship. In other

lius, a Calvinist pastor in Rotterdam, was ejected from his office by the magistrates. Many others experienced the same. However, in 1617 Prince Maurice of Orange put a stop to such actions, defending the Reformed, and, as already mentioned, eventually called a national synod "so that the controversy which had agitated both state and church for at least two decades could finally be settled."[42] Finally, notes Praamsma, at Dort the churches were allowed "to express themselves and make decisions which insured the maintenance of the pure doctrine of the Gospel."[43] Such an opportunity was fitting since, as Phillip Benedict observes, the Calvinists "insisted on the autonomy of the church and its competence in all matters regarding the setting and oversight of doctrine."[44]

Dort's response to the Remonstrants was characterized by the threat they saw to the confessional standards. As mentioned already, scholars like Richard Muller have demonstrated that Arminius was outside the bounds of the Reformed confessions. The same can be said of the Remonstrants who followed. But the point to be made here is not just that their theology strayed outside of the Reformed confessions but also that the Remonstrants held a different view concerning the authority of the confessions themselves. In other words, the Remonstrants, following Arminius, were in favour of confessional revision. Such revision was not of grammar, style or of minor details. On the contrary, the Arminians "had in mind a permanent attitude of openness and freedom" and argued that a "binding confession ultimately conflicted both with the authority of Scripture and with the freedom of the individual conscience."[45] The Calvinists did not disagree that confessional standards cannot replace Scripture or stand on equal authority with Scripture. Nevertheless, the Reformed

---

words, their means of existence, including their daily bread, was taken away. In this manner, under the pretext of public order and tolerance, a systematic oppression of the Reformed Church and its faith was organized" [G. Groen van Prinsterer, *Maurice et Barnevelt (1875)*, 130, as quoted in Praamsma, "The Background of the Arminian Controversy (1586–1618)," 32].

42 Praamsma, "The Background of the Arminian Controversy (1586–1618)," 33.

43 Praamsma, "The Background of the Arminian Controversy (1586–1618)," 33.

44 Benedict, *Christ's Churches Purely Reformed*, 306.

45 Praamsma, "The Background of the Arminian Controversy (1586–1618)," 28.

viewed the confessional standards as essential in order to maintain ecclesiastical unity as well as to guard against heresy. The confessional standards as binding documents were not meant to trump Scripture but to assist the church in guarding against sects and heretics who contradict Scripture.

The Remonstrant effort to modify the Reformed confessions only exposed a question not without centrality at the synod, namely, should the Reformed churches be liberal or confessional? As Praamsma asks, "Was it to be a church with unity in doctrine or one which allowed large freedom for differing views?"[46] It became increasingly evident as the Synod of Dort proceeded that the Arminians desired the liberty to change doctrine as they pleased, as opposed to the Calvinists who were insistent that the Reformed confessions were not only faithful to Scripture, but also served the churches in preserving "doctrinal unity and stability."[47]

Conclusion

While the Remonstrant doctrines continued to have an effect wherever the Arminians went, Jonathan Israel observes, "The Calvinist revolution of the Counter-Remonstrants altered the political balance within the Republic, made the Dutch Reformed Church a bastion of Calvinist orthodoxy, and changed the tone of Dutch life in the short and medium term."[48] Israel concludes that Dort, even if only temporarily, "made the United Provinces the hub of international Calvinism."[49] It is to the Canons of Dort that we now turn, with a particular focus on the piety and spirituality they fostered.

---

46 Praamsma, "The Background of the Arminian Controversy (1586–1618)," 28.
47 Praamsma, "The Background of the Arminian Controversy (1586–1618)," 28.
48 Israel, *The Dutch Republic*, 465.
49 Israel, *The Dutch Republic*, 465.

Jesus answered them, "I told you, and you do not believe. The works that I do in my Father's name bear witness about me, but you do not believe because you are not part of my flock."—JOHN 10:25-26

And when the Gentiles heard this, they began rejoicing and glorifying the word of the Lord, and as many as were appointed to eternal life believed.—ACTS 13:48

What shall we say then? Is there injustice on God's part? By no means! For he says to Moses, "I will have mercy on whom I have mercy, and I will have compassion on whom I have compassion." So then it depends not on human will or exertion, but on God, who has mercy. For the Scripture says to Pharaoh, "For this very purpose I have raised you up, that I might show my power in you, and that my name might be proclaimed in all the earth." So then he has mercy on whomever he wills, and he hardens whomever he wills.—ROMANS 9:14-18

Blessed be the God and Father of our Lord Jesus Christ, who has blessed us in Christ with every spiritual blessing in the heavenly places, even as he chose us in him before the foundation of the world, that we should be holy and blameless before him. In love he predestined us for adoption as sons through Jesus Christ, according to the purpose of his will, to the praise of his glorious grace, with which he has blessed us in the Beloved.
In him we have redemption through his blood, the forgiveness of our trespasses, according to the riches of his grace, which he lavished upon us, in all wisdom and insight making known to us the mystery of his will, according to his purpose, which he set forth in Christ as a plan for the fullness of time, to unite all things in him, things in heaven and things on earth. In him we have obtained an inheritance, having been predestined according to the purpose of him who works all things according to the counsel of his will, so that we who were the first to hope in Christ might be to the praise of his glory.—EPHESIANS 1:3-12

Divine predestination
Source of assurance, humility and holiness

Introduction

What is the purpose of the doctrine of predestination? According to the apostle Paul, God "chose us in him before the foundation of the world, that we should be holy and blameless before him" (Ephesians 1:4). Moreover, according to Paul, as a consequence of being predestined by God we have been blessed in Christ with "every spiritual blessing in the heavenly places" (Ephesians 1:3). Holiness, blamelessness, spiritual blessing—these are not the typical words one hears when engaging in discussions over the doctrine of predestination. But they should be. As important as it is to realize that election is unconditional, we must not lose sight of the grand and glorious truth that the purpose of our election is that we should be holy and blameless before the Father.

Dort acknowledged these purposes of election as well. The Canons of Dort showed that election is designed by God not only to save us but also to lead us into a life of godliness. Furthermore, they argued that election, if truly understood, does not leave the believer with a smug attitude of self-importance but a humble, meek and awe-stricken attitude of reverence before a sovereign God. The Calvinist understands that since election is unconditional, there is nothing within him to boast about. Indeed, all boasting is excluded! Instead, what results is gratitude, praise, thanksgiving and worship. Therefore, the words "pride" and "Calvinist" never belong in the same sentence. How can one be prideful when it was God's pure, undeserved mercy and good pleasure alone, rather than something man did, which moved him to elect sinners? Therefore, Calvinists, out of all people, should be the most humble. As A.N. Martin explains, "The expression, a proud Calvinist, is a misnomer. If a Calvinist is a man who has seen God as he is high and lifted up, enthroned, then he is a man who has been brought to brokenness before that throne as was Isaiah."[1] As we will discover in the present chapter, the Synod of Dort treasured humility and godliness, viewing them as the natural consequence of unconditional election.

The Remonstrant doctrine of conditional election

The Arminians began their Remonstrance with the decree of predestination (1.1). God, they said, has not decreed or decided to "elect anyone to eternal life" nor has he decided to reject anyone from having eternal life without any consideration of man's "preceding obedience or disobedience."[2] Here we see the first strike to the Calvinist. The Arminians are very clear, election is not unconditional. The Arminians elaborate all the more when they say that not only is election not without any consideration of man's preceding obedience or disobedi-

---

1   "A carnal Calvinist? Another misnomer. The enthroned one is the holy one, and he dwells in conscious communion with those who are rightly related to him as the enthroned one and as the holy one" [A.N. Martin, "The Practical Implications of True Calvinism: 1," *The Banner of Truth* 120 (1973): 18].

2   "Appendix H: The Opinions of the Remonstrants," 1.1, in *Crisis in the Reformed Churches: Essays in Commemoration of the Great Synod of Dort, 1618–1619*, ed. Peter Y. De Jong (Grand Rapids: Reformed Fellowship, 1968), 222.

ence but so also it is not: (a) prior to the decree to create humankind, (b) based solely on God's good pleasure, (c) based solely on the "glory of His mercy and justice," or (d) based solely on "His absolute power and domination."[3] Any type of unconditionality, whereby God elects purely with his own glory, mercy, justice, power and domination in mind, is ruled out by the Arminians. God's decree is not made exclusively on the basis of anything in him, but is conditioned on that which is outside of him, namely, the will of man.

In 1.2 of the Remonstrance, the Arminians continue to explain their position more extensively. God's decree to elect unto salvation or perdition, is also not a decree of "the end absolutely intended."[4] Consequently, "neither are such means subordinated to that same decree by which the elect and the reprobate are efficaciously and inevitably led to their final destination."[5] The Arminians, in other words, are claiming that God does not exercise absolute, exhaustive and meticulous control in either the salvation or perdition of the sinner. Neither the end, nor the means to that end, fall within the decree of God. Otherwise God would be determining the final destination of each person, including the very means by which they get there, without qualification or condition.

The denial of God's exhaustive and meticulous sovereignty seen in 1.2 is elaborated upon in 1.3. Here the Arminians give a long list of certain doctrines they deny.[6] God has *not*:

1. with this plan created in the one Adam all men in a state of rectitude,
2. ordained the fall and the permission of it,
3. withdrawn from Adam the grace which was necessary and sufficient,

---

3 "Appendix H: The Opinions of the Remonstrants," 1.1, in *Crisis in the Reformed Churches*, 222.

4 "Appendix H: The Opinions of the Remonstrants," 1.2, in *Crisis in the Reformed Churches*, 222.

5 "Appendix H: The Opinions of the Remonstrants," 1.2, in *Crisis in the Reformed Churches*, 222.

6 "Appendix H: The Opinions of the Remonstrants," 1.3, in *Crisis in the Reformed Churches*, 222–223.

8

4. brought it about that the Gospel is preached and that men are externally called,
5. confer[red] on them any gifts of the Holy Spirit by means of which he leads some of them to life, but deprives others of the benefit of life. [7]

The list ends by also claiming that Christ the Mediator is "not solely the executor of election."[8] The point the Remonstrants are trying to make in these six denials is that God does not decree the specific means by which man is either eternally saved or condemned. To do so would mean that God has not only, in eternity past, decreed the fall but in time he has also withdrawn the grace necessary to continue in obedience and deprived those not chosen of the grace necessary to receive the benefit of eternal life. The Arminians clarify such a point when they conclude 1.3 by writing that God's absolute election to eternal life is not the reason why some are efficaciously called, justified, preserved and glorified: "That others are left in the fall, that Christ is not given to them, that they are either not called at all or not efficaciously called—these are not the reasons why they are absolutely rejected from eternal salvation."[9]

The denial of the Calvinist doctrine of predestination continues. The Arminians insist that "God has not decreed to leave the greatest part of men in the fall, excluded from every hope of salvation, apart from intervening actual sins."[10] In fact, no one, they argue, is ever "rejected from life eternal" or from "the means sufficient for it" by an "absolute antecedent decree."[11] This being the case, the "merit of Christ, calling, and all the gifts of the Spirit can be profitable to salvation for all, and

---

7 "Appendix H: The Opinions of the Remonstrants," 1.3, in *Crisis in the Reformed Churches*, 223.

8 "Appendix H: The Opinions of the Remonstrants," 1.3, in *Crisis in the Reformed Churches*, 223.

9 "Appendix H: The Opinions of the Remonstrants," 1.3, in *Crisis in the Reformed Churches*, 223.

10 "Appendix H: The Opinions of the Remonstrants," 1.4, in *Crisis in the Reformed Churches*, 223.

11 "Appendix H: The Opinions of the Remonstrants," 1.6, in *Crisis in the Reformed Churches*, 223.

truly are, unless they themselves by the abuse of these gifts pervert them to their own perdition."[12] Stated another way, if man is rejected from eternal life it has nothing to do with God's absolute decree, but it is entirely and solely because man himself decided to abuse the gifts given to all people. Indeed, no one is ever predestined "to unbelief, to impiety, and to sins, as means and causes of damnation."[13] Again, we see the Arminian denial not only of predestined ends but of means as well. Not only does God not predestine anyone to eternal damnation but neither does he predestine the specific sins (impiety) to that end.

What then is the basis for God's decree to either elect or reject the sinner? According to the Arminians, election of "particular persons is decisive, out of *consideration of faith in Jesus Christ and of perseverance*" as opposed to an election that is *"apart from* a consideration of faith and perseverance in the true faith."[14] God's election is always conditioned upon man's faith and ability to persevere in that belief. Likewise, the same applies to rejection. Rejection is made on the basis of, not apart from, a "consideration of antecedent unbelief and perseverance in unbelief."[15]

The Arminians are simply reiterating what they had written in their Remonstrance of 1610. There we read the same:

12 "Appendix H: The Opinions of the Remonstrants," 1.6, in *Crisis in the Reformed Churches*, 223.

13 "Appendix H: The Opinions of the Remonstrants," 1.6, in *Crisis in the Reformed Churches*, 223.

14 "Appendix H: The Opinions of the Remonstrants," 1.7, in *Crisis in the Reformed Churches*, 223.

15 "Appendix H: The Opinions of the Remonstrants," 1.8, in *Crisis in the Reformed Churches*, 223–224. The Remonstrants conclude their first canon by addressing the salvation of children: "All the children of believers are sanctified in Christ, so that no one of them who leaves this life before the use of reason will perish. By no means, however, are to be considered among the number of the reprobate certain children of believers who leave this life in infancy before they have committed any actual sin in their own person, so that neither the holy bath of Baptism nor the prayers of the church for them can in any way be profitable for their salvation." And again, "No children of believers who have been baptized in the name of the Father, the Son, and the Holy Spirit, living in the state of infancy, are reckoned among the reprobate by an absolute decree" ("Appendix H: The Opinions of the Remonstrants," 1.9–1.10, in *Crisis in the Reformed Churches*, 224).

> God by an eternal and immutable decree has in Jesus Christ his
> Son determined before the foundation of the world to save out
> of the fallen sinful human race those in Christ, for Christ's sake,
> and through Christ who by the grace of the Holy Spirit shall
> believe in this his Son Jesus Christ and persevere in this faith and
> obedience to the end.[16]

Notice, God's eternal decree is determined but it is determined on the
basis of those who will believe in Christ.

Dort's affirmation of unconditional election
The gospel of sovereign grace

Dort's doctrinal response to the Remonstrants is vigorous, filling eigh-
teen Articles and nine Rejection of the Errors (of the Remonstrants)
which constitute the first head or canon. Dort begins where Scripture
itself begins, namely, with the fall of Adam and the hereditary nature
of his sin for all humankind. Dort argues that "all people have sinned
in Adam and have come under the sentence of the curse and eternal
death" and therefore "God would have done no one an injustice if it
had been his will to leave the entire human race in sin and under the
curse, and to condemn them on account of their sin."[17] In support of
such a claim Dort cites three passages, each from the apostle Paul.

> The whole world is liable to the condemnation of God (Romans
> 3:19).

> All have sinned and are deprived of the glory of God (Romans 3:23).

> The wages of sin is death (Romans 6:23).

Following Paul, Dort exposes man's condemnation before a holy God.
Every man sinned in Adam and is under his curse. The consequence

---

16 "Appendix C: The Remonstrance of 1610," in *Crisis in the Reformed Churches*, 208.

17 "Canons of Dort," 1.1, in *Creeds and Confessions of the Reformation Era*, vol. 2 of
Creeds and Confessions of Faith in the Christian Tradition, eds. Jaroslav Pelikan and Valerie
Hotchkiss (New Haven and London: Yale University Press, 2003), 2:571.

is eternal death. Therefore, for God to save no one at all is not unfair but absolutely consistent with his divine justice. God has every right to leave man to perish in his iniquity and deliver him over to condemnation, as Paul makes so clear in Romans 3:19, 3:23, and 6:23.[18]

However, Dort, following the biblical pattern of redemptive history itself, does not stop at man's condemnation but transitions to God's great love for sinners in salvation.[19] While God in no way is obligated to save sinners, out of love he sent his only begotten Son into the world, that whosoever believeth on him should not perish, but have eternal life (cf. 1 John 4:19; John 3:16). Notice, whereas the Remonstrants began with objections to God's sovereign decree, Dort begins with man's depravity, thereby opening the way to introduce the gospel itself.[20]

How is it that sinners, steeped in iniquity and condemnation, are to hear the message of this great gospel of Jesus Christ so that they might believe? Dort answers by affirming that "people may be brought to faith" because "God mercifully sends proclaimers of this very joyful message to the people he wishes and at the time he wishes."[21] It is by the ministry of men who preach the gospel that sinners are "called to repentance and faith in Christ crucified."[22] Dort once again cites Paul who writes, "How shall they believe in him of whom they have not heard? And how shall they hear without someone preaching? And how shall they preach unless they have been sent?" (Romans 10:14–15).[23]

Sinners who do not believe in this gospel only receive the just and awful wrath of God.[24] However, those who receive it and "embrace Jesus the Savior with a true and living faith are delivered through Him from God's anger and from destruction, and receive the gift of eternal life."[25] If one does not believe then the cause or guilt of his unbelief and all his other sins "is not at all in God, but in man."[26] But if man

---

18 "Canons of Dort," 1.1, in *Creeds and Confessions of the Reformation Era*, 2:571.
19 "Canons of Dort," 1.2, in *Creeds and Confessions of the Reformation Era*, 2:571.
20 "Canons of Dort," 1.2, in *Creeds and Confessions of the Reformation Era*, 2:571.
21 "Canons of Dort," 1.3, in *Creeds and Confessions of the Reformation Era*, 2:571.
22 "Canons of Dort," 1.3, in *Creeds and Confessions of the Reformation Era*, 2:571.
23 "Canons of Dort," 1.3, in *Creeds and Confessions of the Reformation Era*, 2:571.
24 "Canons of Dort," 1.4, in *Creeds and Confessions of the Reformation Era*, 2:571.
25 "Canons of Dort," 1.4, in *Creeds and Confessions of the Reformation Era*, 2:571.
26 "Canons of Dort," 1.5, in *Creeds and Confessions of the Reformation Era*, 2:571.

does believe, having faith in Christ, it "is the free gift of God" for Paul says, "It is by grace you have been saved, through faith, and this is not from yourselves; it is a gift of God" (Ephesians 2:8). And again he reminds the Philippians that their faith in Christ was granted to them so that they would indeed believe (Philippians 1:29).[27]

But from where does this gift of faith originate? Dort is clear, "The fact that some receive from God the gift of faith within time, and that others do not, stems from his eternal decision."[28] In other words, it is God himself who determines to whom he will grant the gift of faith. His decree decides man's belief, not the other way around. Scriptural support for such a claim is to be found, says Dort, in Acts 15:18, "For all his works are known to God from eternity" and in Ephesians 1:11, "Who worketh all things after the counsel of his will." From texts like these we learn, says Dort, that God's decree "graciously softens the hearts, however hard, of his chosen ones and inclines them to believe, but by his just judgment he leaves in their wickedness and hardness of heart those who have not been chosen."[29] God is not unfair to bestow his grace on some while denying it to others since bestowing it *at all* is an act of sheer mercy, and to deny it is an act of pure justice. As Dort explains,

> And in this especially is disclosed to us his act-unfathomable, and as merciful as it is just-of distinguishing between people equally lost. This is the well-known decision of election and reprobation revealed in God's word. This decision the wicked, impure, and unstable distort to their own ruin, but it provides holy and godly souls with comfort beyond words.[30]

This brings us to define election in much more detail, which Dort does not fail to do.

---

27 "Canons of Dort," 1.5, in *Creeds and Confessions of the Reformation Era*, 2:571.
28 "Canons of Dort," 1.6, in *Creeds and Confessions of the Reformation Era*, 2:572.
29 "Canons of Dort," 1.6, in *Creeds and Confessions of the Reformation Era*, 2:572.
30 "Canons of Dort," 1.6, in *Creeds and Confessions of the Reformation Era*, 2:572.

Election is the unchangeable purpose of God

When Dort turns to define exactly what divine election is and is not, Dort begins with two significant scriptural passages, Ephesians 1:4–6 and Romans 8:30.[31]

God chose us in Christ, before the foundation of the world, so that we should be holy and blameless before him with love; he predestined us whom he adopted as his children through Jesus Christ, in himself, according to the good pleasure of his will, to the praise of his glorious grace, by which he freely made us pleasing to himself in his beloved (Ephesians 1:4–6).

Those whom he predestined, he also called; and those whom he called, he also justified; and those whom he justified, he also glorified (Romans 8:30).

From Paul's words in both Ephesians and Romans, the Synod of Dort drew several conclusions. (1) Election is the unchangeable and immutable purpose of God.[32] (2) Election is eternal, occurring before

---

31 "Canons of Dort," 1.7, in *Creeds and Confessions of the Reformation Era*, 2:572.

32 "Canons of Dort," 1.7, in *Creeds and Confessions of the Reformation Era*, 2:572. While such a point may seem obvious, it was controversial because the Reformed view of God's decree and will differed considerably from the Arminian view. The Arminians affirmed an antecedent and consequent will. Antecedent to foreseeing who would believe, God wills that all people would be saved. However, consequent to foreseeing that only some would believe God wills to "elect" those whom he foresees will believe and persevere. Therefore, Arminianism distinguishes between the *voluntas antecedens* (antecedent will of God) and the *voluntas consequens* (consequent will of God), which are sometimes called God's primordial benevolence and God's special benevolence. Such a distinction is found in Arminius himself. See Jacob Arminius, "Examination of Dr. Perkins's Pamphlet on Predestination," in *The Writings of James Arminius*, trans. James Nichols (Grand Rapids: Baker, 1956), 3:429–430; William Gene Witt, "Creation, Redemption and Grace in the Theology of Jacob Arminius," (Ph.D. diss., University of Notre Dame, 1993), 2:643–644. See also Stanglin who, quoting Arminius, explains how such a distinction differs so drastically from the Reformed [Keith D. Stanglin, *Arminius on the Assurance of Salvation: the Context, Roots, and Shape of the Leiden Debate, 1603–1609* (Leiden: E. J. Brill, 2007), 225]. On Arminius's view of God's love in relation to his decrees, see William den Boer, "Jacobus Arminius: Theologian of God's Twofold

the foundation of the world. (3) Election overflows from God's "sheer grace" and is according to the "free good pleasure of his will." (4) Those elected "he chose in Christ to salvation" whom He "appointed from eternity to be the Mediator, the Head of all those chosen, and the foundation of their salvation." (5) Those elected "were neither better nor more deserving than the others," but shared with the non-elect one "common misery." (6) Not only has God elected certain sinners in eternity but he has also decreed the means by which they will be saved in time. Dort writes,

> And so he decided [decreed] to give the chosen ones to Christ to be saved, and to call and draw them effectively into Christ's

---

Love," in *Arminius, Arminianism, and Europe: Jacob Arminius (1559/60–1609)*, ed. Marius van Leeuwen, Keith D. Stranglin, and Marijke Tolsma, Brill's Series in Church History 39 (Leiden: E. J. Brill, 2010), 25–50.

Dort, however, rejects this Arminian view because it teaches that "there are various kinds of election of God unto eternal life: the one general and indefinite, the other particular and definite; and that the latter in turn is either incomplete, revocable, non-decisive, and conditional, or complete, irrevocable, decisive, and absolute." Dort continues, "Likewise: That there is one election unto faith and another unto salvation, so that election can be unto justifying faith, without being a decisive election unto salvation" ("Canons of Dort," Rejection of the Errors 1.2, in *Creeds and Confessions of the Reformation Era*, 2:576). Such a rejection matches Dort's statement in canon and article 1.8, "There are not various decrees of election, but one and the same decree respecting all those who shall be saved, both under the Old and the New Testament; since the Scripture declares the good pleasure, purpose, and counsel of the divine will to be one, according to which He has chosen us from eternity, both to grace and to glory, to salvation and to the way of salvation, which He has ordained that we should walk therein (Ephesians 1:4, 5; 2:10)" ("Canons of Dort," 1.8, in *Creeds and Confessions of the Reformation Era*, 2:572–573). Dort also elaborates in Rejection of the Errors 1.3. Dort rejects those who teach that "the good pleasure and purpose of God, of which Scripture makes mention in the doctrine of election, does not consist in this, that God chose certain persons rather than others, but in this, that He chose out of all possible conditions (among which are also the works of the law), or out of the whole order of things, the act of faith which from its very nature is undeserving, as well as its incomplete obedience, as a condition of salvation, and that He would graciously consider this in itself as a complete obedience and count it worthy of the reward of eternal life" ("Canons of Dort," Rejection of the Errors 1.3, in *Creeds and Confessions of the Reformation Era*, 2:571).

fellowship through his word and Spirit. In other words, he decided to grant them true faith in Christ, to justify them, to sanctify them, and finally, after powerfully preserving them in the fellowship of his Son, to glorify them. God did all this in order to demonstrate his mercy, to the praise of the riches of his glorious grace [Eph. 1:4-6].[33]

God decrees not only the ends but the means. These include an effectual call by the Word and Spirit, whereby sinners are drawn into communion with Christ, justified by faith and finally sanctified, which results in glorification due to the preserving hand of God to keep those whom he has elected to the very end. All of these, from election to glorification, occur by God's mercy and for his glory.

Election is unconditional

So far we have seen that for Dort election is purely and solely by God's mercy and grace. Furthermore, Dort rejects the Arminian view which compromises this very mercy and grace.

This same election took place, not on the basis of foreseen faith, of the obedience of faith, of holiness, or of any other good quality and disposition, as though it were based on a prerequisite cause or condition in the person to be chosen, but rather for the purpose of faith, of the obedience of faith, of holiness, and so on.[34]

---

33 "Canons of Dort," 1.7, in *Creeds and Confessions of the Reformation Era*, 2:572.

34 "Canons of Dort," 1.9, in *Creeds and Confessions of the Reformation Era*, 2:573. See also Rejection of the Errors 1.3, 1.4, 1.5, 1.6, and 1.9. For example, Dort says in Rejection of the Errors 1.5 that they reject those who teach that "the incomplete and non-decisive election of particular persons to salvation occurred because of a foreseen faith, conversion, holiness, godliness, which either began or continued for some time; but that the complete and decisive election occurred because of foreseen perseverance unto the end in faith, conversion, holiness, and godliness; and that this is the gracious and evangelical worthiness, for the sake of which he who is chosen is more worthy than he who is not chosen; and that therefore faith, the obedience of faith, holiness, godliness, and perseverance are not fruits of the unchangeable election unto glory: but are conditions, which, being required before hand, were foreseen as being met by those who will be fully elected, and are causes without which the unchangeable elec-

If election is based on foreseen faith, obedience or some quality in man, then grace is no longer grace and election cannot be credited to God's glory alone for man now has a part to play. To the contrary, election is not decided on the basis of what man does, but what man does is the result of whether he is elected. Therefore, election "is the source [fountain] of each of the benefits of salvation. Faith, holiness, and the other saving gifts, and at last eternal life itself, flow forth from election as its fruits and effects."[35] Here Dort is drawing from Ephesians 1:4 once again, arguing that Paul says God has chosen us *that we should be* holy and without blemish before him *not because we were* holy and without blemish before him. Such a distinction may seem minor, but in reality it is the very difference between an Arminian and Calvinist soteriology. The former is a soteriology centred around man's free will decision as opposed to the latter which is a soteriology centred around divine grace.

So if it is not anything in man that grounds God's election, what then is the foundation for divine predestination? Dort once again looks to Scripture, specifically Romans 9:11–13 and Acts 13:48. In Romans 9 we read that before Jacob or Esau had done anything good or bad, God loved Jacob and hated Esau. In other words, God's choice was not made on the basis of anything Jacob or Esau did. The same truth is emphasized in Acts 13:48 where we read, "All who were appointed for eternal life believed." Notice the order of the report. The text does not say as many as believed were ordained to eternal life, as the Arminian must have it. To the contrary, the text says the opposite, namely, that as many as were ordained to eternal life believed. Therefore, Dort concludes, "But the cause of this undeserved election is exclusively the good pleasure of God. This does not

---

tion to glory does not occur." Dort cites in support Romans 9:11, Acts 13:48, Ephesians 1:4, John 15:16, Romans 11:16 and 1 John 4:10. Dort says something similar in regard to the gospel going to certain people and not others. Dort rejects those who teach that "the reason why God sends the gospel to one people rather than to another is not merely and solely the good pleasure of God, but rather the fact that one people is better and worthier than another to which the gospel is not communicated." Dort cites in support Deuteronomy 10:15–16 and Matthew 11:21 ("Canons of Dort," Rejection of the Errors 1.5, in *Creeds and Confessions of the Reformation Era*, 2:577–578).

35 "Canons of Dort," 1.9, in *Creeds and Confessions of the Reformation Era*, 2:573.

involve his choosing certain human qualities or actions from among all those possible as a condition of salvation, but rather involves his adopting certain particular persons from among the common mass of sinners as his own possession."[36] Dort then adds that God is "most wise, unchangeable, all-knowing [omniscient], and almighty [omnipotent]" and therefore his election in no way can be "suspended," "altered, revoked, or annulled." Nor can the elect be "cast off, nor their number be reduced."[37]

Reprobation and the justice of God

Dort insists that its affirmation of the "eternal and undeserved grace of election" is the express testimony of Scripture, which tells us "that not all people have been chosen but that some have not been chosen or have been passed by in God's eternal election."[38] Dort goes on to explain that God,

> on the basis of his entirely free, most just, irreproachable, and unchangeable good pleasure, made the following decision: to leave them in the common misery into which, by their own fault, they have plunged themselves; not to grant them saving faith and the grace of conversion; but finally to condemn and eternally punish them (having been left in their own ways and under his just judgment), not only for their unbelief but also for their other sins, in order to display his justice.[39]

But is God unjust for not electing and granting faith to those whom he could save if he so chooses? If God leaves man in his sin and even

---

36 "Canons of Dort," 1.10, in *Creeds and Confessions of the Reformation Era*, 2:573.

37 "Canons of Dort," 1.11, in *Creeds and Confessions of the Reformation Era*, 2:573.

38 "Canons of Dort," 1.15, in *Creeds and Confessions of the Reformation Era*, 2:574. See also Rejection of the Errors, 1.8 where Dort rejects those who teach that "God, simply by virtue of His righteous will, did not decide either to leave anyone in the fall of Adam and in the common state of sin and condemnation, or to pass anyone by in the communication of grace which is necessary for faith and conversion." Dort cites in support Romans 9:18, Matthew 11:25–26 and 13:22 ("Canons of Dort," Rejection of the Errors 1.8, in *Creeds and Confessions of the Reformation Era*, 2:578–579).

39 "Canons of Dort," 1.15, in *Creeds and Confessions of the Reformation Era*, 2:574.

ordains the very sin he is left in from eternity pass, does this not make God the author of sin? Absolutely not, says Dort. The decree of repro-bation "does not at all make God the author of sin (a blasphemous thought!) but rather its fearful, irreproachable, just judge and avenger."[40] Dort highlights the biblical truth that God is a righteous judge and avenger, an emphasis we saw earlier. As judge and avenger God is not obligated to save anyone and the fact that he does save anyone at all is pure mercy and grace. Therefore, for God to leave a sinner in his sin is not unfair but perfectly just, as all men are by nature children of wrath, dead in their trespasses and sins, deserving nothing but eternal condemnation (Ephesians 2:1–5).

Dort responds to those "who complain about this grace of an unde-served election and about the severity of a just reprobation" by agree-ing with Christ Jesus when he says, "Have I no right to do what I want with my own?" (Matthew 20:15) and also with the apostle Paul, "Who are you, O man, to talk back to God? (Romans 9:20).[41] Dort concludes by submitting to the mystery God himself has left us with.[42] As Paul says in Romans 11:33–36,

> Oh, the depths of the riches both of the wisdom and the know-ledge of God! How unsearchable are his judgments, and his ways beyond tracing out! For who has known the mind of the Lord? Or who has been his counselor? Or who has first given to God, that God should repay him? For from him and through him and to him are all things. To him be the glory forever! Amen.

The Arminians felt it an excuse to appeal to mystery when asked why, if not on the basis of man's faith, God chooses some and not others. However, Dort's appeal to divine mystery is perfectly in line with Scripture as seen in Romans 11:33–36.[43] We can answer, as Scripture

---

40 "Canons of Dort," 1.15, in *Creeds and Confessions of the Reformation Era*, 2:574. For an extensive treatment of reprobation in 1.15 and in the Canons as a whole see Donald W. Sinema, "Reprobation at the Synod of Dort (1618–19) in Light of the History of This Doctrine," (Ph.D. diss., University of St. Michael's College, 1985).

41 "Canons of Dort," 1.18, in *Creeds and Confessions of the Reformation Era*, 2:575.

42 "Canons of Dort," 1.18, in *Creeds and Confessions of the Reformation Era*, 2:575.

43 "Canons of Dort," 1.18, in *Creeds and Confessions of the Reformation Era*, 2:575.

does, that election is based solely on God's good pleasure and will. As to why he chooses one person and not another, Scripture is silent, so we must be content with God's revelation. God's reason is his own and is in accord with his seamless goodness, mercy, justice, and righteousness and of this we can have full assurance.[44]

Divine predestination: source of assurance, humility and holiness
Unspeakable consolation

Now that divine predestination as defined by Dort has been explained, it is necessary to return to the Canons once again to discuss how certain articles draw an explicit connection from election to personal and corporate spirituality. We begin with 1.6 where we read the following,

> The fact that some receive from God the gift of faith within time, and that others do not, stems from his eternal decision. For "all his works are known to God from eternity" [Acts 15:18; Ephesians 1:11]. In accordance with his decision he graciously softens the hearts, however hard, of his chosen ones and inclines them

---

44 "Canons of Dort," 1.18, in *Creeds and Confessions of the Reformation Era*, 2:575. It is significant to observe the language Dort uses, especially in canon 1.15. Those whom God does not elect are "*passed by* in God's eternal election" for he has decreed "*to leave* them in the common misery into which, by their own fault, they have plunged themselves; not to grant them saving faith and the grace of conversion; but finally to condemn and eternally punish them (having been *left* in their own ways and under his just judgment), not only for their unbelief but also for all their other sins, in order to display his justice" ("Canons of Dort," 1.15, in *Creeds and Confessions of the Reformation Era*, 2:574). One must detect the indirect language used here when referring to reprobation: "passed by," "to leave" and "left." J.V. Fesko notes that all of the delegations (except for Gomarus and south Holland) "spoke of reprobation in Augustinian terms of preterition, or non-election, rather than in terms of predestination as Calvin does in his *Institutes*" [J.V. Fesko, *Diversity Within the Reformed Tradition: Supra- and Infralapsarianism in Calvin, Dort, and Westminster* (Greenville: Reformed Academic Press, 20001), 196–197 (cf. 198)]. For a comparison of Calvin and Dort on predestination, see S.J. Hayhow, "Calvin and the Synod of Dort," *The Banner of Truth* 330 (1991): 11–15; John Murray, "Calvin, Dort and Westminster—a comparative study," in *Crisis in the Reformed Churches*, 150–160. See Appendix 1 on whether or not Dort assumed supra- or infralapsarianism.

to believe, but by his just judgment he leaves in their wickedness and hardness of heart those who have not been chosen. And in this especially is disclosed to us his act—unfathomable, and as merciful as it is just—of distinguishing between people equally lost. This is the well-known decision of election and reprobation revealed in God's word. This decision the wicked, impure, and unstable distort to their own ruin, but it provides holy and godly souls with comfort beyond words.[45]

It is in canon 1.6 that we first see a glimpse of how Calvinism has massive implications for personal piety and spirituality. The wicked deserve reprobation, and God's decision to leave them in their wickedness and hardness of heart the impure and unstable distort to their own ruin. However, for the elect predestination is the cause of great comfort, so great a comfort that words are insufficient for the holy and godly soul. Exactly what type of comfort Dort has in mind is seen in canon 1.12, where we read that assurance of one's eternal and unchangeable election is something that comes in due time, "though by various stages and in differing measures."[46] Such an assurance, however, is not received or attained by "inquisitive searching into the hidden and deep things of God, but by noticing within themselves, with spiritual joy and holy delight, the unmistakable fruits of election pointed out in God's word."[47] What are these infallible fruits in God's Word? They are "true faith in Christ, a child-like fear of God, a godly sorrow for their sin, a hunger and thirst for righteousness."[48]

Assurance of salvation in Christ is the great comfort that comes in affirming the doctrine of unconditional election.[49] Election is to

---

45 "Canons of Dort," 1.6, in *Creeds and Confessions of the Reformation Era*, 2:572.
46 "Canons of Dort," 1.12, in *Creeds and Confessions of the Reformation Era*, 2:573.
47 "Canons of Dort," 1.12, in *Creeds and Confessions of the Reformation Era*, 2:573.
48 "Canons of Dort," 1.12, in *Creeds and Confessions of the Reformation Era*, 2:573.
49 Joel Beeke defines assurance as follows: "Assurance of faith is the believer's conviction that, by God's grace, he belongs to Christ, has received full pardon for all sins, and will inherit eternal life. Someone who has true assurance not only believes in Christ for salvation but also knows that he believes and is graciously loved by God. Such assurance includes freedom from guilt, joy in God, and a sense of belonging to the family of God." Beeke continues, "Assurance is dynamic; it varies

remind the believer that he is safe in the arms of God, for God has chosen him before the foundation of the world.[50] However, Dort is quick to qualify the serenity of the comfort that comes with assurance. Not all receive assurance in equal measure nor do all receive assurance all at once. Rather assurance comes "by various stages and in differing measures."[51] Such a qualification is key lest a saint despair because he does not feel the assurance he previously delighted in. Nevertheless, though assurance may come in differing stages and measures, it is to be found in the believer by noticing the unmistakable and infallible fruits.[52] When the believer recognizes the presence of these fruits of election, he will undoubtedly be moved to "spiritual joy" and "holy delight [pleasure]," as he is assured of his salvation in Christ.[53]

---

according to conditions and is capable of growing in force and fruitfulness" [Joel R. Beeke, *Living for God's Glory: An Introduction to Calvinism* (Grand Rapids: Reformation Heritage, 2008), 119]. It is not the purpose of this essay to explore definitions of assurance or the debate over where there is continuity or discontinuity between Calvin and the later Calvinists in their understanding of assurance. However, I am in agreement with Beeke (contra R.T. Kendall and Basil Hall) in his thesis that "Calvinism's wrestlings with assurance were quantitatively beyond, but not qualitatively contradictory to that of Calvin." See Joel R. Beeke, *The Quest for Full Assurance: The Legacy of Calvin and His Successors* (Edinburgh: Banner of Truth, 1999), 3. I would argue that the same is true of the divines at Dort. For the case for continuity on other Reformed issues, see Richard A. Muller, *Christ and the Decree: Christology and Predestination in Reformed Theology from Calvin to Perkins* (Grand Rapids: Baker, 1988); Richard A. Muller, *Post-Reformation Reformed Dogmatics*, 4 vols. (Grand Rapids: Baker, 2003); Richard A. Muller, *After Calvin: Studies in the Development of a Theological Tradition* (Oxford and New York: Oxford University Press, 2003); Paul Helm, *Calvin and the Calvinists* (Edinburgh: Banner of Truth, 1982).

50 Puritanism as a whole grounded the believer's assurance in election. "English Puritan divines like…William Perkins and Richard Sibbes…took the Reformed doctrine of election to heart, fostering an 'experimental predestinarianism' that encouraged the believer to seek assurance that they were chosen by God for salvation" [John Coffey and Paul C.H. Lim, "Introduction," in *The Cambridge Companion to Puritanism* (Cambridge: Cambridge University Press, 2008), 4].

51 "Canons of Dort," 1.12, in *Creeds and Confessions of the Reformation Era*, 2:573.

52 "Canons of Dort," 1.12, in *Creeds and Confessions of the Reformation Era*, 2:573.

53 "Canons of Dort," 1.12, in Creeds and Confessions of the Reformation Era, 2:573.

Daily humiliation and ardent love

However, as if to guard the Christian from becoming arrogant in recognizing his own election and fruitfulness, Dort explains the type of attitude assurance should engender:

> In their awareness and assurance of this election God's children daily find greater cause to humble themselves before God, to adore the fathomless depth of his mercies, to cleanse themselves, and to give fervent love in return to him who first so greatly loved them. This is far from saying that this teaching concerning election, and reflection upon it, make God's children lax in observing his commandments or carnally self-assured. By God's just judgment this does usually happen to those who casually take for granted the grace of election or engage in idle and brazen talk about it but are unwilling to walk in the ways of the chosen.[54]

The child of God, aware and confident of his election, is moved by such assurance on a daily basis to find greater cause to humble himself before God because he recognizes that his election and even the assurance of his election are not due to his own righteousness but due entirely to the sovereign grace and mercy of God. If election were conditional, the child of God would find reason in himself to boast and humility would be lost. However, since God's election is not based on anything foreseen within man and man's assurance is a gift from God, there is no response fitting except that of Christian humility and thanksgiving. Children of God, therefore, have every reason for adoring the depth of his mercies, for cleansing themselves, and rendering grateful returns of ardent love to him who first manifested so great a love toward them.[55] Once again, unconditional election is the very basis not only for comfort and assurance but for humility, praise, worship and love, as the believer fathoms God's mercy, loves his Saviour and seeks to rid himself of sin.

Furthermore, Dort anticipates the objection that unconditional election leads the elect to be lax in observing God's commandments

---

54 "Canons of Dort," 1.13, in *Creeds and Confessions of the Reformation Era*, 2:574.
55 "Canons of Dort," 1.13, in *Creeds and Confessions of the Reformation Era*, 2:574.

or carnally self-assured. Dort counters by arguing that this does happen to those who are casual and presumptuous, taking for granted electing grace and engaging themselves in idle and foolish talk about grace.[56] They are unwilling to walk in the ways of the elect. In other words, if one does become lax, fostering a carnal self-assurance, he is living inconsistently with the doctrine of unconditional election itself. Election, in Scripture, is never an excuse for lax carnality but proactive deeds in holiness.[57] It is only when the elect seek daily obedience to Christ, trusting in the gospel promises of the cross, that they can have a proper assurance of their election. Edwin Palmer, reflecting on Dort, insightfully remarks,

> Clarification: It is true that if one is elected, he can never be lost; and that once saved, always saved. But how does a person know whether or not he is elected? He has no secret access into the hidden counsel of God. There is, however, a divinely ordained way for everyone to know: his present possession of faith. If one believes, such faith is an infallible sign that God loved and chose him, for faith is the gift of God's electing love.[58]

Palmer continues, "If anyone should think that he was elected and should reason that it makes no difference whether or not he continues to believe, he would be rationalizing and departing from the clear teaching of Scripture. For although the Bible teaches eternal security, it never proclaims carnal security."[59] Palmer is on solid ground in pointing to 1 Peter 1:1–5 and 2 Peter 1:10 to verify such a claim. These passages read as follows,

> Peter, an apostle of Jesus Christ, To those who are elect exiles of the dispersion in Pontus, Galatia, Cappadocia, Asia, and Bithynia, according to the foreknowledge of God the Father, in the sancti-

56 "Canons of Dort," 1.13, in *Creeds and Confessions of the Reformation Era*, 2:574.

57 "Canons of Dort," 1.13, in *Creeds and Confessions of the Reformation Era*, 2:574.

58 Edwin H. Palmer, "The Significance of the Canons for Pastoral Work," in *Crisis in the Reformed Churches*, 144.

59 Palmer, "The Significance of the Canons for Pastoral Work," 146.

fication of the Spirit, for obedience to Jesus Christ and for sprin-
kling with his blood: May grace and peace be multiplied to you.
Blessed be the God and Father of our Lord Jesus Christ! According to his great mercy, he has caused us to be born again to a
living hope through the resurrection of Jesus Christ from the
dead, to an inheritance that is imperishable, undefiled, and
unfading, kept in heaven for you, who by God's power are being
guarded through faith for a salvation ready to be revealed in the
last time (1 Peter 1:1–5).

Therefore, brothers, be all the more diligent to make your calling
and election sure, for if you practice theses [godly] qualities you
will never fall (2 Peter 1:10).

Elsewhere Palmer helpfully elaborates,

Moreover, when correctly understood, the teachings of the Canons of Dort do not feed the flames of indolence and sin, but, on
the contrary, induce one to be a better Christian. It is precisely
the Calvinist who, knowing that by nature he has not an iota of
a good thought, desire or deed; and realizing that he has been
saved by grace all the way through, even to the extent of receiving
the ability to believe on Christ—it is exactly such a Christian who
will become more humble, increasingly filled with praise and
more determined to live a holier life out of thankfulness. For he
has more to be thankful for than one who thinks he is only par-
tially bad.[60]

Palmer points us to two passages:

Put on then, as God's chosen ones, holy and beloved, compas-
sionate hearts, kindness, humility, meekness, and patience, bear-
ing with one another and, if one has a complaint against another,
forgiving each other; as the Lord has forgiven you, so you also
must forgive (Colossians 3:12–13).

---

60 Palmer, "The Significance of the Canons for Pastoral Work," 146.

But since we belong to the day, let us be sober, having put on the breastplate of faith and love, and for a helmet the hope of salvation. For God has not destined us for wrath, but to obtain salvation through our Lord Jesus Christ, who died for us so that whether we are awake or asleep we might live with him. Therefore encourage one another and build one another up, just as you are doing (1 Thessalonians 5:8–11).

Having these passages in mind, he writes, "Strikingly—contrary to popular opinion—the Bible reasons in the exact opposite way for those who think that the teaching of election leads to moral indifference. Paul appeals to election as a motivation for greater exertion!"[61]

The measure of holiness and faith

Nonetheless, Dort is not so naïve as to believe that all the elect experience assurance in the same measure. For many, assurance is lacking. Dort identifies and addresses three types of people. First, there are those who do not yet actively experience within themselves a "living faith in Christ" or an "assured confidence of heart."[62] These lack a peace of conscience, a zeal for childlike obedience and a "glorying in God through Christ." Despite all this they nevertheless use "the means by which God has promised to work these things [graces] in us."[63] Dort's counsel to such Christians is that they should not be "alarmed at the mention of reprobation" nor "count themselves among the reprobate."[64] In other words, though they lack peace, zeal and passion, they should not despair, contemplating whether they should be counted among the wicked. Rather, Dort advises them to press on, persistently using the means God has promised to use to work spiritual fruit within. By doing so they should fervently desire for a time to come when they will experience God's grace in fuller measure. Moreover, while waiting for such grace they should do so in reverence and humility knowing that the God who predestines is the same God who

---

61 Palmer, "The Significance of the Canons for Pastoral Work," 146.

62 "Canons of Dort," 1.16, in *Creeds and Confessions of the Reformation Era*, 2:575.

63 "Canons of Dort," 1.16, in *Creeds and Confessions of the Reformation Era*, 2:575.

64 "Canons of Dort," 1.16, in *Creeds and Confessions of the Reformation Era*, 2:575.

will provide a time of assurance. Dort's emphasis on assurance as the fruit of predestination leads Cornelis P. Venema to conclude,

> A fair-minded reader of the Canons could scour every nook and cranny of the five heads of doctrine, contemplating every article in turn, and discover an absence of any evidence for the kind of fatalism or uncertainty of salvation that they allegedly encourage. Because salvation does not hang upon the thin thread of their own initiative and perseverance, but upon the solid chain of God's electing purpose in Christ, believers may be assured of their salvation. Sovereign and merciful election furnishes believers with the occasion to give thanks to God on the one hand, and rest confidently in his gracious favor in Christ on the other."[65]

The second group of people Dort identifies are those who desire to turn to God, please God and be delivered from sin, but are not yet able to "make such progress along the way of godliness and faith as they would like."[66] This second group of believers seems to possess the desire and zeal that the first group lacked. However, due to the constant struggle with sin they often fail to turn to God and find their satisfaction in him alone. They want to "be delivered from the body of death" but are impeded in making progress in godliness and faith as they desire.[67] Should such a person fear that he is one of the reprobate rather than the elect? No, they should not fear the teaching of reprobation, for God is merciful and he has promised to be faithful to his elect, not snuffing them out (like a smoldering wick) or breaking them apart (like a bruised reed), but advancing them in godliness in due time.[68]

The third group, unlike the first two, receives no assurance or comfort for they have forgotten God and Jesus Christ the Saviour, abandon-

---

65 Venema points to Kaajan who argues that Dort had this pastoral emphasis by design [H. Kaajan, *De Groote Synode van Dordrecht in 1618–1619* (Amersterdam: De Standaard, n. d.), 175]. See Cornelis P. Venema, "The Election and Salvation of the Children of Believers Who Die in Infancy: A Study of Article I/17 of the Canons of Dort," *Mid-America Journal of Theology* 17 (2006): 58.

66 "Canons of Dort," 1.16, in *Creeds and Confessions of the Reformation Era*, 2:575.

67 "Canons of Dort," 1.16, in *Creeds and Confessions of the Reformation Era*, 2:575.

68 "Canons of Dort," 1.16, in *Creeds and Confessions of the Reformation Era*, 2:575.

ing themselves to the "pleasures of the flesh" and the "cares of the world."[69] They have every reason to fear the teaching of reprobation "as long as they do not seriously turn to God."[70] Indeed, the teaching of reprobation serves them as a warning to turn to God lest they perish in their sins.

The spirit of discretion and piety

The teacher of such hard doctrines as predestination and reprobation must keep these three types of people in mind, setting forth his teaching with reverence, "in the spirit of discretion and piety, for the glory of God's most holy Name, and for enlivening and comforting His people, without vainly attempting to investigate the secret ways of the Most High (Acts 20:27; Rom. 11:33–34; 12:3; Heb. 6:17–18)."[71] Additionally, teachers and pastors must utilize a mind of humility, in order to "deal with this teaching in a godly [pious] and reverent manner, in the academic institutions as well as in the churches" whether it be in speaking or in writing.[72] The purpose is to teach predestination "with a view to the glory of God's name, holiness of life, and the comfort of anxious [afflicted] souls."[73]

Finally, Dort concludes canon 1 with Rejection of the Errors (of the Remonstrants), two of which are particularly important for our purposes here. In Rejection I.6, Dort argues that to agree with the

---

69 "Canons of Dort," 1.16, in *Creeds and Confessions of the Reformation Era*, 2:575.

70 "Canons of Dort," 1.16, in *Creeds and Confessions of the Reformation Era*, 2:575.

71 The fact that Dort turns to address the teacher and how he should instruct his students on these issues reveals the ecclesiological method the Synod of Dort took in writing the canons. As Godfrey states, "When the time came to write the canons, the synod had to choose between these two methods of presentation: between the scholastic mode, that is, the technical form of a theological school lecture, and a more popular manner, addressed to the church as a whole for its edification. Delegates decided that it would be most fruitful to frame the canons so that they might be easily understood by and edifying to the churches. Hence the canons are not scholastic but simple and straightforward in format" [W. Robert Godfrey, *Reformation Sketches: Insights into Luther, Calvin, and the Confessions* (Phillipsburg: P & R, 2003), 131].

72 "Canons of Dort," Conclusion: Rejection of False Accusations, in *Creeds and Confessions of the Reformation Era*, 2:599.

73 "Canons of Dort," Conclusion: Rejection of False Accusations, in *Creeds and Confessions of the Reformation Era*, 2:599.

Arminians that "not every election to salvation is unchangeable, but that some of the chosen can perish and do in fact perish eternally, with no decision of God to prevent it" is not only a "gross error" that robs God of his glory in preserving his elect, but it is to "destroy the comfort of the godly concerning the steadfastness of their election," which is contrary to the Scriptures.[74] The Scriptures Dort has in mind include Matthew 24:24 which teaches that "the elect cannot be led astray," and John 6:39 where we learn that "Christ does not lose those given to him by the Father," and finally Romans 8:30 where we discover that "those whom God predestined, called and justified, he also glorifies."[75] Therefore, the synod rejects the errors of those who teach that in this life there is "no fruit, no awareness, and no assurance of one's unchangeable election to glory, except as conditional upon something changeable and contingent [uncertain]."[76] Dort explains that not only is this "absurd to speak of an uncertain assurance," but these things also militate against how the Bible describes the Christian's experience. Christians can rejoice with the apostle Paul (Ephesians 1:4) because they have "an awareness of their election."[77] Likewise, according to Christ's admonition, Christians can celebrate, as Christ's disciples did, that "their names have been written in heaven (Luke 10:20)."[78] Moreover, Christians are able to "hold up against the flaming arrows of the devil's temptations the awareness of their election, with the question, 'Who will bring any charge against those whom God has chosen?' [Romans 8:33)."[79] It is this last reference that is of particular importance, namely, that believers are able to hold up their awareness of election against

74 "Canons of Dort," Rejection of the Errors I.6, in *Creeds and Confessions of the Reformation Era*, 2:578.

75 "Canons of Dort," Rejection of the Errors I.6, in *Creeds and Confessions of the Reformation Era*, 2:578.

76 "Canons of Dort," Rejection of the Errors I.7, in *Creeds and Confessions of the Reformation Era*, 2:578.

77 "Canons of Dort," Rejection of the Errors I.7, in *Creeds and Confessions of the Reformation Era*, 2:578.

78 "Canons of Dort," Rejection of the Errors I.7, in *Creeds and Confessions of the Reformation Era*, 2:578.

79 "Canons of Dort," Rejection of the Errors I.7, in *Creeds and Confessions of the Reformation Era*, 2:578.

the flaming arrows of the devil's temptations. One's awareness of his election is a two-edged sword: (1) it is reason to rejoice and (2) it is to be shoved in the face of Satan, as a shield against his fiery arrows that seek to tempt and destroy faith.

Conclusion

Dort's conclusion to the canons is most illuminating. Dort detests those who argue that the Reformed doctrine of predestination "leads off the minds of men from all piety and religion," that it is used by Satan who "lies in wait for all, and from which he wounds multitudes, and mortally strikes through many with darts both of despair and security," and that it "renders men carnally secure, since they are persuaded by it that nothing can hinder the salvation of the elect" and can "live as they please" and therefore may "safely perpetrate every species of the most atrocious crimes."[80] To the contrary, as demonstrated in this chapter, the Synod of Dort showed from Scripture that the doctrine of divine predestination actually establishes the Christian's assurance of salvation, comforting troubled souls that the God who has elected them will preserve them to the end without fail. Predestination is not a motivator for laxity and carnality but the very source of good works and the ammunition needed to shield the believer from the fiery darts of the devil, which seek to lead the believer's conscience to despair.

---

80 "Canons of Dort," Conclusion: Rejection of False Accusations, in *Creeds and Confessions of the Reformation Era*, 2:598–599.

"I am the good shepherd. The good shepherd lays down his life for the sheep."
—JOHN 10:11

"I am praying for them. I am not praying for the world but for those whom you have given me, for they are yours."—JOHN 17:9

Husbands, love your wives, as Christ loved the church and gave himself up for her, that he might sanctify her, having cleansed her by the washing of water with the word, so that he might present the church to himself in splendor, without spot or wrinkle or any such thing, that she might be holy and without blemish.—EPHESIANS 5:25–27

Since therefore the children share in flesh and blood, he himself likewise partook of the same things, that through death he might destroy the one who has the power of death, that is, the devil, and deliver all those who through fear of death were subject to lifelong slavery. For surely it is not angels that he helps, but he helps the offspring of Abraham.—HEBREWS 2:14–16

And they sang a new song, saying,

"Worthy are you to take the scroll
and to open its seals,
for you were slain, and by your blood you ransomed people for God
from every tribe and language and people and nation,
and you have made them a kingdom and priests to our God,
and they shall reign on the earth."—REVELATION 5:9–10

4

Particular atonement
Cause for personal and corporate worship

Introduction

For the Calvinist, few doctrines are as precious and personal as limited atonement, the belief that Christ purchased the redemption of the elect. Why is this the case? If, argues the Calvinist, Christ died for all people without exception, not actually securing salvation for anyone in particular, but merely making salvation a possibility, then the love of Christ is not in any way special for the elect. Rather, it is equal for all, elect and non-elect alike. In order to understand how disheartening such a view is one must turn to the apostle Paul in Ephesians 5 where we read, "Husbands, love your wives, as Christ loved the church and gave himself up for her, that he might sanctify her, having cleansed her by the washing of water with the word, so that he might present the church to himself in splendor, without spot or wrinkle or any such thing, that she might be holy and without blemish" (Ephesians 5:25–27). Here Paul describes a special love Christ has only for his church. This special love is exemplified in a husband's love for his wife. A husband does not love all women equally. Imagine how insulting it would be for a husband to tell his wife that while he loves her, he does not love her in a way that is any different than his love for all women. Indeed, he says, he loves all women equally! Thankfully, this is not the case with Christ. Christ has a special love for his bride, the church. Therefore, when he goes to the cross it is specifically for her (John 10:11; 17:9; Hebrews 2:14–16). How sweet and precious this love is for those who belong to Christ! For believers, Christ's love is not general and generic, but personal and particular to them. It is on the basis of this love that the believer has a certain confidence that before the throne of God he is without spot or wrinkle, thanks to the atoning work of Christ on the cross. Consequently, it is the doctrine of particular atonement that the framers of the Canons of Dort believed should elicit persistent love and worship of Christ, both here and in eternity.

The Remonstrant doctrine of universal atonement

In *The Opinions of the Remonstrants*, the Arminians begin by getting right to the point concerning the universality of the merit of the death of Christ. The "price of the redemption which Christ offered to God the Father is not only in itself and by itself sufficient for the redemption of the whole human race but has also been paid for all men and for every man, according to the decree, will, and grace of God the Father."[1] Therefore, "no one is absolutely excluded from the participation in the fruits of Christ's death by an absolute and antecedent decree of God."[2] Stated otherwise, the atonement paid for the sins of every man, without exception. This was the very intention of God, says the Arminian, because it was according to his decree, will and grace that Christ should die on behalf of every man.

---

1   "Appendix H: The Opinions of the Remonstrants," 2.1, in *Crisis in the Reformed Churches: Essays in Commemoration of the Great Synod of Dort, 1618–1619*, ed. Peter Y. De Jong (Grand Rapids: Reformed Fellowship, 1968), 224.

2   "Appendix H: The Opinions of the Remonstrants," 2.1, in *Crisis in the Reformed Churches*, 224.

While 2.1 uses the language of "redemption" to say Christ paid the price for all men, 2.2 uses the language of "merit" and "reconciliation." The Remonstrants argue that "Christ has, by the merit of his death, so reconciled God the Father to the whole human race that the Father, on account of that merit, without giving up His righteousness and truth, has been able and has willed to make and confirm a new covenant of grace with sinners and men liable to damnation."[3] In other words, the covenant of grace itself is dependent upon the merit of Christ's death for every man. It is because Christ has reconciled God the Father to all of mankind that he is also able to confirm and establish this covenant with those doomed to condemnation.

However, the Remonstrants were not universalists, believing that because Christ has atoned for every man so also will every man be saved. To the contrary, the Remonstrants qualify their previous articles by stating in 2.3 that even though Christ has "merited reconciliation with God and remission of sins for all men and for every man, yet no one, according to the pact of the new and gracious covenant, becomes a true partaker of the benefits obtained by the death of Christ in any other way than by faith."[4] Here we see the conditionality of the atonement. Just as election is conditioned upon faith, so also is the efficacy of the atonement merited by Christ. While Christ merited reconciliation and the remission of sins for every person, its efficiency is void unless man wills to embrace it by faith. The Remonstrants go on to explain, while Christ merited the remission of sins, man's sins are not forgiven until he actually and truly believes in Christ.[5] Therefore, it is essential to observe that while the Calvinist may limit the *extent* of the atonement (as we have yet to see), the Arminian limits the *efficacy* of the atonement. Or as Peter Feenstra states, "The Arminians limit and restrict Christ's work of atonement so that little or nothing is accomplished without the will of man. If man does not choose for God,

---

3 "Appendix H: The Opinions of the Remonstrants," 2.2, in *Crisis in the Reformed Churches*, 224.

4 "Appendix H: The Opinions of the Remonstrants," 2.3, in *Crisis in the Reformed Churches*, 224–225.

5 "Appendix H: The Opinions of the Remonstrants," 2.3, in *Crisis in the Reformed Churches*, 225.

atonement is powerless. Christ's work really only gives the possibility of salvation."[6]

The Reformed affirmation of particular atonement
Tension and agreement

As the Synod of Dort gathered to write its response to the second canon there was a Reformed consensus that affirmed the particularity and efficacy of the atonement. As Robert Godfrey explains,

> They were all part of the Reformed consensus which held that Christ had died with a particular intention for the elect. They were convinced that there was nothing novel or strange about this doctrine, but that it was an important clarification of the doctrine of the work of Christ. They knew that it had been taught by the fathers of Reformed Christianity and was to be found implicitly or explicitly in the writings of Christians throughout the centuries. They were agreed that the Arminians who rejected this doctrine tended toward the quicksand of Popery, Pelagianism and Socinianism.[7]

However, despite this strong tradition from which they were to draw, there were unforeseen challenges. As Godfrey observes, all the "members of the Synod agreed that the Remonstrants' theses were completely unacceptable, but they found that they could not agree so easily on an acceptable orthodox reply to the Remonstrant position."[8] Tension and quarrels resulted.[9]

---

6   Peter G. Feenstra, *Unspeakable Comfort: A Commentary on The Canons of Dort* (Winnipeg: Premier, 1997), 66.

7   William Robert Godfrey, "Tensions Within International Calvinism: The Debate on the Atonement at the Synod of Dort, 1618–1619," (Ph.D., diss., Stanford University, 1974), 130.

8   Godfrey, "Tensions Within International Calvinism," 151.

9   For example, John Hales' letter of January 15, 1619, shows that a debate ensued over whether or not Christ is the *Fundamentum Electionis*, namely, the author of election or only the executor. Martinius affirmed Christ as the author and Gomarus became so enraged that he challenged Martinius to a duel! Bogerman successfully calmed Gomarus. Godfrey explains the theological dilemma, "For Gomarus the question of

Problems first began when Martinius of Breme expressed his modi-
fications of the Reformed understanding of the extent of the atonement. We discover from John Hales,

> Martinius, as it seems, is somewhat favourable to some Tenants
> of the Remonstrants concerning Reprobation, the latitude of
> Christ's merit, the Salvation of Infants, etc. and to bring him to
> some conformity was there a private meeting of the Foreign
> Divines upon Wednesday morning in my Lord Bishop's Lodging,
> in which thus much was obtain'd, that though he would not leave
> his Conclusions, yet he promised moderation and temper in such
> manner, that there would be no dissention in the Synod by reason
> of any opinion of his.[10]

Martinius's promise that his moderate views would not cause dissen-
tion was only temporarily reassuring, for his views on the atonement
soon became the central issue in the debate. Again we read of the
conversations between Bishop Carleton and Martinius,

> My Lord Bishop of late hath taken some pains with Martinius of
> Breme, to bring him from his opinion of Universal Grace. By
> chance I came to see his Letter written to Martinius in which he
> expounded that place in the third of John, God so loved the world,

---

Christ as *Fundamentum Electionis* was a familiar Remonstrant evasion. By declaring
Christ to be the Author of election, the Remonstrants thought they could strengthen
their contention that the sacrifice on the cross preceded the decree of election. On
the other hand, the strict Calvinists saw that by declaring that the work of Christ was
simply to fulfil the antecedent decree of election, they could more easily defend their
position. Martinius, as a foreign delegate from Bremen, was probably unfamiliar with
the background of this debate. Undoubtedly he was only trying to re-enforce the
centrality of Christ in the process of election and salvation" (Godfrey, "Tensions Within
International Calvinism," 152).

10 John Hales, *Golden Remains of the Ever Memorable Mr. John Hales of Eton College*
(London, 1659), 72, as quoted in Godfrey, "Tensions Within International Calvinism,"
153. See also Homer C. Hoeksema, *The Voice of Our Fathers* (Grand Rapids: Reformed
Free, 1980), 23–25.

that he gave his only begotten Son etc. which is the strongest ground upon which Martinius rests himself.[11]

However, Martinius was not alone in his views. He would eventually be joined by Samuel Ward of the English delegation and John Davenant as well, who appealed to the Thirty Nine Articles of the Church of England. Ward, for example, "stressed the general as well as the particular significance of the death of Christ."[12] The responsibility then fell to Bishop Carleton and George Balcanqual to make peace and also to write to England to discover the official position.[13]

The English delegation was divided at first. "Some of the English delegates supported the moderate position of Martinius while others favored the firm position clearly espoused by the majority at the Synod."[14] Godfrey outlines the three issues of debate among the English delegation: (1) The first revolves around the sufficiency and efficiency of the atonement and whether such a distinction should be affirmed. In short, this distinction maintained that while Christ's death is of infinite value, sufficient for the sins of the whole world, nevertheless, it is intended to be efficacious only for the elect. Many strict Calvinists "wished to abandon the distinction despite the fact, as Balcanqual noted, that the idea of sufficiency was taught by most of the Reformed Doctors and the Bishop of Salisbury."[15] (2) Also,

---

11 Hales, *Golden Remains*, 72, as quoted in Godfrey, "Tensions Within International Calvinism," 154. However, Godfrey later qualifies the position of Martinius by arguing that he still affirmed that there was a special decree only for the elect by which the saving benefits of the atonement were applied. Likewise, Martinius maintained that faith is a gift from God only given to the elect. "These theses revealed that however much Martinius, like Davenant, wished to expand the notion of sufficiency beyond the bounds that most of the strict Calvinists were willing to accept, he maintained the Calvinist position that all efficacy in the process of salvation came from God alone. Thus, in no sense could Martinius rightly be associated with the Remonstrants or a 'semi-Remonstrant' cause" (Godfrey, "Tensions Within International Calvinism," 198).

12 Godfrey, "Tensions Within International Calvinism," 176.

13 Hales, *Golden Remains*, appendix, 2–3.

14 Godfrey, "Tensions Within International Calvinism," 167; Hales, *Golden Remains*, appendix, 2.

15 Godfrey, "Tensions Within International Calvinism," 172. One such delegation was the Genevan delegates who "implicitly rejected the distinction commonly made

should the sufficiency of the atonement be broadened in its meaning, beyond the intrinsic worth of the atonement? Martinius answered that it should. (3) Finally, does the phrase the "whole world" (*totius mundi*) refer to all men or only the elect? Godfrey notes that Balcanqual's interpretation of Matthew 26:28 and Augustine's Epistle 48 limit the "whole world" to the elect.[16] Ultimately, some in the English delegation were uncertain, which led them to wonder whether they should simply refrain from commenting on such an issue.

The final submission of the English *Judicium* included six propositions and three rejections of errors.[17] Here we see the Reformed view of limited atonement affirmed but not without certain concessions to satisfy the more moderate English delegates. In the first two propositions the traditional Calvinist position is upheld, as expressed by Bishop Carleton, Balcanqual and Thomas Goad. "They emphasized the strict Calvinist position that Christ died efficaciously for the elect to give them faith and all other gifts necessary for salvation."[18] It was obvious that this was the "majority feeling." However, King James would never allow division within the English delegation, which the delegates knew all too well. Therefore, it was the last four propositions that gave "significant concession to the consciences of Davenant and Ward."[19] For example, not only was a special, saving love for the elect affirmed but so also was a general love toward all of creation.[20] Also,

---

between sufficiency and efficiency." "Their nearest approximation of that distinction occurred in proposition two where they spoke of the 'infinite value of his death.' Except for this one reference, all the propositions remained completely within the realm of the efficient" (Godfrey, "Tensions Within International Calvinism," 195). The same seems to be the case with the Emden delegation (Godfrey, "Tensions Within International Calvinism," 203). For a more extensive study of the Genevan delegates, see Nicolas Fornerod, "'The Canons of the Synod Had Shot Off the Advocate's Head': A Reappraisal of the Genevan Delegation at the Synod of Dordt," in *Revisiting the Synod of Dordt (1618–1619)*, eds. Aza Goudriaan and Fred van Lieburg (Leiden: Brill, 2011), 181–216.

16 Godfrey, "Tensions Within International Calvinism," 172.
17 For an extensive treatment of who wrote each proposition, see Godfrey, "Tensions Within International Calvinism," 165–224.
18 Godfrey, "Tensions Within International Calvinism," 177.
19 Godfrey, "Tensions Within International Calvinism," 177.
20 *The Collegiate Suffrage of the Divines of Great Britain Concerning the Five Articles*

as we have yet to explore, they sought to address the issue of "sufficiency" as well, stating that Christ's death is of infinite value and worth, even though the intention of the atonement is only designed to make remission for the sins of the elect. Finally, the Rejection of Errors seems to use the language of compromise. As Godfrey explains, the "received distinction between sufficiency and efficiency and the received restriction of 'totum mundum' to the elect were maintained, but in a much broader and inclusive sense than is true of most of the Theses of other delegations."[21]

On March 17, 1619, news from England finally arrived, though far too late as the English delegation had already presented their thesis on the atonement. One letter was from Archbishop Abbot and the other from Sir Robert Naunton, Secretary of State. Abbot consulted King James who concluded that "the delegates should support the traditional Reformed doctrine."[22] Naunton's letter advised moderation. Ultimately, no contradiction was seen between the limited atonement view of the majority of representatives at Dort and the Thirty-Nine Articles.[23]

Even after the final draft of canon two was presented for discussion on April 16, debate continued among the English delegation, delaying final approval of the canon. However, after one last debate, compromise was met on April 18, as a consensus not only rejected the Arminian view of universal atonement but affirmed the Reformed view of particular atonement.[24] It is to the specifics of this Reformed view that we now turn our attention.

The satisfaction of divine wrath by Christ

Dort's second canon responds to the Arminian doctrine of universal atonement. However, like canon 1 on predestination, Dort once again begins with the redemptive-historical framework of Scripture in mind.

Controverted in the Low Countries... (London, 1629), 43–64. See also Godfrey, "Tensions Within International Calvinism," 177.

21 Godfrey, "Tensions Within International Calvinism," 178.

22 Godfrey, "Tensions Within International Calvinism," 159.

23 Godfrey, "Tensions Within International Calvinism," 175.

24 See Packer on the articulation of limited atonement by later Puritans, especially John Owen. J.I. Packer, *A Quest for Godliness: The Puritan Vision of the Christian Life* (Wheaton: Crossway, 1990), 125–148.

Before addressing the atonement, Dort starts with who God is in light of man's sin.

> God is not only supremely merciful, but also supremely just. His justice requires (as he has revealed himself in the word) that the sins we have committed against his infinite mercy be punished with both temporal and eternal punishments, of soul as well as body. We cannot escape these punishments unless satisfaction is given to God's justice.[25]

Dort could not begin in a more strategic place. Arminianism often takes as its starting point God's universal love and draws theological implications to the atonement from there. However, Dort begins by reminding us that not only is he a God of mercy but he is a God of justice, indeed, *supreme* justice.[26] Therefore, his justice, as evident in Scripture, requires that sin, a violation of his "infinite majesty," must be punished if he is to remain holy. Notice, the "presupposition of this first article is that you cannot say anything about redemption without saying something about the Redeemer-God, and that your conception of the latter determines your conception of the former."[27] The Remonstrants, however, differed significantly in their presuppositions. As Hoeksema explains,

> The Arminians themselves adopted a certain theological starting point. They loved to emphasize God's love and God's mercy to the exclusion of His righteousness and justice. Accordingly, they enjoyed accusing Reformed men of having a hard and cold con-

---

25 "Canons of Dort," 2.1, in *Creeds and Confessions of the Reformation Era*, vol. 2 of *Creeds and Confessions of Faith in the Christian Tradition*, eds. Jaroslav Pelikan and Valerie Hotchkiss (New Haven and London: Yale University Press, 2003), 2:579.

26 Feenstra argues that Dort's language here is very similar to the Heidelberg Catechism, Lord's Days 4 and 5 (Feenstra, *Unspeakable Comfort*, 68). Klooster also points to Q. 10–18, as well as the Belgic Confession, Art. 16–20 [Fred H. Klooster, "The Doctrinal Deliverances of Dort," in *Crisis in the Reformed Churches: Essays in Commemoration of the Great Synod of Dort, 1618–1619*, ed. Peter Y. De Jong (Grand Rapids: Reformed Fellowship, 1968), 74 n.23].

27 Hoeksema, *The Voice of Our Fathers*, 328–329.

ception of God as an inexorably severe and just God, a Judge who knew no mercy.... The Arminians posited a conflict in God between His justice and His mercy, a conflict in which divine mercy was victorious and overcame divine justice. According to His mercy, so they teach, God yearns for the happiness of the sinner and cannot cause suffering and misery to him. And though His justice requires that the sinner be stricken with the curse and be killed, God cannot exercise His justice without doing violence to His mercy. Hence, His mercy prevails. He denies His justice, and without the satisfaction of His justice bestows upon the sinner forgiveness and eternal life. [28]

Hoeksema continues, explaining the problem Dort saw in such a conception.

The fundamental error in this conception lies in the fact that it denies the unity and simplicity of God, and denies the essential unity of His attributes. It makes a separation between God's attributes. It posits a schism in God. Now we must not imagine that the fathers of Dordrecht go to the opposite extreme and maintain God's justice in preference to His mercy. Not at all; but they maintain both divine justice and divine mercy, not, however, in irreconcilable conflict with one another, but in essential unity. ... Never is there in God a mercy which is not just, nor a justice which is not essentially merciful. His justice, therefore, never functions without His mercy, and His mercy never operates apart from His justice. There is no conflict in God![29]

For Dort, justice and mercy kiss in the cross of Christ. The only way we, as sinners, can escape punishment is if another satisfies divine wrath on our behalf. As Dort says in 2.2, "Since, however, we ourselves cannot give this satisfaction or deliver ourselves from God's anger, God in his boundless mercy has given us as a guarantee his only-begotten Son, who was made to be sin and a curse for us, in our place, on the

---

28 Hoeksema, *The Voice of Our Fathers*, 328–329.
29 Hoeksema, *The Voice of Our Fathers*, 328–329.

cross, in order that he might give satisfaction for us."[30] Dort exposes the
essence of the cross in what today is labeled "penal substitutionary
atonement," a doctrine the Arminian too often overlooks in debates over
the extent of the atonement. As Dort points out, man is a sinner condemned before a holy God who must meet his justice with due wrath.
We, as sinners, cannot satisfy or deliver ourselves from divine wrath as
we are enslaved to sin and absolutely guilty before God, owing a debt of
infinite measure. Yet, God has given his one and only Son, out of his
"boundless mercy" and love to be a curse in our place, satisfying the
wrath of God in our stead (i.e. propitiation) so that we are redeemed.[31]

The infinite value of Christ's death
Before entering into the issue of the extent of Christ's atonement, Dort
is careful to add the preliminary observation that the actual value of
Christ's death is immeasurable. Against the charge that the Calvinists
denied the infinite value of the atonement, Dort argued, "This death
of God's Son is the only and entirely complete sacrifice and satisfaction for sins; it is of infinite value and worth, more than sufficient to
atone for the sins of the whole world."[32] The infinite worth of Christ's
atonement is again explained in 2.4,

> This death is of such great value and worth for the reason that
> the person who suffered it is—as was necessary to be our Sav-
> ior—not only a true and perfectly holy man, but also the only-
> begotten Son of God, of the same eternal and infinite essence
> with the Father and the Holy Spirit.[33]

30 "Canons of Dort," 2.2, in *Creeds and Confessions of the Reformation Era*, 2:579.

31 This is not to say God is anger while Jesus is love, setting the two against one
another as many do. Rather, while God's justice is exhibited at the cross, we must
remember that it was God himself who sent Christ to the cross out of love for us. In
other words, Christ died for us because God is merciful and loving. For contemporary
treatments of penal substitution, see Steve Jeffery, Michael Ovey, Andrew Sach, *Pierced
for Our Transgressions: Rediscovering the Glory of Penal Substitution* (Wheaton: Crossway,
2007); J.I. Packer and Mark Dever, *In My Place Condemned He Stood* (Wheaton: Crossway, 2007); John R.W. Stott, *The Cross of Christ* (Downers Grove: InterVarsity, 2006).

32 "Canons of Dort," 2.3, in *Creeds and Confessions of the Reformation Era*, 2:580.

33 Dort adds, "Another reason is that this death was accompanied by the experience

Two observations must be made. First, the infinite value of Christ's death is due to both the person and the work of Christ. It is due to the person of Christ because he is not only fully man, whose humanity is essential to our salvation, but because he is the one and only Son of God who is of the same eternal and infinite essence as the Father and the Spirit. But the infinite value is also due to the perfect and holy life Christ lived in obedience to his Father, fulfilling the law in every way. As Feenstra states, "Not only does our Saviour and Mediator need to be a true man, He must also be completely exempt from sin. Jesus of Nazareth met this criterion as well. The law of God was written upon His heart."[34]

Second, because Christ's death is of infinite value and worth, it would be more than sufficient to atone for the sins of the whole world. Whether his death was actually intended to atone for the sins of the whole world is another question still to be answered. Indeed, as we will see, Dort in no way affirms a general or universal atonement but denies it. Christ's atonement is only for the elect. Nevertheless, as Dort maintains, while Christ actually made satisfaction only for the elect, technically, due to the infinite value of Christ himself, his death would be sufficient to atone for the whole world, though in reality God executed Christ's death only on behalf of his elect.[35] Or as Fred Klooster writes, Dort can "speak of Christ's death as 'abundantly sufficient to expiate the sins of the whole world,' but they do not teach that Christ's death did actually expiate the sins of the whole world."[36] The purpose in Dort going to such length in affirming the sufficiency of Christ's death is to maintain against its objectors that there is nothing deficient with Christ's work, but rather it is the sovereign prerogative of God to decide that Christ's atonement should only be made for his children.[37] As Klooster states, the "Synod did not affirm limited

---

of God's anger and curse, which we by our sins had fully deserved." "Canons of Dort," 2.4, in *Creeds and Confessions of the Reformation Era*, 2:580.

34 Feenstra, *Unspeakable Comfort*, 80.

35 One should not conclude from this that Dort affirmed "hypothetical universalism." This is certainly not the case, when Dort's view of election and atonement are considered together.

36 Klooster, "Doctrinal Deliverences," 75.

37 "It means that the sacrifice and satisfaction of Christ *when considered by itself*, that is, apart from God's elective decree and apart from the intent and purpose of

atonement because there were inherent limits in Christ's sacrifice." In other words, the "definite or particular focus of the atonement stems from the sovereign will and design of God himself, not from inherent limitations in Christ's work."[38]

The universal proclamation of the gospel

Dort transitions from the infinite value and worth of Christ's death to the mandate to proclaim the gospel to all people. It is "the promise of the gospel that whoever believes in Christ crucified shall not perish but have eternal life."[39] This promise, "together with the command to repent and believe, ought to be announced and declared without differentiation or discrimination to all nations and people, to whom God in his good pleasure sends the gospel."[40] Notice, for Dort there is no conflict or tension between the well-meant offer of the gospel and the doctrine of particular atonement, which we will come to shortly. Both of these truths are taught in Scripture and Dort simply affirms them both.[41]

Dort elaborates upon this well-meant, free offer of the gospel by explaining the difference between belief and unbelief. Those "called through the gospel" who "do not repent or believe in Christ but perish

---

Christ's death and apart from the fact that Christ actually represented in His death only the elect, *would have been* sufficient to expiate the sins of the entire human race, yea, of several more worlds. There is nothing defective in that death itself, nothing lacking in the value of the sacrifice, which would compel its atoning efficiency to be limited to the elect alone. The latter limitation is not due to a limited value of Christ's death: for His death was in itself abundantly sufficient, infinite in value. But the limitation to the elect alone is a sovereign limitation by God's elective will, the will with which Christ was in perfect harmony when He gave Himself to the death of the cross" (Hoeksema, *The Voice of Our Fathers*, 341).

38 Klooster, "Doctrinal Deliverences," 74.

39 "Canons of Dort," 2.5, in *Creeds and Confessions of the Reformation Era*, 2:580.

40 "Canons of Dort," 2.5, in *Creeds and Confessions of the Reformation Era*, 2:580. Statements like these highlight Dort's emphasis on the necessity of missions. See Anthony A. Hoekema, "The Missionary Focus of the Canons of Dort," *Calvin Theological Journal* 7, no. 2 (1972): 209–220. See also Kenneth J. Stewart, "Calvinism and Missions: The Contested Relationship Revisited," *Themelios* 34, no. 1 (2009): 63–78.

41 "Whatever paradox there may be between limited atonement and the universal call of the gospel, the Synod of Dort affirmed both and curtailed neither—convinced that this was scriptural" (Klooster, "Doctrinal Deliverences," 76).

in unbelief" cannot blame Christ, as if "the sacrifice of Christ offered on the cross is deficient or insufficient."[42] To the contrary, their refusal to repent and believe is "because they themselves are at fault."[43] However, "all who genuinely believe and are delivered and saved by Christ's death from their sins and from destruction receive this favor solely from God's grace—which he owes to no one—given to them in Christ from eternity."[44] The significance of this last sentence should not be lost. God owes his grace to no one and is in no way obligated to redeem anyone by the blood of his Son. Therefore, when some do believe and are saved by Christ's death, it is due *entirely* to his eternal mercy and grace.[45]

The efficacy of Christ's death

Though Dort insists that Christ's death is of infinite value, nevertheless, this does not mean that God intended for Christ to die for all people. To the contrary, while his death is of infinite worth, it is only intended

---

42 "Canons of Dort," 2.6, in *Creeds and Confessions of the Reformation Era*, 2:580.

43 "Canons of Dort," 2.6, in *Creeds and Confessions of the Reformation Era*, 2:580.

44 "Canons of Dort," 2.7, in *Creeds and Confessions of the Reformation Era*, 2:580.

45 Before moving into Dort's exposition of the efficacy and particularity of the atonement, it is significant to note that some, like Homer Hoeksema, have misinterpreted Dort's affirmation of the well-meant offer of the gospel in articles five through seven. As seen above, Dort is straightforward in stating that the gospel is to be freely offered to all people, with the promise of eternal life to all who believe ("Canons of Dort," 2.5, in *Creeds and Confessions of the Reformation Era*, 2:580). Hoeksema, a hyper-Calvinist who denies the well-meant offer of the gospel to all people, rejects such an interpretation of Dort. Hoeksema argues that Dort does "not intend to teach a general, well-meant offer of salvation or a general promise of salvation" (Hoeksema, *The Voice of Our Fathers*, 356). But as we have seen already, nothing could be further from the truth, especially when Dort says, without any qualification, "This promise, together with the command to repent and believe, ought to be announced and declared without differentiation or discrimination to all nations and people, to whom God in his good pleasure sends the gospel" ("Canons of Dort," 2.5, in *Creeds and Confessions of the Reformation Era*, 2:580). What is evident in article five is that with the gospel comes the command to repent and believe, a command which is not secretly given to the elect but indiscriminately proclaimed to all people. As Matthew 4:17 records, "From that time Jesus began to preach, saying, '*Repent*, for the kingdom of heaven is at hand.'" Dort is simply following the example of Christ himself who offered and commanded the repentance of all sinners for eternal life. (Because Hoeksema's hyper-Calvinism tends to discolour Dort's articles at several points, I have chosen not to rely on Hoeksema's work extensively.)

and accomplished for the elect. Jan Rohls, commenting on Dort, explains, "God's saving intention is thus not universal, but particular, so that Christ's sacrifice, although in itself it is sufficient to save *all* sinners, is only the means to save *some* sinners."[46] In 2.8 Dort explains,

> For it was the entirely free plan and very gracious will and intention of God the Father that the enlivening and saving effectiveness of his Son's costly death should work itself out in all his chosen ones, in order that he might grant justifying faith to them only and thereby lead them without fail to salvation.[47]

Dort goes on to articulate the matter in much more detail,

> In other words, it was God's will that Christ through the blood of the cross (by which he confirmed the new covenant) should effectively redeem from every people, tribe, nation, and language all those and only those who were chosen from eternity to salvation and given to him by the Father; that he should grant them faith (which, like the Holy Spirit's other saving gifts, he acquired for them by his death); that he should cleanse them by his blood from all their sins, both original and actual, whether committed before or after their coming to faith; that he should faithfully preserve them to the very end; and that he should finally present them to himself, a glorious people without spot or wrinkle.[48]

Dort's affirmation of particular atonement is explicit. Christ shed his blood on the cross, thereby confirming the new covenant to "effectively redeem" those and only those "who were chosen from eternity to salvation and given to him by the Father." These elect for whom Christ died come from every tribe and nation. Therefore, Christ's death is not for all without *exception* but it is for all without *distinction*.

---

46 Jan Rohls, *Reformed Confessions: Theology from Zurich to Barmen*, trans. John Hoffmeyer, Columbia Series in Reformed Theology (Louisville: Westminster John Knox, 1997), 162.

47 "Canons of Dort," 2.8, in *Creeds and Confessions of the Reformation Era*, 2:580–581.

48 "Canons of Dort," 2.8, in *Creeds and Confessions of the Reformation Era*, 2:580–581.

Furthermore, it is the efficacy and particularity of Christ's shed blood that guarantees that the Spirit will grant the elect faith. In other words, Christ, by his death, "acquired for them" the very faith that the Spirit would apply within. And it is also by Christ's death that the elect sinner is cleansed by Christ's blood from all his sins, both original sin and actual sin, both before conversion and during sanctification. But Dort does not stop there. Dort goes on to draw the connection not only between Christ's death and the irresistible application of faith but also between Christ's death and the preservation of the saints. Just as Christ's death acquired for his elect saving faith, so also does his death acquire for the elect perseverance in the faith. Because of Christ's atoning work God can "faithfully preserve them to the very end" and "finally present them to himself, a glorious people without spot or wrinkle."[49]

The particularity and efficacy of the atonement is again evident in Dort's Rejection of Errors. As already seen, the Arminian view of universal atonement does not actually save anyone but merely makes man savable. It is not actually efficacious in and of itself but is dependent upon man's free will for its efficacy.[50] Dort, however, rejects those who

teach that God the Father appointed his Son to death on the cross without a fixed and definite plan to save anyone by name, so that the necessity, usefulness, and worth of what Christ's death obtained could have stood intact and altogether perfect, com-

---

49 "Canons of Dort," 2.8, in *Creeds and Confessions of the Reformation Era*, 2:580–581.

50 As Godfrey states, "Their basic notion was that Christ made salvation possible for all men, but that this salvation was actualized in men only by their response of faith" (Godfrey, "Tensions Within International Calvinism," 151). For the Calvinists, such a view succumbed to Pelagianism and Socinianism. "This position was both Pelagian and Socinian: Pelagian because man must actualize, with his own powers, the possibility of salvation, and Socinian because no real benefits were actually accomplished for man on the cross. If there were truly a universal efficacy in Christ's death, then all would be actually saved. This 'Huberian falsity' had been rejected by the orthodox since the classic struggle between Beza and Huberus" (Godfrey, "Tensions Within International Calvinism," 190). Feenstra makes a similar point, "When we say that Christ opened to us the possibility of reconciliation and atonement we in fact proclaim ourselves to be our own saviours" (Feenstra, *Unspeakable Comfort*, 68).

plete, and whole, even if the redemption that was obtained had never in actual fact been applied to any individual.[51]

Dort finds such a view an "insult to the wisdom of God the Father and to the merit of Jesus Christ" as it is "contrary to Scripture" itself. Notice, says Dort, how Jesus speaks of his atoning death when he proclaims, "I lay down my life for the sheep, and I know them" (John 10:15,27). We do not see here a universal atonement that simply makes salvation possible for all, but a particular atonement ("for the sheep") on the very basis of the fact that Christ knows them in a saving way. Isaiah 53:10 tells us the same, "When he shall make himself an offering for sin, he shall see his offspring, he shall prolong his days, and the will of Jehovah shall prosper in his hand." The offering for sin is not made for all but only for "his offspring," that is, the offspring of the Messiah. Other passages also demonstrate the limited extent of the atonement. Dort cites the following:

Christ loved me and gave himself up for me (Galatians 2:20).

Who will bring any charge against those whom God has chosen? It is God who justifies. Who is he that condemns? It is Christ who died, that is, for them (Romans 8:33–34).

"I lay down my life for the sheep" (John 10:15).

"My command is this: Love one another as I have loved you. Greater love has no one than this, that one lay down his life for his friends" (John 15:12–13).[52]

While Dort first and foremost observes how the Arminian view contradicts Scripture, Dort adds that such a view "undermines the article of

---

51 "Canons of Dort," Rejection of the Errors 2.1, in *Creeds and Confessions of the Reformation Era*, 2:581.

52 "Canons of Dort," Rejection of the Errors 2.7, in *Creeds and Confessions of the Reformation Era*, 2:583.

the creed in which we confess what we believe concerning the church."[53]
Dort focuses more attention on the efficacy of Christ's death in
Rejection of Errors 2.2. Dort rejects those that teach that the "purpose
of Christ's death was not to establish in actual fact a new covenant of
grace by his blood, but only to acquire for the Father the mere right
to enter once more into a covenant with men, whether of grace or of
works."[54] Again, such a view contradicts passages like Hebrews 7:22
and 9:15 where are told that Jesus "has become the guarantee and
mediator of a better—that is, a new covenant." The author of Hebrews
goes on to write,

> And for this cause he is the mediator of the new testament, that
> by means of death, for the redemption of the transgressions that
> were under the first testament, they which are called might
> receive the promise of eternal inheritance. For where a testament
> is, there must also of necessity be the death of the testator. For a
> testament is of force after men are dead: otherwise it is of no
> strength at all while the testator liveth. Whereupon neither the
> first testament was dedicated without blood. For when Moses
> had spoken every precept to all the people according to the law,
> he took the blood of calves and of goats, with water, and scarlet
> wool, and hyssop, and sprinkled both the book, and all the people,
> Saying, "This is the blood of the testament which God hath
> enjoined unto you" (Hebrews 9:15–20).

This passage demonstrates that the blood of Christ establishes and
guarantees a new, better covenant. This new covenant is not merely
made available, conditioned upon man's free will, but it is actually
purchased by the blood of Christ and irresistibly applied to the elect
by the sovereign work of the Spirit.[55] The will or covenant is actually

---

53 "Canons of Dort," Rejection of the Errors 2.1, in *Creeds and Confessions of the Reformation Era*, 2:581.

54 "Canons of Dort," Rejection of the Errors 2.2, in *Creeds and Confessions of the Reformation Era*, 2:582.

55 "The Arminians taught that as a result of Christ's universal atonement, 'all men have been accepted unto the state of reconciliation and unto the grace of the covenant, so that no one is worthy of condemnation on account of original sin, and that no one

enacted and ratified at the death of Christ. Such efficacy is due, as Hebrews 7:22 tells us, to Christ our surety. He is our high priest, after the order of Melchizedek (Hebrews 5:6). Dort's emphasis on Christ our mediator and high priest is very similar to that of John Calvin who wrote, "For as has been said, we or our prayers have no access to God unless Christ, as our High Priest, having washed away our sins, sanctifies us and obtains for us that grace from which the uncleanness of our transgressions and vices debars us." Calvin concludes, "Thus we see that we must begin from the death of Christ in order that the efficacy and benefit of His priesthood may reach us."[56]

The unconditionality of Christ's atonement is again evident in 2.3 of Dort's Rejection and Errors. Dort rejects those who teach that

> Christ, by the satisfaction which he gave, did not certainly merit for anyone salvation itself and the faith by which this satisfaction of Christ is effectively applied to salvation, but only acquired for the Father the authority or plenary will to relate in a new way with men and to impose such new conditions as he chose, and that the satisfying of these conditions depends on the free choice of man; consequently, that it was possible that either all or none would fulfill them.[57]

---

shall be condemned because of it, but that all are free from the guilt of original sin.' This teaching is specifically rejected by the synod in II, Par. 5. Dort held that by the death of Christ, God has *confirmed* the new covenant of grace through Christ's blood, but rejects the teaching that as a result of Christ's death God has established an entirely new covenant including all men in which are prescribed new conditions dependent upon the free will of man (II, Par. 2, 3). The Arminians held that Christ had paid for the sins of all men by his death, so that the guilt of original sin is now removed for all, and all come into a new state of reconciliation and into a new covenant of grace. Thus they contended that the one sin for which man could be condemned was the sin of unbelief—rejecting the message that Christ died for them" (Klooster, "Doctrinal Deliverences," in *Crisis in the Reformed Churches*, 75).

56 John Calvin, *Institutes of the Christian Religion*, ed. John T. McNeil, trans. Ford Lewis Battles, LCC, vols. 20–21 (Philadelphia: Westminster, 1960), 2.15.6. This observation is made by Feenstra, *Unspeakable Comfort*, 77.

57 "Canons of Dort," Rejection of the Errors 2.3, in *Creeds and Confessions of the Reformation Era*, 2:582.

In the Arminian view, it was hypothetically possible that even though Christ had made an atonement, due to man's free will no man would choose to believe and receive the benefits of the atonement. Such a possibility is due to the fact that the atonement of Christ, for the Arminian, does not "certainly merit for anyone salvation itself."[58] Nor does Christ's death and satisfaction guarantee faith for anyone in particular. Consequently, the efficacy of the cross is emptied of its power, all at the expense of man's "free choice."[59] Dort concludes, "For they have too low an opinion of the death of Christ, do not at all acknowledge the foremost fruit or benefit which it brings forth, and summon back from hell the Pelagian error."[60]

Dort once again exposes the exaltation of man's free will by the Arminians at the expense of the efficacy of the atonement when Dort says it rejects those who "make use of the distinction between obtaining and applying in order to instill in the unwary and inexperienced

---

58 "Canons of Dort," Rejection of the Errors 2.3, in *Creeds and Confessions of the Reformation Era*, 2:582.

59 "Canons of Dort," Rejection of the Errors 2.3, in *Creeds and Confessions of the Reformation Era*, 2:582.

60 "Canons of Dort," Rejection of the Errors 2.3, in *Creeds and Confessions of the Reformation Era*, 2:582. Dort also makes the connection between the death of Christ and justification, accusing the Arminians of distorting a biblical view of justification by grace through faith. In Rejection of Errors 2.4, Dort rejects those who "teach that what is involved in the new covenant of grace which God the Father made with men through the intervening of Christ's death is not that we are justified before God and saved through faith, insofar as it accepts Christ's merit, but rather that God, having withdrawn his demand for perfect obedience to the law, counts faith itself, and the imperfect obedience of faith, as perfect obedience to the law, and graciously looks upon this as worthy of the reward of eternal life. For they contradict Scripture: 'They are justified freely by his grace through the redemption that came by Jesus Christ, whom God presented as a sacrifice of atonement, through faith in his blood.' [Romans 3:24–25] And along with the ungodly Socinus, they introduce a new and foreign justification of man before God, against the consensus of the whole church." And again, in Rejection of Errors 2.5, "Who teach that all people have been received into the state of reconciliation and into the grace of the covenant, so that no one on account of original sin is liable to condemnation, or is to be condemned, but that all are free from the guilt of this sin. For this opinion conflicts with Scripture which asserts that we are by nature children of wrath [Ephesians 2:3]" ("Canons of Dort," Rejection of the Errors 2.4–2.5, in *Creeds and Confessions of the Reformation Era*, 2:582).

the opinion that God, as far as he is concerned, wished to bestow equally upon all people the benefits which are gained by Christ's death."[61] Such a view claims that "the distinction by which some rather than others come to share in the forgiveness of sins and eternal life depends on their own free choice (which applies itself to the grace offered indiscriminately), but does not depend on the unique gift of mercy which effectively works in them, so that they, rather than others, apply that grace to themselves."[62] The distinction Dort speaks of is the Arminian distinction between Christ obtaining and the Spirit applying redemption. The former obtains the possibility of redemption for all people equally, while the latter applies redemption to those who, by their own free will, decide for themselves whether or not they will take advantage of it. Notice, the efficacy of Christ's atonement and its benefits are completely and entirely dependent upon man's will to accept or reject it. The major problem with such a view, however, is that grace "does not depend on the unique gift of mercy which effectively works in them, so that they, rather than others, apply that grace to themselves."[63] Whether or not what Christ accomplished is made effectual is dependent upon man's will rather than God's.

The Emden delegates, in particular, reacted strongly to this Arminian view, calling it blasphemous, because they believed it made Christ an "incomplete Saviour."[64] Dort labels such a view of grace the "deadly poison of Pelagianism" which ruins the people of God. Moreover, the reason such a view makes Christ an "incomplete Saviour" is because it separates the death of Christ from the work of the Spirit. For Dort, the application of Christ's work by the Spirit in regeneration and faith

---

61 "Canons of Dort," Rejection of the Errors 2.6, in *Creeds and Confessions of the Reformation Era*, 2:583.

62 "Canons of Dort," Rejection of the Errors 2.6, in *Creeds and Confessions of the Reformation Era*, 2:583.

63 "Canons of Dort," Rejection of the Errors 2.6, in *Creeds and Confessions of the Reformation Era*, 2:583.

64 For a more extensive treatment of the Emden delegates and their contribution, see Godfrey, "Tensions Within International Calvinism," 202. The delegates from Utrecht seem to say the same (Godfrey, "Tensions Within International Calvinism," 214–215).

is actually purchased in the atonement for the elect. For the Arminians, the application of Christ's work is merely made a possibility due to the atonement but ultimately it is not guaranteed but dependent upon man's will. Klooster explains the significance of this difference,

> The Canons do not view the application of redemption as some-thing divorced from or distinct from the atonement. The atone-ment describes what God intended (willed) and what Christ actually achieved by his death. While the Arminians viewed the atonement as obtaining redemption and the forgiveness of sins for all men so that all are now brought into a state of reconcili-ation and salvation is available for all, they did not regard the application of redemption as included in the atonement. The atonement does not insure saving efficacy. Hence they taught universal atonement but particular redemption. The Canons specifically reject this view. Dort views the atonement as including effective application. Hence Dort here teaches a definite or particular atonement which includes definite or particular redemption.[65]

Klooster reminds us that for Dort there is an interrelatedness between unconditional election, definite atonement, irresistible grace and the preservation of the saints. "Efficacy, application, salva-tion, perseverance, and glorification are unitedly willed by God in his good pleasure and achieved, obtained, purchased by Christ in his atoning death." In other words, "All the saving gifts which the Holy Spirit applies to the elect were purchased by the Son and decreed by God. There is no disunity, only harmony and unity, in the work of the Father, the Son, and the Holy Spirit in man's salvation."[66] There-fore, both the "efficacy" and the "application" are included in Christ's atoning work.

---

65 Klooster, "Doctrinal Deliverances of Dort," 77–78.
66 Klooster, "Doctrinal Deliverances of Dort," 78.

The gates of hell seeking vainly to prevail

Dort's affirmation of the particularity and efficacy of the atonement exalts the sovereign, immutable hand of God in accomplishing redemption through his Son Jesus Christ. Such a biblical emphasis as this is highlighted by Dort in 2.9, "This plan, arising out of God's eternal love for his chosen ones, from the beginning of the world to the present time has been powerfully carried out and will also be carried out in the future, the gates of hell seeking vainly to prevail against it."[67] Nothing can frustrate or prevent the redemptive plan of God, which originates in eternity and is carried out to the present time with the promise and guarantee of its fulfilment in the future. Feenstra explains the matter precisely,

> God's counsel (His plan with man) will not be thwarted but accomplished. He will fulfil His purpose. Christ died for His people and He will see to it that the benefits of His atonement will be applied to them. We do not have to face the future in fear but with confidence. The church would be wiped off the globe if God's electing work was not being fulfilled or it was dependent on man's decision.[68]

What a tremendous comfort the believer has in trusting in the sovereignty of God! From election, to the atonement of Christ, to regeneration and sanctification by the Spirit, God's saving purposes for his church are undefeatable and insuperable.

Particular atonement: cause for personal and corporate worship

In Dort's exposition of election and reprobation the implications for individual piety and holiness are explicit. However, in Dort's articulation of particular atonement the implications for piety are more subtle, yet still apparent. As seen already in 2.5, Dort's emphasis on the particularity of Christ's atonement comes from its understanding that in Scripture while God has a general love for all people (e.g., his gospel

---

67 "Canons of Dort," 2.9, in *Creeds and Confessions of the Reformation Era*, 2:581.

68 Feenstra, *Unspeakable Comfort*, 89.

is freely preached and offered to all), he has a special, definite and
saving love meant only for his elect, whom Scripture calls his sheep
(John 10:15,27; cf. 15:12–13) and offspring (Isaiah 53:10).[69] Therefore,
Dort can say in 2.9,

> This plan, arising out of God's eternal love for his chosen ones,
> from the beginning of the world to the present time has been
> powerfully carried out and will also be carried out in the future,
> the gates of hell seeking vainly to prevail against it. As a result
> the chosen are gathered into one, all in their own time, and there
> is always a church of believers founded on Christ's blood, a
> church which steadfastly loves, persistently worships, and—here
> and in all eternity—praises him as her Savior who laid down his
> life for her on the cross, as a bridegroom for his bride.[70]

These elect children are purchased by the blood of the lamb, and it is
their sins that are paid for in full at the cross. Dort is overt: the
response from the church, both here and in eternity, is praise and
worship, because the Saviour has laid down his life for her on the cross,
"as a bridegroom for his bride."[71]

Therefore, it is the doctrine of limited atonement that sweetly
reminds us that the church, and only the church, is the bride of Christ,
for he has paid for her with his blood. It is this doctrine that Dort
believes should elicit persistent love and worship of Christ, both here
and in eternity. Therefore, Venema is right when he states that the
key notes throughout the canons are "praise toward the Triune God
for his amazing, undeserved grace in Christ, and a remarkable confidence in his invincible favor."[72]

---

69 "Canons of Dort," 2.5, in *Creeds and Confessions of the Reformation Era*, 2:580.

70 "Canons of Dort," 2.9, in *Creeds and Confessions of the Reformation Era*, 2:581.

71 "Canons of Dort," 2.9, in *Creeds and Confessions of the Reformation Era*, 2:581. See
also Ephesians 5:25–27.

72 Cornelis P. Venema, "The Election and Salvation of the Children of Believers
Who Die in Infancy: A Study of Article I/17 of the Canons of Dort," *Mid-America Journal
of Theology* 17 (2006): 58.

Conclusion

While the first canon showed us how the doctrine of election was a great cause for personal comfort, assurance, humility and godliness, this second canon has demonstrated that for Dort the doctrine of limited atonement is a cause for corporate spirituality as the body of Christ extols her Saviour for laying down his life and securing redemption.

Jesus answered them, "Truly, truly, I say to you, everyone who commits sin is a slave to sin."—JOHN 8:34

None is righteous, no, not one.—ROMANS 3:10

And you were dead in the trespasses and sins in which you once walked, following the course of this world, following the prince of the power of the air, the spirit that is now at work in the sons of disobedience.—EPHESIANS 2:1-2

Jesus answered, "Truly, truly, I say to you, unless one is born of water and the Spirit, he cannot enter the kingdom of God. That which is born of the flesh is flesh, and that which is born of the Spirit is spirit. Do not marvel that I said to you, 'You must be born again.' The wind blows where it wishes, and you hear its sound, but you do not know where it comes from or where it goes. So it is with everyone who is born of the Spirit."—JOHN 3:5-8

"No one can come to me unless the Father who sent me draws him. And I will raise him up on the last day."—JOHN 6:44

One who heard us was a woman named Lydia, from the city of Thyatira, a seller of purple goods, who was a worshiper of God. The Lord opened her heart to pay attention to what was said by Paul.—ACTS 16:14

And those whom he predestined he also called, and those whom he called he also justified, and those whom he justified he also glorified.—ROMANS 8:30

Blessed be the God and Father of our Lord Jesus Christ! According to his great mercy, he has caused us to be born again to a living hope through the resurrection of Jesus Christ from the dead, to an inheritance that is imperishable, undefiled, and unfading, kept in heaven for you, who by God's power are being guarded through faith for a salvation ready to be revealed in the last time.—1 PETER 1:3-5

But you are a chosen race, a royal priesthood, a holy nation, a people for his own possession, that you may proclaim the excellencies of him who called you out of darkness into his marvelous light.—1 PETER 2:9

Total depravity and effectual grace
Humble gratitude and the death of pride

Introduction

"A biblical belief in the sovereignty of God smashes, not cultivates, human pride."[1] These words by Ian Hamilton make up the very argument of this chapter. Hamilton elaborates,

> Calvinism challenges the residual pride in human hearts. We are naturally and natively far more comfortable with Arminianism, which allows us to make a contribution to our salvation. To be confronted by the truth of our total inability is deeply humbling, but it is the truth of God's own Word, not a notion that John Calvin concocted in Geneva. Becoming persuaded of

---

1   Ian Hamilton, "Winsome Calvinism," *The Banner of Truth* 526 (2007): 4.

this and casting ourselves solely on God's mercy in Christ knocks (in large measure) the pride out of us and teaches us to live as men and women who glory in the God of grace. This is simply another way of saying that Calvinism puts God where he belongs and puts us where we belong. This is the text of authentic, biblical Christianity.[2]

It is hard to improve upon Hamilton's words. Sovereign grace fosters Christian humility and is the antidote to pride. Therefore, Hamilton is exactly right to conclude that a "proud Calvinist is an oxymoron."[3] However, long before Hamilton penned these words, the Synod of Dort made exactly the same point. It is the purpose of this chapter to unveil the connection Dort makes between sovereign grace in effectual calling and Christian humility and gratitude.[4]

Arminian synergism

Contrary to popular opinion, the Arminian Remonstrants did affirm the doctrines of total depravity and the bondage of the will.[5] As they argue in 3.1, "Man does not have saving faith of himself, nor out of the powers of his free will, since in the state of sin he is able of himself and by himself neither to think, will, or do any good (which would indeed be saving good, the most prominent of which is saving faith)."[6] Or consider 3.4, "The will in the fallen state, before calling, does not have the power and the freedom to will any saving good. And therefore we deny that the freedom to will saving good as well as evil is present

---

2   Hamilton, "Winsome Calvinism," *The Banner of Truth* 526 (2007): 5.

3   Hamilton, "Winsome Calvinism," *The Banner of Truth* 526 (2007): 4.

4   For a more extensive study of effectual calling and regeneration, see Matthew Barrett, *Salvation by Grace: The Case for Effectual Calling and Regeneration* (Phillipsburg: P & R, 2013). Portions of this chapter are taken from that study with permission.

5   For an extensive study of the Remonstrants's anthropology, see Aza Goudriaan, "The Synod of Dordt on Arminian Anthropology," in *Revisiting the Synod of Dordt (1618–1619)*, eds. Asa Goudriaan and Fred van Lieburg (Leiden: Brill, 2011), 81–106.

6   "Appendix H: The Opinions of the Remonstrants," 3.1, in *Crisis in the Reformed Churches: Essays in Commemoration of the Great Synod of Dort, 1618–1619*, ed. Peter Y. De Jong (Grand Rapids: Reformed Fellowship, 1968), 225.

to the will in every state."[7] Consequently, man is in need of divine grace if he is to be lifted out of this state of inability. "It is necessary therefore that by God in Christ through His Holy Spirit he be regenerated and renewed in intellect, affections, will, and in all his powers, so that he might be able to understand, reflect upon, will and carry out the good things which pertain to salvation."[8] Such grace, argue the Remonstrants, is not only the beginning but the progression and completion of "every good, so much so that even the regenerate himself is unable to think, will, or do the good, or to resist any temptations to evil, apart from that preceding or prevenient, awakening, following and cooperating grace."[9] Therefore, "all good works and actions which anyone by cogitation is able to comprehend are to be ascribed to the grace of God."[10]

However, notice the type of grace the Remonstrants identify as that which is necessary to regenerate fallen man. As 3.2 makes clear, it is a "prevenient" or "cooperating" grace.[11] In other words, while grace is necessary to deliver man out of his state of depravity and bondage, nevertheless, grace is synergistic, meaning man must cooperate with it. As the Remonstrants state in 3.5, "The efficacious grace by which anyone is converted is not irresistible."[12] In other words, "though God

---

7 "Appendix H: The Opinions of the Remonstrants," 3.4, in *Crisis in the Reformed Churches*, 226.

8 "Appendix H: The Opinions of the Remonstrants," 3.1, in *Crisis in the Reformed Churches*, 225.

9 "Appendix H: The Opinions of the Remonstrants," 3.2, in *Crisis in the Reformed Churches*, 225.

10 "Appendix H: The Opinions of the Remonstrants," 3.2, in *Crisis in the Reformed Churches*, 225. The Remonstrants go on to state in 3.3, "Yet we do not believe that all zeal, care, and diligence applied to the obtaining of salvation before faith itself and the Spirit of renewal are vain and ineffectual—indeed, rather harmful to man than useful and fruitful. On the contrary, we hold that to hear the Word of God, to be sorry for sins committed, to desire saving grace and the Spirit of renewal (none of which things man is able to do without grace) are not only not harmful and useless, but rather most useful and most necessary for the obtaining of faith and or the Spirit of renewal."

11 "Appendix H: The Opinions of the Remonstrants," 3.2, in *Crisis in the Reformed Churches*, 225.

12 "Appendix H: The Opinions of the Remonstrants," 3.5, in *Crisis in the Reformed Churches*, 226.

so influences the will by the Word and the internal operation of His Spirit that He both confers the strength to believe or supernatural powers, and actually causes man to believe—yet man is able of himself to despise that grace and not to believe, and therefore to perish through his own fault."[13] While man is dependent upon God to initiate grace (i.e., prevenient grace), ultimately man himself reserves the right to resist and thwart God's saving purposes.

Furthermore, not only is this grace resistible but it is equally distributed to all to whom the Word is preached. The Holy Spirit confers "as much grace to all men and to each man to whom the Word of God is preached as is sufficient for promoting the conversion of men in its steps."[14] Therefore, sufficient grace "for faith and conversion falls to the lot not only of those whom God is said to will to save according to the decree of absolute election, but also of those who are not actually converted."[15] The Arminians reject the Calvinist who believes "God calls certain ones externally whom He does not will to call internally, that is, as truly converted, even before the grace of calling has been rejected."[16] If he did, then his call, says the Arminian, could not be "seriously" meant and "completely unhypocritical" in its intention and will to save.[17]

The Arminian concern in arguing against the distinction between an *external* gospel call to all people and an *internal* effectual call only for the elect, is rooted in the Arminian rejection of a secret and a revealed will in God. "There is not in God a secret will which so contradicts the will of the same revealed in the Word that according to it (that is, the secret will) He does not will the conversion and salvation of the greatest part of those whom He seriously calls and invites by

---

13 "Appendix H: The Opinions of the Remonstrants," 3.5, in *Crisis in the Reformed Churches*, 226.

14 "Appendix H: The Opinions of the Remonstrants," 3.6, in *Crisis in the Reformed Churches*, 226.

15 "Appendix H: The Opinions of the Remonstrants," 3.6, in *Crisis in the Reformed Churches*, 226.

16 "Appendix H: The Opinions of the Remonstrants," 3.8, in *Crisis in the Reformed Churches*, 226–227.

17 "Appendix H: The Opinions of the Remonstrants," 3.8, in *Crisis in the Reformed Churches*, 226–227.

the Word of the Gospel and by His revealed will."[18] If this were the case, say the Remonstrants, then there would be in God a "double person" or "holy simulation."[19]

To conclude, for the Remonstrants, while grace is necessary it is not effectual. While God initiates grace, man can thwart the Spirit's purpose to save. It is exactly such a view of grace that the Calvinists at Dort would identify as contrary to the Scriptures where we read that God calls his elect in a different manner than he calls all people in general, namely, by an effectual and invincible grace.

Dort's affirmation of total depravity and effectual grace
Total depravity

Dort begins canons 3–4 by describing the pervasiveness of depravity. Man has inherited from Adam a corrupt nature so that after the Fall, every man is a slave to sin. "Man," says Dort, "was originally created in the image of God and was furnished in his mind with a true and salutary knowledge of his Creator and things spiritual, in his will and heart with righteousness, and in all his emotions with purity; indeed, the whole man was holy."[20] However, "rebelling against God

---

18 "Appendix H: The Opinions of the Remonstrants," 3.9, in *Crisis in the Reformed Churches*, 227.

19 "Appendix H: The Opinions of the Remonstrants," 3.9, in *Crisis in the Reformed Churches*, 227. The Remonstrants go on to object, "It is not true that all things, not only good but also bad, necessarily occur, from the power and efficacy of the secret will or decree of God, and that indeed those who sin, out of consideration of the decree of God, are not able to sin; that God wills to determine and to bring about the sins of men, their insane, foolish, and cruel works, and the sacrilegious blasphemy of His name – in fact, to move the tongues of men to blasphemy, and so on." And again in 3.12, "To us the following is false and horrible: that God impels men to sins which He openly prohibits; that those who sin do not act contrary to the will of God properly named; that what is unrighteous (that is, what is contrary to His precept) is in agreement with the will of God; indeed, that it is truly a capital crime to do the will of God" ("Appendix H: The Opinions of the Remonstrants," 3.11–3.12, in *Crisis in the Reformed Churches*, 227).

20 "Canons of Dort," 3-4.1, in *Creeds and Confessions of the Reformation Era*, vol. 2 of *Creeds and Confessions of Faith in the Christian Tradition*, eds. Jaroslav Pelikan and Valerie Hotchkiss (New Haven and London: Yale University Press, 2003), 2:583.

at the devil's instigation and by his own free will, he deprived himself of these outstanding gifts."[21] What did he replace these "outstanding gifts" with? Dort answers, "in their place he brought upon himself blindness, terrible darkness, futility, and distortion of judgment in his mind; perversity, defiance, and hardness in his heart and will; and finally impurity in all his emotions."[22] The consequence for Adam's progeny was deadly to say the least. After the Fall, Adam's children were born with a corrupt nature. "That is to say, being corrupt he brought forth corrupt children. The corruption spread, by God's just judgment, from Adam to all his descendants—except for Christ alone—not by way of imitation (as in former times the Pelagians would have it) but by way of the propagation of his perverted nature."[23] Dort argues that their view, in contrast to the Remonstrant view, is supported by Scripture.

> [Dort rejects those] Who teach that, properly speaking, it cannot be said that original sin itself is enough to condemn the whole human race or to warrant temporal and eternal punishments. For they contradict the apostle when he says: "Sin entered the world through one man, and death through sin, and in this way death passed on to all men because all sinned" [Romans 5:12]; also "The guilt followed one sin and brought condemnation" [Romans 5:16]; likewise: "The wages of sin is death" [Romans 6:23].[24]

All people, therefore, are conceived in sin, born under the wrath of God, "unfit for any saving good, inclined to evil, dead in their sins, and slaves to sin."[25] Consequently, "without the grace of the regenerating Holy Spirit they are neither willing nor able to return to God, to reform their distorted nature, or even to dispose themselves to such reform."[26] Again, Dort argues that the Scriptures are on their side.

---

21 "Canons of Dort," 3–4.1, in *Creeds and Confessions of the Reformation Era*, 2:583.

22 "Canons of Dort," 3–4.1, in *Creeds and Confessions of the Reformation Era*, 2:583.

23 "Canons of Dort," 3–4.2, in *Creeds and Confessions of the Reformation Era*, 2:584.

24 "Canons of Dort," Rejection of the Errors 3–4.2, in *Creeds and Confessions of the Reformation Era*, 2:588–589.

25 "Canons of Dort," 3–4.3, in *Creeds and Confessions of the Reformation Era*, 2:584.

26 "Canons of Dort," 3–4.3, in *Creeds and Confessions of the Reformation Era*, 2:584.

[Dort rejects those] Who teach that in spiritual death the spiritual gifts have not been separated from man's will, since the will in itself has never been corrupted but only hindered by the darkness of the mind and the unruliness of the emotions, and since the will is able to exercise its innate free capacity once these hindrances are removed, which is to say it is able of itself to will or choose whatever good is set before it—or else not to will or choose it. This is a novel idea and an error and has the effect of elevating the power of free choice, contrary to the words of Jeremiah the prophet: "The heart itself is deceitful above all things and wicked" [Jeremiah 17:9]; and of the words of the apostle: "All of us also lived among them [the sons of disobedience] at one time in the passions of our flesh, following the will of our flesh and thoughts" [Ephesians 2:3].

And again,

[Dort rejects those] Who teach that unregenerate man is not strictly or totally dead in his sins or deprived of all capacity for spiritual good but is able to hunger and thirst for righteousness or life and to offer the sacrifice of a broken and contrite spirit which is pleasing to God. For these views are opposed to the plain testimonies of Scripture: "You were dead in your transgressions and sins" [Ephesians 2:1,5]; "The imagination of the thoughts of man's heart is only evil all the time" [Genesis 6:5, 8:21]. Besides, to hunger and thirst for deliverance from misery and for life, and to offer God the sacrifice of a broken spirit is characteristic only of the regenerate and of those called blessed [Psalm 51:17; Matthew 5:6].[27]

In these first three articles it is evident Dort affirms that (1) man's depravity pervades every aspect of his being (will, mind, affections), (2) man is dead, a slave to his sinful nature, and (3) man is in no way

---

27 "Canons of Dort," Rejection of the Errors 3–4.4, in *Creeds and Confessions of the Reformation Era*, 2:589.

willing to return to God or reform his distorted nature. He is in total reliance upon the saving power of God.[28]

Effectual grace

Despite man's ruin, God has revealed himself to man both in the Old Testament and in the New Testament. In the Old Testament God "revealed this secret of his will to a small number" while in the New Testament he "discloses it to a large number," without any "distinction between peoples."[29] His saving revelation, however, was not motivated by anything in man, as if Israel in the Old Testament was any greater than the other nations. Nor was it due to certain men using the light of nature better than others. To the contrary, his saving revelation was due "to the free good pleasure and undeserved love of God" himself.

Moreover, those who receive this gospel revelation are seriously called. "For seriously and most genuinely God makes known in his word what is pleasing to him: that those who are called should come to him. Seriously he also promises rest for their souls and eternal life to all who come to him and believe [Matthew 11:28–29]."[30] Here Dort is responding to the objection of the Remonstrants who argued, as already seen, that the Calvinist God was hypocritical to call all people

---

28 Dort goes on to argue in 3–4. 4 that though there remains within man "a certain light of nature" in which he "retains some notions about God, natural things, and the difference between what is moral and immoral," nevertheless, this light of nature "is far from enabling man to come to a saving knowledge of God" nor is it able to convert him. To the contrary, man distorts the light and "suppresses it in unrighteousness" and in so doing "he renders himself without excuse before God." Just as the light of nature is inadequate so also is the Law. "For man cannot obtain saving grace through the Decalogue, because, although it does expose the magnitude of his sin and increasingly convict him of his guilt, yet it does not offer a remedy or enable him to escape from his misery, and, indeed, weakened as it is by the flesh, leaves the offender under the curse." See 3–4.5 for a fuller statement. Article 6 provides the solution, "What, therefore, neither the light of nature nor the law can do, God accomplishes by the power of the Holy Spirit, through the word or the ministry of reconciliation. This is the gospel about the Messiah, through which it has pleased God to save believers, in both the Old and New Testament" ("Canons of Dort," 3–4.4, in *Creeds and Confessions of the Reformation Era*, 2:584).
29 "Canons of Dort," 3–4.7, in *Creeds and Confessions of the Reformation Era*, 2:585.
30 "Canons of Dort," 3–4.8, in *Creeds and Confessions of the Reformation Era*, 2:585.

by his gospel when he would effectually save only his elect. Dort rejects such a charge. Scripture is clear; God does indeed call all externally though according to his decretive will he only chooses to internally convert his elect. God is in no way hypocritical for he only holds out to the sinner that which he could have (eternal life) if he would believe. However, the sinner not only cannot believe but he will *not* believe. Therefore, as Dort argues in 3–4.9, the fact that the sinner does not believe is nobody's fault but his own.[31]

However, when a sinner does hear the gospel and believes, God and God alone receives all of the credit, for he is the one who first gave the sinner new life to believe. Dort states in 3–4.10,

> The fact that others who are called through the ministry of the gospel do come and are brought to conversion must not be credited to man, as though one distinguishes himself by free choice from others who are furnished with equal or sufficient grace for faith and conversion (as the proud heresy of Pelagius maintains). No, it must be credited to God: just as from eternity he chose his own in Christ, so within time he effectively calls them, grants them faith and repentance, and, having rescued them from the dominion of darkness, brings them into the kingdom of his Son [Colossians 1:13], in order that they may declare the wonderful deeds of him who called them out of darkness into this marvelous light [1 Peter 2:9], and may boast not in themselves, but in the Lord, as apostolic words frequently testify in Scripture [1 Corinthians 1:31].[32]

---

31 "The fact that many who are called through the ministry of the gospel do not come and are not brought to conversion must not be blamed on the gospel, nor on Christ, who is offered through the gospel, nor on God, who calls them through the gospel and even bestows various gifts on them, but on the people themselves who are called. Some in self-assurance do not even entertain the word of life; others do entertain it but do not take it to heart, and for that reason, after the fleeting joy of a temporary faith, they relapse; others choke the seed of the word with the thorns of life's cares and with the pleasures of the world and bring forth no fruits. This our Savior teaches in the parable of the sower [Matthew 13]" ("Canons of Dort," 3–4.9, in *Creeds and Confessions of the Reformation Era*, 2:585).

32 "Canons of Dort," 3–4.10, in *Creeds and Confessions of the Reformation Era*, 2:585–586.

For the sinner to believe, God must irresistibly and effectually, by the power of the Spirit, call that elect sinner to himself and awaken him to new life. Therefore, when God works true conversion in his elect,

> he not only sees to it that the gospel is proclaimed to them out-
> wardly, and enlightens their minds powerfully by the Holy Spirit
> so that they may rightly understand and discern the things of the
> Spirit of God, but, by the effective operation of the same regen-
> erating Spirit, he also penetrates into the inmost being of man,
> opens the closed heart, softens the hard heart, and circumcises
> the heart that is uncircumcised.[33]

Dort continues, "He infuses new qualities into the will, making the dead will alive, the evil one good, the unwilling one willing, and the stubborn one compliant; he activates and strengthens the will so that, like a good tree, it may be enabled to produce the fruits of good deeds."[34] According to Dort, no mere moral persuasion will do, but unfailing resurrection to spiritual life is necessary. God works this new creation in us "without our help."[35] It is not by mere "outward teaching, by moral persuasion, or by such a way of working that, after God has done his work, it remains in man's power whether or not to be reborn or converted."[36] To the contrary,

> it is an entirely supernatural work, one that is at the same time
> most powerful and most pleasing, a marvelous, hidden, and
> inexpressible work, which is not lesser than or inferior in power

---

33 "Canons of Dort," 3–4.11, in *Creeds and Confessions of the Reformation Era*, 2:586.

34 "Canons of Dort," 3–4.11, in *Creeds and Confessions of the Reformation Era*, 2:586. Horton argues that this infusion of new qualities is "not a medieval notion of infused habits, but simply a manner of expressing the impartation of new life from a source external to the person who is 'dead in sins.' ...[regeneration] is not represented here as accomplished apart from or prior to the external preaching of the gospel" [Michael S. Horton, *Covenant and Salvation: Union with Christ* (Louisville: Westminster John Knox, 2007), 203, n.83].

35 "Canons of Dort," 3–4.12, in *Creeds and Confessions of the Reformation Era*, 2:586.

36 "Canons of Dort," 3–4.12, in *Creeds and Confessions of the Reformation Era*, 2:586.

to that of creation or of raising the dead, as Scripture (inspired by the author of this work) teaches.[37]

What is the result of this spiritual resurrection from the dead? Answer: "all those in whose hearts God works in this marvelous way are certainly, unfailingly, and effectively reborn and do actually believe."[38] Rebirth, moreover, includes the renewal of the will as well. After rebirth the will, "now renewed, is not only activated and motivated by God but in being activated by God is also itself active" and for this reason "man himself, by that grace which he has received, is also rightly said to believe and to repent."[39]

Perhaps no confession since Dort has spent so much space articulating the monergistic nature of grace. Notice, in article 12, Dort is unambiguous: God works regeneration before any act of faith on our part and apart from our help (*contra* Arminianism).[40] Such a work of God, not upon all but only upon his elect, is irresistible, effectual and always successful, bringing the sinner from death to new life.[41] As Ezekiel 36:26 demonstrates, God's work is not by mere moral persuasion nor is it conditioned upon "man's power whether or not to be reborn or converted."[42] Rather, it is a work equivalent to raising the

---

37 "Canons of Dort," 3–4.12, in *Creeds and Confessions of the Reformation Era*, 2:586.
38 "Canons of Dort," 3–4.12, in *Creeds and Confessions of the Reformation Era*, 2:586.
39 "Canons of Dort," 3–4.12, in *Creeds and Confessions of the Reformation Era*, 2:586.
40 "Canons of Dort," 3–4.12, in *Creeds and Confessions of the Reformation Era*, 2:586.
41 Dort rejects a universal grace that is contingent upon the will of man. "Having set forth the orthodox teaching, the synod rejects the errors of those … 5. Who teach that corrupt and natural man can make such good use of common grace (by which they mean the light of nature) or of the gifts remaining after the fall that he is able thereby gradually to obtain a greater grace—evangelical or saving grace—as well as salvation itself; and that in this way God, for his part, shows himself ready to reveal Christ to all people, since he provides to all, to a sufficient extent and in an effective manner, the means necessary for the revealing of Christ, for faith, and for repentance." Dort cites Psalm 147:19–20, Acts 14:16 and Acts 16:6–7 in support. See "Canons of Dort," Rejection of the Errors 3–4.5, in *Creeds and Confessions of the Reformation Era*, 2:589–590.
42 "Canons of Dort," 3–4.12, in *Creeds and Confessions of the Reformation Era*, 2:586. Dort rejects a mere persuasion, "Having set forth the orthodox teaching, the synod rejects the errors of those … 7. Who teach that the grace by which we are converted

dead. Indeed, God's act of rebirth is always certain, unfailing and effective, so that those whom God chooses to specially call and regenerate "do actually believe." Bavinck summarizes Dort well,

> God is the primary actor in the work of redemption. He gives a new heart, apart from any merit or condition having been achieved from our side, merely and only according to His good pleasure. He enlightens the understanding, bends the will, governs the impulses, regenerates, awakens, vivifies, and He does that within us quite apart from our doing.... No consent of our intellect, no decision of our will, no desire of our heart comes in between. God accomplishes this work within our hearts through His Spirit, and He does this directly, internally, invincibly. [43]

Appealing to Ephesians 1:19; 2 Thessalonians 1:11, and 2 Peter 1:3, Dort's rejection of synergism is also evident in Rejections of Errors 3–4.8, rebuffing the Arminians who believe that

> God in regenerating man does not bring to bear that power of his omnipotence whereby he may powerfully and unfailingly bend man's will to faith and conversion, but that even when God has accomplished all the works of grace which he uses for man's conversion, man nevertheless can, and in actual fact often does,

---

to God is nothing but a gentle persuasion, or (as others explain it) that the way of God's acting in man's conversion that is most noble and suited to human nature is that which happens by persuasion, and that nothing prevents this grace of moral suasion even by itself from making natural men spiritual; indeed, that God does not produce the assent of the will except in this manner of moral suasion, and that the effectiveness of God's work by which it surpasses the work of Satan consists in the fact that God promises eternal benefits while Satan promises temporal ones." Dort goes on to say that such a teaching is Pelagian and contradicts Ezekiel 36:26. See "Canons of Dort," Rejection of the Errors 3–4.7, in *Creeds and Confessions of the Reformation Era*, 2:590.

43 Herman Bavinck, *Saved by Grace: The Holy Spirit's Work in Calling and Regeneration*, ed. J. Mark Beach, trans. Nelson D. Kloosterman (Grand Rapids: Reformation Heritage, 2008), 29. For a detailed description of Dort's articulation of grace against the Remonstrants, see pages 41–65.

so resist God and the Spirit in their intent and will to regenerate him, that man completely thwarts his own rebirth; and, indeed, that it remains in his own power whether or not to be reborn.[44]

According to Dort, such a view as this "does away with all effective functioning of God's grace in our conversion and subjects the activity of Almighty God to the will of man."[45] Furthermore, such a view is

contrary to the apostles, who teach that we believe by virtue of the effective working of God's mighty strength, and that God fulfills the undeserved good will of his kindness and the work of faith in us with power, and likewise that his divine power has given us everything we need for life and godliness.[46]

Notice the emphasis Dort places on making sure it is God, not man, who receives all of the credit and glory (1 Corinthians 1:31). To reverse the order is to rob God of his glory and give man grounds to boast.

If, as Dort argues, man's faith is the result of God's effectual call and regenerative work, then it also follows that faith itself is a gift. However, Dort is very careful to avoid an Arminian definition of faith. Having Jeremiah 31:18 and 33, Isaiah 44:3 and Romans 5:5 in mind, article 14 states, "In this way, therefore, faith is a gift of God, not in the sense that it is offered by God for man to choose, but that

---

44 "Canons of Dort," Rejection of the Errors 3–4.8, in *Creeds and Confessions of the Reformation Era*, 2:590–591.

45 "Canons of Dort," Rejection of the Errors 3–4.8, in *Creeds and Confessions of the Reformation Era*, 2:591.

46 "Canons of Dort," Rejection of the Errors 3–4.8, in *Creeds and Confessions of the Reformation Era*, 2:591. Dort also states in Rejection 9, "Having set forth the orthodox teaching, the synod rejects the errors of those… 9. Who teach that grace and free choice are concurrent partial causes which cooperate to initiate conversion, and that grace does not precede—in the order of causality—the effective influence of the will; that is to say, that God does not effectively help man's will to come to conversion before man's will itself motivates and determines itself." Dort goes on to argue that the church condemned the Pelagians for such an error. Dort cites Romans 9:16, 1 Corinthians 4:7, and Philippians 2:13 in support. See "Canons of Dort," Rejection of the Errors 3–4.9, in *Creeds and Confessions of the Reformation Era*, 2:591.

it is in actual fact bestowed on man, breathed and infused into him."[47] Dort continues,

> Nor is it a gift in the sense that God bestows only the potential to believe, but then awaits assent—the act of believing—from man's choice; rather, it is a gift in the sense that he who works both willing and acting and, indeed, works all things in all people produces in man both the will to believe and the belief itself.[48]

In other words, the Arminian defines faith in such a way that it is a gift but only in the sense that it is *offered* so that whether or not it becomes *actual* is man's choice, not God's. To the contrary, faith is a gift that God wills to implant within the dead, lifeless sinner so that upon granting the dead sinner new life he believes *necessarily*. As Dort states, God produces "in man both the will to believe and the belief itself" (3–4.14). Peter Toon correctly concludes that, on the basis of article 14, Dort taught "that regeneration precedes faith and is the cause of faith."[49]

Dort, however, is aware of two objections. First, the Arminian objects that if it is only God who can do this effectual and irresistible work so that without it no man can believe, then God is unjust and unfair to limit his saving work to only some rather than all. But Dort responds to this objection in the tradition of the apostle Paul in Romans 9. "God does not owe this grace to anyone. For what could

---

47 "Canons of Dort," 3–4.14, in *Creeds and Confessions of the Reformation Era*, 2:587.

48 "Canons of Dort," 3–4.14, in *Creeds and Confessions of the Reformation Era*, 2:587. Likewise, Rejection 6 states, "Having set forth the orthodox teaching, the synod rejects the errors of those... 6. Who teach that in the true conversion of man new qualities, dispositions, or gifts cannot be infused or poured into his will by God, and indeed that the faith [or believing] by which we first come to conversion and from which we receive the name 'believers' is not a quality or gift infused by God, but only an act of man, and that it cannot be called a gift except in respect to the power of attaining faith." Dort cites Jeremiah 31:33, Isaiah 44:3, Romans 5:5 and Jeremiah 31:18 in support ("Canons of Dort," Rejection of Errors 3–4.6, in *Creeds and Confessions of the Reformation Era*, 2:590).

49 Peter Toon, *Born Again: A Biblical and Theological Study of Regeneration* (Grand Rapids: Baker, 1987), 123.

God owe to one who has nothing to give that can be paid back? Indeed, what could God owe to one who has nothing of his own to give but sin and falsehood?"[50] Man has nothing to offer but sin and guilt. Therefore, it is pure mercy for God to call and regenerate anyone at all. To level the charge of injustice against God is to miss this point entirely.

Second, the Remonstrants also objected that if grace is irresistible, not just providing the opportunity to believe but actually providing the will to believe, then man is reduced to a block or stone, stripped of his personal agency. Dort responds insightfully.

> However, just as by the fall man did not cease to be man, endowed with intellect and will, and just as sin, which has spread through the whole human race, did not abolish the nature of the human race but distorted and spiritually killed it, so also this divine grace of regeneration does not act in people as if they were blocks and stones.[51]

Dort continues, "nor does it abolish the will and its properties or coerce a reluctant will by force, but spiritually revives, heals, reforms, and—in a manner at once pleasing and powerful—bends it back."[52] Consequently, "a ready and sincere obedience of the Spirit now begins to prevail where before the rebellion and resistance of the flesh were completely dominant. It is in this that the true spiritual restoration and freedom of our will consists."[53] Dort concludes, "Thus, if the marvelous Maker of every good thing were not dealing with us, man would have no hope of getting up from his fall by his free choice, by which he plunged himself into ruin when still standing upright."[54]

In summary, the grace of regeneration works upon the will not to abolish it or coerce it, but rather in a way that revives, heals and reforms it, bending it back to love God rather than sin. Notice exactly how God revives, heals, reforms and bends the will: it is in a "manner

---

50 "Canons of Dort," 3–4.15, in *Creeds and Confessions of the Reformation Era*, 2:587.
51 "Canons of Dort," 3–4.16, in *Creeds and Confessions of the Reformation Era*, 2:587.
52 "Canons of Dort," 3–4.16, in *Creeds and Confessions of the Reformation Era*, 2:587.
53 "Canons of Dort," 3–4.16, in *Creeds and Confessions of the Reformation Era*, 2:587.
54 "Canons of Dort," 3–4.16, in *Creeds and Confessions of the Reformation Era*, 2:587.

at once pleasing and powerful."⁵⁵ It is pleasing because man is a sinner, deserving only wrath. It is powerful in that God does not leave salvation up to man's will but brings him into union with Christ without fail, accomplishing the redemption he intended.

Humble gratitude and the death of pride

In order to see how Dort connects the doctrine of effectual grace to spiritual humility and gratitude we must return to articles 7 and 15. In 3–4.7 Dort argues, as we already saw, that the revelation of the gospel is due to his free mercy alone and not to anything in man. Why the gospel is made effective in some and not in others is not due to one man's ability to use the light of nature better than another nor is it due to any intrinsic worth in one man that makes him more worthy than another. To the contrary, it is due to "the free good pleasure and undeserved love of God."⁵⁶ What then should the attitude of those who receive this grace be? Dort answers, "those who receive so much grace, beyond and in spite of all they deserve, ought to acknowledge it with humble and thankful hearts."⁵⁷ God does not save the elect sinner because of anything in him, but actually in spite of everything in him. Consequently, the only suitable and worthy response from the sinner is humility, praise and thanksgiving toward God.

The same emphasis is again seen in article 15 where Dort responds to the Arminian objection that if it is only God who can do this effectual and irresistible work so that without it no man can believe, then God is unjust and unfair to limit his saving work to only some rather than all. Dort replies,

> God does not owe this grace to anyone. For what could God owe to one who has nothing to give that can be paid back? Indeed, what could God owe to one who has nothing of his own to give but sin and falsehood? Therefore the person who receives this grace owes and gives eternal thanks to God alone; the person who does not receive it either does not care at all about these

---

55 "Canons of Dort," 3–4.16, in *Creeds and Confessions of the Reformation Era*, 2:587.
56 "Canons of Dort," 3–4.7, in *Creeds and Confessions of the Reformation Era*, 2:585.
57 "Canons of Dort," 3–4.7, in *Creeds and Confessions of the Reformation Era*, 2:585.

spiritual things and is satisfied with himself in his condition, or else in self-assurance foolishly boasts about having something which he lacks. Furthermore, following the example of the apostles, we are to think and to speak in the most favorable way about those who outwardly profess their faith and better their lives, for the inner chambers of the heart are unknown to us. But for others who have not yet been called, we are to pray to God who calls things that do not exist as though they did. In no way, however, are we to pride ourselves as better than they, as though we had distinguished ourselves from them.[58]

The divide then between the believer saved by grace and the unbeliever justly condemned shows itself in external manifestations. The believer has nothing to say but thanksgiving and praise to his Saviour, while the unbeliever either cares nothing for the things of God or, in a haughty and boastful spirit, is under a false assurance of salvation. Dort is not silent on how Christians should approach these two types of people. First, Dort states that since we do not know the "inner chambers of the heart" we must "speak in the most favorable way" about those who outwardly confess Christ and seek to grow in sanctification.[59] Second, concerning those who have not yet been effectually called, we are to pray earnestly to God on their behalf, for God and God alone is the one "who calls things that do not exist as though they did."[60] Here we see the connection between divine sovereignty and evangelism. God alone can call and change a heart of stone to a heart of flesh (Ezekiel 36:25–27). However, the Christian is to pray for these unbelievers and ask God to call them to himself. Just as God calls light out of darkness, so also can God call a dead, depraved sinner into the light of the life of Christ (2 Corinthians 4:6). Yet, God instructs us to pray for unbelievers, for our prayers are the very means to this salvific end.

Moreover, Dort not only reminds the believer to pray fervently for the unbeliever, but Dort warns the believer that in no way should we

58 "Canons of Dort," 3–4.15, in *Creeds and Confessions of the Reformation Era*, 2:587.
59 "Canons of Dort," 3–4.15, in *Creeds and Confessions of the Reformation Era*, 2:587.
60 "Canons of Dort," 3–4.15, in *Creeds and Confessions of the Reformation Era*, 2:587.

"pride ourselves as better than they, as though we had distinguished ourselves from them."[61] For the Calvinist, man contributes absolutely nothing to his salvation, not even the slightest cooperation of his free will. It is God alone who works to effectually call and regenerate the dead and depraved sinner, bringing life out of death (cf. John 3:5–8). Consequently, the believer has no right whatsoever to then, out of a proud heart, turn with contempt upon an unbeliever. To do so, as Dort says, is to act as if something in us made us more worthy of salvation than they. But there is nothing to be found. The saved sinner, as Edwin Palmer remarks, is left to say: "Truly, Lord, except for thy grace, I would have done the same evil." Consequently, "Calvinism produces humility."[62] Such humility is accompanied by sheer gratitude to God and a life of obedience.[63] Additionally, the Christian's interaction with unbelievers must be characterized by meekness, for only then is he consistent with the doctrine of sovereign grace. True piety and holiness, as well as a love for the lost soul, comes from the heart that realizes that it was nothing within that moved God to save, but wholly and completely the grace and mercy of God through Christ.

Finally, Dort's biblical affirmation of irresistible grace is a motivator of pastoral hope in hopeless cases. Whereas Arminianism advocates a God whose saving grace is contingent upon man's will to save, Dort's Calvinism looks to a God whose will to save a dead sinner cannot be thwarted (John 6:44). Irresistible grace is a reminder that no human method or strategy can save a sinner. It is not the case that the lost simply need more convincing due to their indifference. It is not as if one must simply be persuasive enough to get the sinner to react. As Palmer states,

> For the man is spiritually dead. He cannot say Yes while he does not have life. He is totally depraved, that is, utterly unable to desire salvation unless the Spirit first of all makes him alive. The man must be born from above, born a second time, spiritually

---

61 "Canons of Dort," 3–4.15, in *Creeds and Confessions of the Reformation Era*, 2:587.

62 Edwin H. Palmer, "The Significance of the Canons for Pastoral Work," in *Crisis in the Reformed Churches*, 140.

63 Henry Petersen, *The Canons of Dort* (Grand Rapids: Baker, 1968), 73.

resurrected, made alive again in Christ Jesus. And how else can that be done except that God does it? The pastor knows he has tried every human means to no avail. But when he remembers that God in his electing love works irresistibly, then he can take hope. Although the pastor cannot touch the lost man's life, God can. If he could regenerate Paul, the Christ-hater, then he can touch today's hardened or indifferent man. God's election and the irresistible grace bring hope as the minister deals with the "hopeless" cases.[64]

Dort provides hope to the tired and wearied pastor by reminding him that it is not his own human efforts, whatever they may be, but the power of God to work irresistibly within a dead man's heart that saves. Irresistible grace gives the pastor confidence to preach the word and evangelize, knowing that God will save his elect. If anything, the pastor is "made to depend upon God more."[65]

Conclusion

"Calvinism cannot ever be proud, cold, clinical and censorious, and that for one main reason: You cannot 'see the King' [Isaiah 6:5] in his exalted majesty, and have your sinful heart laid bare before him and yourself, and still remain proud."[66] This truth stated by Ian Hamilton is vividly expressed in the Canons of Dort. For Dort, the doctrines of total depravity and sovereign grace do not produce pride but humility. Those who have had their eyes opened to the omnipotence of regenerating grace see the King high and lifted up. Witnessing the majesty of a sovereign God does not lead one to be puffed up in himself but cast down to the ground, to his knees, in gratitude and self-effacement. As Hamilton continues to explain, "Authentic Calvinism is so far from trampling on humility and promoting pride that it actually breeds by its nature a meek and lowly spirit. How can you or I be savingly united to the meek and lowly Saviour, and be proud, clinical, or metallic in

---

64 Palmer, "The Significance of the Canons for Pastoral Work," 139.
65 Palmer, "The Significance of the Canons for Pastoral Work," 140.
66 Hamilton, "Proud Calvinism," *The Banner of Truth* 496 (2005): 16.

our Christianity? Proud Calvinism is the ultimate oxymoron."[67] The "proud Calvinist" Hamilton speaks of cannot be found in the Canons of Dort. Rather, when one reads the Canons one discovers that sovereign grace is a tool in the hands of a mighty God by which he brings about true, authentic Christian humility. Therefore, Calvinists are to be the meekest of all people. Hamilton once again explains,

> Authentic Calvinism is natively meek-spirited. To claim to believe that God is the Sovereign King, that you owe all you are to his distinguishing grace and love, that you are and ever will be a "debtor to mercy alone," while behaving proudly and treating other sinners, and even worse, Christian brothers, with supercilious disdain, is not to expose yourself as an inauthentic Calvinist, but to expose yourself as an inauthentic Christian![68]

Dort sees authentic Christians as debtors to mercy alone. The only proper response to divine mercy is gratitude and praise.

---

67 Hamilton, "Proud Calvinism," *The Banner of Truth* 496 (2005): 19.
68 Hamilton, "Proud Calvinism," *The Banner of Truth* 496 (2005): 17–18.

"And this is the will of him who sent me, that I should lose nothing of all that he has given me, but raise it up on the last day."—JOHN 6:39

"My sheep hear my voice, and I know them, and they follow me. I give them eternal life, and they will never perish, and no one will snatch them out of my hand."—JOHN 10:27-28

What then shall we say to these things? If God is for us, who can be against us? He who did not spare his own Son but gave him up for us all, how will he not also with him graciously give us all things? Who shall bring any charge against God's elect? It is God who justifies. Who is to condemn? Christ Jesus is the one who died—more than that, who was raised—who is at the right hand of God, who indeed is interceding for us. Who shall separate us from the love of Christ? Shall tribulation, or distress, or persecution, or famine, or nakedness, or danger, or sword? As it is written, "For your sake we are being killed all the day long; we are regarded as sheep to be slaughtered." No, in all these things we are more than conquerors through him who loved us. For I am sure that neither death nor life, nor angels nor rulers, nor things present nor things to come, nor powers, nor height nor depth, nor anything else in all creation, will be able to separate us from the love of God in Christ Jesus our Lord.—ROMANS 8:31-39

And I am sure of this, that he who began a good work in you will bring it to completion at the day of Jesus Christ.—PHILIPPIANS 1:6

Having purified your souls by your obedience to the truth for a sincere brotherly love, love one another earnestly from a pure heart, since you have been born again, not of perishable seed but of imperishable, through the living and abiding word of God.—1 PETER 1:22-23

The perseverance of the saints
Incentive to holy living

Introduction

"If your understanding of Calvinistic thinking has led you to the place where you can, as it were, boast in your liberty and use it as an occasion for licence, then you have never become a biblical Calvinist."[1] When it comes to the doctrine of the perseverance of the saints, these words by A.N. Martin could not describe the Synod of Dort better. When God regenerates a depraved sinner, the believer receives new affections. Whereas before he only desired the pleasures of the flesh, now that he has been awakened by the Spirit he desires Christ above all things. Whereas before he was a slave to sin, now that he has been

---

1   A.N. Martin, "The Practical Implications of True Calvinism: 1," *The Banner of Truth* 120 (1973): 19.

born again by the Spirit he treasures his Saviour more than life itself. Therefore, God's promise to preserve those whom the Son has died for and the Spirit has regenerated unto glory is an incentive to holy living. God does not regenerate the dead sinner, resurrecting him to newness of life by the power of his Spirit and then leave him to work out his salvation from that point on by himself. By no means! On the contrary, the same Spirit that brought new life into a dead corpse, continues to work on a daily basis deeds of holiness pleasing in God's sight. Those redeemed by the blood of the Lamb, therefore, do not see the Spirit's work as an excuse to live in sin but as the very grace they need to fight against sin. Moreover, the believer indwelt by the Spirit has the Spirit as a guarantee that he will persevere to the end. No wonder the apostle Paul could write, "And I am sure of this, that he who began a good work in you will bring it to completion at the day of Jesus Christ" (Philippians 1:6). The Reformed doctrine of the perseverance of the saints serves not as a barrier but as an incentive and prop for godliness. It is to the Synod of Dort's articulation of this doctrine, as well as the Remonstrant argument against it, that we now turn.

Arminianism and the loss of salvation

What did the Remonstrants believe concerning the believer's perseverance in the faith? Can someone who trusted in Christ lose his salvation by choosing to walk away from the faith despite God's efforts to keep him in Christ? The Arminians, in their Remonstrance of 1610 cannot confidently answer this question. They write in article 5,

> But whether they can through negligence fall away from the first principle of their life in Christ, again embrace the present world, depart from the pure doctrine once given to them, lose the good conscience, and neglect grace, must first be more carefully determined from the Holy Scriptures before we shall be able to teach this with the full persuasion of our heart.[2]

---

2 "Appendix C: The Remonstrance of 1610," in *Crisis in the Reformed Churches: Essays in Commemoration of the Great Synod of Dort, 1618–1619*, ed. Peter Y. De Jong (Grand Rapids: Reformed Fellowship, 1968), 209.

However, in the Opinions of the Remonstrance of 1618 we see a fuller, more decisive answer given to the Calvinists on this subject. The Arminians begin by denying that the perseverance of believers in the faith is "an effect of that absolute decree by which God is said to have chosen singular persons defined by no condition of obedience."[3] God's involvement, however, does include his provision of grace, or at least "as much grace and supernatural powers as He judges, according to His infinite wisdom, to be sufficient for persevering and for overcoming the temptations of the devil, the flesh, and the world."[4] Whether or not the believer chooses to use this grace is determined not by God but by man's free will. Consequently, "it is never to be charged to God's account that they do not persevere."[5] The Remonstrants then declare without hesitation: "True believers can fall from true faith and can fall into such sins as cannot be consistent with true and justifying faith."[6] Moreover, "not only is it possible for this to happen, but it even happens frequently."[7] Stated otherwise, "True believers are able to fall through their own fault into shameful and atrocious deeds, to persevere and to die in them; and therefore finally to fall and to perish."[8]

---

3 "Appendix H: The Opinions of the Remonstrants," 5.1, in *Crisis in the Reformed Churches*, 228.

4 "Appendix H: The Opinions of the Remonstrants," 5.2, in *Crisis in the Reformed Churches*, 228.

5 "Appendix H: The Opinions of the Remonstrants," 5.2, in *Crisis in the Reformed Churches*, 228.

6 "Appendix H: The Opinions of the Remonstrants," 5.3, in *Crisis in the Reformed Churches*, 228.

7 "Appendix H: The Opinions of the Remonstrants," 5.3, in *Crisis in the Reformed Churches*, 228.

8 "Appendix H: The Opinions of the Remonstrants," 5.4, in *Crisis in the Reformed Churches*, 228. Likewise, 5.6 says, "The following dogmas, therefore, which by public writings are being scattered among the people, we reject with our whole mind and heart as harmful to piety and good morals: namely, (1) True believers are not able to sin deliberately, but only out of ignorance and weakness. (2) True believers through no sins can fall out of the grace of God. (3) A thousand sins, even all the sins of the whole world, are not able to render election invalid.... (4) To believers and to the elect no sins, however great and grave they can be, are imputed; but all present and future sins have already been remitted. (5) True believers, having fallen into destructive

Despite the reality that many true believers fall into sin and become unbelievers once again, the Remonstrants insist that God, "according to the multitude of His mercies, may recall them through His grace to repentance."[9] Such a reversal, they claim, "happens not infrequently, although we cannot be persuaded that this will certainly and indubitably happen."[10]

According to the Remonstrants, a true believer can lose his salvation, regain it by the grace of God and possibly lose it again. Can he then, at any one time, have a certainty or assurance? The Remonstrants insist that he can: "A true believer, as for the present time he can be certain about his faith and the integrity of his conscience, and thus also concerning his salvation and the saving benevolence of God toward him, for that time can be and ought to be certain."[11] Notice, however, that the Remonstrants qualify such certainty and assurance by saying that it is possible to have such comfort "as for the present time."[12] The Arminian cannot guarantee any assurance and certainty for the future because it is very possible and often common that true believers fall into damnation. What the true believer can be certain of for the future is that "he is able, by diligent watchfulness, through prayers, and through other holy exercises, to persevere in true faith, and he ought also to be certain that divine grace for persevering will never be lacking."[13] In other words, while the believer cannot be

heresies, into grave and most atrocious sins, like adultery and homicide, on account of which the church, after the justification of Christ, is compelled to testify that it is not able to tolerate them in its external communion and that they will have no part in the kingdom of Christ unless they are converted, nevertheless are not able to fall from faith totally and finally" ("Appendix H: The Opinions of the Remonstrants," 5.6, in *Crisis in the Reformed Churches*, 228–229).

9 "Appendix H: The Opinions of the Remonstrants," 5.5, in *Crisis in the Reformed Churches*, 228.

10 "Appendix H: The Opinions of the Remonstrants," 5.5, in *Crisis in the Reformed Churches*, 228.

11 "Appendix H: The Opinions of the Remonstrants," 5.7, in *Crisis in the Reformed Churches*, 229.

12 "Appendix H: The Opinions of the Remonstrants," 5.7, in *Crisis in the Reformed Churches*, 229.

13 "Appendix H: The Opinions of the Remonstrants," 5.8, in *Crisis in the Reformed Churches*, 229.

certain or guaranteed that he will persevere, nevertheless, he can be confident that (1) he has the ability to persevere if he so chooses through means such as watchfulness, prayers and other "holy exercises" and (2) God will always make divine grace available (it "will never be lacking") so that he can choose for himself whether or not he will persevere in that grace. Despite the availability of these gracious resources, nevertheless, "we do not see how he can be certain that he will never afterwards be remiss in his duty but that he will preserve in faith and in those works of piety and love which are fitting for a believer in this school of Christian warfare."[14] Indeed, we do not "deem it necessary that concerning this thing a believer should be certain."[15] Here again we see the Remonstrant view presented, namely, that the believer can have no final, ultimate or future certainty and assurance that he will preserve in faith or continue in those "works of piety and love" needed to finish the race.[16]

The preservation and perseverance of the saints
The Calvinists or Counter-Remonstrants rejected the Arminian view entirely. While the Christian life is a real battle against sin, the believer can have a genuine and certain assurance of his salvation, not just that he will persevere in the moment but for the future as well. In other words, while the Christian continues to wage war against sin, he can be confident that the sovereign God who saved him from damnation will not let him fall away from true faith and perish eternally. God is faithful to his promises, and he will not lose any of his children nor allow anyone, including the devil himself, to pluck them out of the hand of his Son.

We see such a strong affirmation of divine preservation in canon 5. Dort is not satisfied with the Arminian view that while the believer cannot be certain he will finally persevere he can at least be certain

---

14 "Appendix H: The Opinions of the Remonstrants," 5.8, in *Crisis in the Reformed Churches*, 229.

15 "Appendix H: The Opinions of the Remonstrants," 5.8, in *Crisis in the Reformed Churches*, 229.

16 "Appendix H: The Opinions of the Remonstrants," 5.8, in *Crisis in the Reformed Churches*, 229.

that the resources to do so will be available. Dort responds,

> Because of these remnants of sin dwelling in them and also because of the temptations of the world and Satan, those who have been converted could not remain standing in this grace if left to their own resources. But God is faithful, mercifully strengthening them in the grace once conferred on them and powerfully preserving them in it to the end.[17]

In other words, if man is left to these resources the only guarantee is that he will *not* persevere to the end. But this is not the case. To the contrary, God does not merely give man the resources he needs and then leave it up to his own free will as to whether or not he will use the grace he has been given to persevere.[18] Rather, as 1 Corinthians 1:8 makes clear, God actually makes sure his children will persevere to the end. His grace is not merely provisionary but effectual and powerful. It is here that we see the dividing line between the Arminian and the Calvinist. For the Arminian, God makes available what is needed but he will not intervene out of fear that he might violate man's free will. For the Calvinist, however, God is far more personally involved. His power is not at the mercy of the sinner but the sinner is at the mercy of his power. God is not merely available but he actually intercedes on the sinner's behalf, strengthening him in grace and faithfully

---

17 "Canons of Dort," 5.3, in *Creeds and Confessions of the Reformation Era*, vol. 2 of *Creeds and Confessions of Faith in the Christian Tradition*, eds. Jaroslav Pelikan and Valerie Hotchkiss (New Haven and London: Yale University Press, 2003), 592.

18 As Dort states in Rejection of the Errors 2, they reject those who "teach that God does provide the believer with sufficient strength to persevere and is ready to preserve this strength in him if he performs his duty, but that even with all those things in place which are necessary to persevere in faith and which God is pleased to use to persevere faith, it still always depends on the choice of man's will whether or not he perseveres. For this view is obviously Pelagian; and though it intends to make men free it makes them sacrilegious. It is against the enduring consensus of evangelical teaching which takes from man all cause for boasting and ascribes the praise for this benefit only to God's grace. It is also against the testimony of the apostle: It is God who keeps us strong to the end, so that we will be blameless on the day of our Lord Jesus Christ [1 Corinthians 1:8]" ("Canons of Dort," Rejection of the Errors 5.2, in *Creeds and Confessions of the Reformation Era*, 2:595).

fulfilling his promise to preserve him to the very end. The difference, in other words, is between a God who is powerless to save and a God who is powerful to save.

It is also important to recognize how Dort connects election to the perseverance of the saints. In Rejection of the Errors (of the Remonstrants) at the end of canon 5, Dort says it rejects the errors of those who "teach that the perseverance of true believers is not an effect of election or a gift of God produced by Christ's death, but a condition of the new covenant which man, before what they call his 'peremptory' election and justification, must fulfill by his free will."[19] For the Remonstrants, perseverance is the condition the covenant man must fulfil by his own free will if he is to be elected. In other words, God conditions his election upon whether or not he foresees the sinner not only having faith but persevering in that faith till the end. Therefore, election is conditioned upon perseverance. Just the opposite is true for Dort. Perseverance does not determine election but election determines perseverance. In other words, perseverance is the fruit and result of God's unconditional choice. Dort explains, "For Holy Scripture testifies that perseverance *follows from* election and is granted to the chosen by virtue of Christ's death, resurrection, and intercession."[20]

It is at this point that Dort turns to Scripture for support. Citing Romans 11:7, Dort writes, "The chosen obtained it; the others were hardened." Dort also cites Romans 8:32–35,

> He who did not spare his own Son, but gave him up for us all— how will he not, along with him, grant us all things? Who will bring any charge against those whom God has chosen? It is God who justifies. Who is he that condemns? It is Christ Jesus who died—more than that, who was raised—who also sits at the right hand of God, and is also interceding for us. Who shall separate us from the love of Christ?

---

19 "Canons of Dort," Rejection of the Errors 5.1, in *Creeds and Confessions of the Reformation Era*, 2:595.

20 Emphasis added. "Canons of Dort," Rejection of the Errors 5.1, in *Creeds and Confessions of the Reformation Era*, 2:595. See also Peter G. Feenstra, *Unspeakable Comfort: A Commentary on The Canons of Dort* (Winnipeg: Premier, 1997), 165.

Dort is on solid ground to reject the Arminian view, for Paul testifies that Christ himself intercedes for us and therefore nothing can separate us from his love. Feenstra summarizes Dort well when he writes, "the God who elects is also the God who causes the saints to persevere." In other words, "Take away the doctrine of election and the doctrine of the perseverance of the saints falls to the ground. The perseverance of the saints is a fruit of election."[21]

Dort appeals to other passages of Scripture as well. Dort rejects those who "teach that those who truly believe and have been born again not only can forfeit justifying faith as well as grace and salvation totally and to the end, but also in actual fact do often forfeit them and are lost forever."[22] Such a view "nullifies the very grace of justification and regeneration as well as the continual preservation by Christ."[23] Biblical support is found in the following passages, says Dort:

> If Christ died for us while we were still sinners, we will therefore much more be saved from God's wrath through him, since we have now been justified by his blood (Romans 5:8–9).

> No one who is born of God is intent on sin, because God's seed remains in him, nor can he sin, because he has been born of God (1 John 3:9).

> I give eternal life to my sheep, and they shall never perish; no one can snatch them out of my hand. My Father, who has given them to me, is greater than all; no one can snatch them out of my Father's hand (John 10:28–29).

In these passages we see that once a sinner has been regenerated and justified he is now *in Christ* and therefore the Father will not let anyone tear asunder that union with Christ.

---

21 Feenstra, *Unspeakable Comfort*, 146–147.

22 "Canons of Dort," Rejection of the Errors 5.3, in *Creeds and Confessions of the Reformation Era*, 2:596.

23 "Canons of Dort," Rejection of the Errors 5.3, in *Creeds and Confessions of the Reformation Era*, 2:596.

Dort continues, addressing both regeneration and justification more specifically. Concerning justification Dort rejects those who teach "that the faith of those who believe only temporarily does not differ from justifying and saving faith except in duration alone."[24] How can this be when Christ himself says in Matthew 13 and Luke 8 that "the former receive the seed on rocky ground, and the latter receive it in good ground, or a good heart" and again "the former have no root, and the latter are firmly rooted; the former have no fruit, and the latter produce fruit in varying measure, with steadfastness, or perseverance"? Clearly, says Dort, Christ distinguishes "between temporary and true believers," the former of which turn out not to be true believers at all.[25]

Concerning regeneration, Dort rejects those who "teach that it is not absurd that a person, after losing his former regeneration, should once again, indeed quite often, be reborn."[26] In reality, says Dort, it is the Arminian position that is "absurd"! How many times must a man be born again and again and again before he is secure in Christ? Is the work of the Spirit in regeneration so incomplete and impotent that it can so easily be reversed by the will of man? Does the Spirit not only work omnipotently in regeneration but in sanctification and perseverance as well? "For by this teaching they deny the imperishable nature of God's seed by which we are born again," contrary to what the apostle Peter says, "Born again, not of perishable seed, but of imperishable" (1 Peter 1:23).[27] Or consider other passages as well:

"I [Christ] have prayed for you, Peter, that your faith may not fail" (Luke 22:32).

---

24 "Canons of Dort," Rejection of the Errors 5.7, in *Creeds and Confessions of the Reformation Era*, 2:597.

25 "Canons of Dort," Rejection of the Errors 5.7, in *Creeds and Confessions of the Reformation Era*, 2:597.

26 "Canons of Dort," Rejection of the Errors 5.8, in *Creeds and Confessions of the Reformation Era*, 2:597.

27 "Canons of Dort," Rejection of the Errors 5.8, in *Creeds and Confessions of the Reformation Era*, 2:597.

"Holy Father, preserve them ["not only for the apostles, but also for all those who were to believe"] in your name" (John 17:11; cf. 17:20).

"My prayer is not that you take them out of the world, but that you preserve them from the evil one" (John 17:15).

Has the Father failed to answer the prayer of his Son to preserve his children from the evil one? Certainly not! Once again, Dort demonstrates that the Arminian position is deeply in conflict with Scripture.

Dort also addresses the issue of the unpardonable sin. Dort rejects those who teach "that those who truly believe and have been born again can commit the sin that leads to death (the sin against the Holy Spirit)."[28] The sin against the Holy Spirit is a sin that only an unbeliever can commit. Justification for such a claim comes from 1 John 5:16–17 and 1 John 5:18 where we read,

If any man see his brother sin a sin which is not unto death, he shall ask, and he shall give him life for them that sin not unto death. There is a sin unto death: I do not say that he shall pray for it. All unrighteousness is sin: and there is a sin not unto death (1 John 5:16–17).

We know that anyone born of God does not commit sin [that is, that kind of sin], but the one who was born of God keeps himself safe, and the evil one does not touch him (1 John 5:18).

Christ himself keeps those born of God from sin that leads to death.

Perseverance and preservation: the incentive to holy living
Holy exercises of godliness
Out of the five canons articulated by Dort, it is the fifth and final canon which has the most to say about Christian piety. Dort begins canon 5

by describing the regenerate believer's situation, namely, as one who is *simul iustus et peccator* (simultaneously righteous and a sinner). Those whom God has called to Christ and the Spirit has regenerated, God has also set free from the "reign and slavery of sin, though in this life not entirely from the flesh and from the body of sin."[29] In other words, sin's grip has been broken, having no condemning power over the justified believer, but this side of heaven the regenerate man continues to wage warfare against sin (Romans 6:1–6).

> Hence daily sins of weakness arise, and blemishes cling to even the best works of God's people, giving them continual cause to humble themselves before God, to flee for refuge to Christ crucified, to put the flesh to death more and more by the Spirit of supplication and by holy exercises of godliness [piety], and to strain toward the goal of perfection, until they are freed from this body of death and reign with the Lamb of God in heaven.[30]

There is not a hint of perfectionism in these words. Dort, realizing the believer's ongoing battle with sin, reminds the Christian that blemishes are a continual cause of godly humiliation before a holy God. However, it is not condemnation that awaits the believer but forgiveness at the cross of Christ, for Dort exhorts the believer to "flee for refuge to Christ crucified."

Note, Dort's first reaction for the Christian sinner is to look upon the *objective* work of Christ, where redemption has been accomplished and secured and where forgiveness flows for all eternity for those for whom Christ died. However, Dort does not stay there, but secondarily turns to the *subjective*, namely, the sin within the believer himself, encouraging him to mortify the flesh by putting it to death "more and more by the Spirit of supplication and by holy exercises of godliness." By the negative practice of mortification and the positive practice of putting on godliness, the believer is able to "strain toward the goal of perfection," which is finally acquired when the believer reigns with

---

29 "Canons of Dort," 5.1, in *Creeds and Confessions of the Reformation Era*, 2:591.

30 "Canons of Dort," 5.2, in *Creeds and Confessions of the Reformation Era*, 2:591–592.

the Lamb of God in heaven. Here is a clear reference to Paul's words in Philippians 3:14, "I press on toward the goal for the prize of the upward call of God in Christ Jesus."

The spirit is willing, but the flesh is weak

Unlike the Arminian, the Calvinist is not left without the promise that those whom the Father has called, Christ will indeed keep to the end. God is faithful, mercifully strengthening his children in grace, powerfully preserving them to the end.[31] However, Dort does not believe that simply because God has promised to keep those whom he has chosen, man is perfectly motivated and excited at all times in treasuring Christ. Rather, though secure in Christ, believers can and do fall into sin, failing to trust in Christ when temptation comes.

> Although that power of God strengthening and preserving true believers in grace is more than a match for the flesh, yet those converted are not always so activated and motivated by God that in certain specific actions they cannot by their own fault depart from the leading of grace, be led astray by the desires of the flesh, and give in to them.[32]

Dort continues,

> For this reason they must constantly watch and pray that they may not be led into temptations [Matthew 26:41]. When they fail to do this, not only can they be carried away by the flesh, the world, and Satan into sins, even serious and outrageous ones, but also by God's just permission they sometimes are so carried away —witness the sad cases, described in Scripture, of David, Peter, and other saints falling into sins."[33]

---

31 See "Canons of Dort," 5.3, in *Creeds and Confessions of the Reformation Era*, 2:592.

32 "Canons of Dort," 5.4, in *Creeds and Confessions of the Reformation Era*, 2:592.

33 "Canons of Dort," 5.4, in *Creeds and Confessions of the Reformation Era*, 2:592. For a very similar statement, see Chapters 17.3 and 18.4 of the Westminster Confession of Faith.

According to Dort, sin is a real threat, so that believers, by no fault but their own, "depart from the leading grace," being led astray by the sinful pleasures of the flesh. Dort's solution is biblical, turning to Matthew 26:41, "Watch and pray that you may not enter into temptation. The spirit indeed is willing, but the flesh is weak." Again, the instruction is both defensive (i.e. watch; be on guard against sin) and offensive (i.e. seek God's help daily through prayer). If the Christian fails to "watch and pray" they can very well be seduced by the flesh, the world, or Satan, committing not only minor sins but "serious and outrageous ones."

However, the believer falls into no such sin, minuscule or serious, apart from "God's just permission." Just as it is God who preserves the believer to glory so also is it God who controls and permits the believer's fall into sin. Here again is an example of how Calvinism for Dort is inseparable from the Christian's progression in sanctification or his digression from holiness. God is in sovereign control, and he will not fail to preserve every sinner his Son has died for. Yet, such divine sovereignty is not a *general* sovereignty as the Remonstrants believed, conditioning God's providence upon man's free will. Rather, God's sovereign control is both *exhaustive and meticulous*. With regard to the believer's sanctification, this means that God is in control not only of the believer's success in holiness but also of his lapse into sin and temptation. Nevertheless, Dort is careful, refusing to fall prey to the Arminian accusation that such a view of God's sovereignty makes God guilty of sin. Dort frames its discussion by the word "permission." When the Christian is "carried away" into sin, he does so by "God's just permission." Dort notes that Scripture is very clear in affirming such a just permission as evidenced in the lives of David (2 Samuel 11–12) and Peter (Matthew 26:34,74).

The grace of a reconciled God

Nonetheless, though God permits a Christian's lapse into sin, God takes the believer's fault very seriously and the consequences are costly.

By such monstrous sins, however, they greatly offend God, deserve the sentence of death, grieve the Holy Spirit, suspend the exercise of faith, severely wound the conscience, and sometimes lose the awareness of grace for a time—until, after they have returned to the way of genuine repentance, God's fatherly face again shines upon them.[34]

Dort's list of deadly consequences (offend God, deserve death, grieve the Spirit, suspend the exercise of faith, severely wound the conscience, and temporarily lose an awareness of grace) is not to be taken lightly. These consequences will increase until the Christian turns in "genuine repentance." Yet, even though the Christian has committed such sins and is in danger of God's discipline, when he repents he finds "God's fatherly face" shining upon him. Moreover, in the Christian's turning from sin to the Father, who is it Dort points to as the one who receives the credit and praise for such a recovery and continuance in the faith? Dort is emphatic that it is God who is to be praised and recognized for his preservation of believers, working within them once again "heartfelt and godly sorrow for the sins they have committed" and renewing them to repentance.[35]

Dort explains the matter more thoroughly, making two significant points. First, "God preserves in those saints when they fall his imperishable seed from which they have been born again, lest it perish or be dislodged."[36] Second, "by his word and Spirit he certainly and effectively renews them to repentance."[37] Dort lists five results this effectual and certain renewal to repentance has.[38] They

1. have a heartfelt and godly sorrow for the sins they have committed
2. seek and obtain, through faith and with a contrite heart, forgiveness in the blood of the Mediator
3. experience again the grace of a reconciled God
4. through faith adore his mercies
5. more eagerly work out their own salvation with fear and trembling.[39]

---

34 "Canons of Dort," 5.5, in *Creeds and Confessions of the Reformation Era*, 2:592.
35 "Canons of Dort," 5.7, in *Creeds and Confessions of the Reformation Era*, 2:593.
36 "Canons of Dort," 5.7, in *Creeds and Confessions of the Reformation Era*, 2:593.
37 "Canons of Dort," 5.7, in *Creeds and Confessions of the Reformation Era*, 2:593.
38 "Canons of Dort," 5.7, in *Creeds and Confessions of the Reformation Era*, 2:593.
39 "Canons of Dort," 5.7, in *Creeds and Confessions of the Reformation Era*, 2:593.

Furthermore, Dort assures the believer that when the Christian falls into sin, God never takes away his Holy Spirit from his own completely, for if he did he would forfeit his rich mercy and unchangeable purpose of election.[40] Not only is the Spirit's presence not compromised but God also does not "let them fall down so far that they forfeit the grace of adoption and the state of justification, or commit the sin which leads to death (the sin against the Holy Spirit), and plunge themselves, entirely forsaken by him, into eternal ruin."[41] Rather, God, by his Word and Spirit, keeps them in his hand and at the proper time restores them so that they "seek and obtain, through faith and with a contrite heart, forgiveness in the blood of the Mediator."[42] Believers experience the "grace of a reconciled God" and through faith "adore his mercies" so that they "eagerly work out their salvation with fear and trembling" (cf. Philippians 2:12).[43]

Again, it is essential to recognize that God's glory and power are behind the believer's perseverance in the faith. Dort makes this clear, "So it is not by their own merits or strength but by God's undeserved mercy that they neither forfeit faith and grace totally nor remain in their downfalls to the end and are lost."[44] If it were left up to the believer, as the Arminian maintains, falling away from Christ "not only easily could happen, but also undoubtedly would happen."[45] However, while the believer does play an important role in persevering, ultimately it is God who is behind it all. Therefore, since our sanctification and progression in holiness is God's doing, falling away from faith in Christ

cannot possibly happen, since his plan cannot be changed, his promise cannot fail, the calling according to his purpose cannot be revoked, the merit of Christ as well as his interceding and preserving cannot be nullified, and the sealing of the Holy Spirit can neither be invalidated nor wiped out.[46]

40 "Canons of Dort," 5.6, in Creeds and Confessions of the Reformation Era, 2:592.
41 "Canons of Dort," 5.6, in Creeds and Confessions of the Reformation Era, 2:592.
42 "Canons of Dort," 5.7, in Creeds and Confessions of the Reformation Era, 2:593.
43 "Canons of Dort," 5.7, in Creeds and Confessions of the Reformation Era, 2:593.
44 "Canons of Dort," 5.8, in Creeds and Confessions of the Reformation Era, 2:593.
45 "Canons of Dort," 5.8, in Creeds and Confessions of the Reformation Era, 2:593.
46 "Canons of Dort," 5.8, in Creeds and Confessions of the Reformation Era, 2:593.

Edwin Palmer, commenting on Dort, recognizes the massive implications Dort's doctrine of perseverance and assurance has for pastoral ministry.

> The pastor, however, is able to show the timid that salvation depends ultimately not upon man's perseverance but upon God's love toward man. He can go on to demonstrate that this God is not chameleon-like, changing with man's varying moods. But rather, as he wrote, "I, the Lord, change not" (Malachi 3:6). Once the all-knowing God has sovereignly and lovingly determined to save a person, he will not change—Arminian-wise—because of an unforeseen wickedness in man. For he never chose a person in the first place because of any foreseen faith. And what God begins, God finishes. "I am persuaded of this one thing: he who started a good work in you will complete it at the day of Christ Jesus" (Philippians 1:6). If a person believes, the Bible says he has eternal life—eternal, that is, not temporary.[47]

Palmer concludes,

> Therefore, a pastor can give real encouragement to his parishioners who worry continually about their future salvation. Such knowledge is of practical importance. Otherwise, fearful ones will concentrate so much on "laying again a foundation of repentance from dead works and of faith toward God" that they will not be able to go on to perfection (Hebrews 6:1–2). Such meek ones must be taught to rely on God's eternal, unchanging love and then to press on toward the goal of their high calling in Christ Jesus.[48]

Palmer's pastoral insight is astute. It is because God will indeed preserve those whom he has chosen to the end that the pastor can confidently point the doubting and struggling believer away from himself

---

47 Edwin H. Palmer, "The Significance of the Canons for Pastoral Work," in *Crisis in the Reformed Churches*, 142.

48 Palmer, "The Significance of the Canons for Pastoral Work," 142.

and instead direct his attention upward to the cross of Christ and the sovereign God who has promised to protect him.

Assurance and the troubled conscience

It is no surprise that Dort would next move to provide hope for the Christian of a troubled conscience. First, Dort addresses the assurance that *can* come from God's preservation. Dort recognizes that "believers themselves can and do become assured in accordance with the measure of their faith, by which they firmly believe that they are and always will remain true and living members of the church, and that they have the forgiveness of sins and eternal life."[49] So if it is the case, as Dort says it is, that the believer can become assured "in accordance with the measure of their faith," from where does this assurance originate? Dort answers,

> this assurance does not derive from some private revelation beyond or outside the word, but from faith in the promises of God which he has very plentifully revealed in his word for our comfort, from the testimony of the Holy Spirit testifying with our spirit that we are God's children and heirs, and finally from a serious and holy pursuit of a clear conscience and of good works.[50]

---

49 "Canons of Dort," 5.9, in *Creeds and Confessions of the Reformation Era*, 2:593. "The Canons affirm here [5.9] that believers 'may and do' obtain assurance of their perseverance. That assurance, however, is grounded in 'the preservation of the elect unto salvation'. Take away those words, and every conscientious believer would despair. For, if the believer grounds assurance solely in his own activity, he must confess that he so often fails in his duty to God and to his neighbour that such activity more often leads to doubt than to assurance. By speaking first of God's election and preservation, the Canons of Dort show that assurance and its fruits are rooted in God's sovereign grace and promises-yes, in God himself. These promises are the foundation of both assurance and perseverance" [Joel R. Beeke, "Perseverance and Assurance," *The Banner of Truth* 517 (2006): 3].

50 "Canons of Dort," 5.10, in *Creeds and Confessions of the Reformation Era*, 2:593. "Assurance serves perseverance through sanctification. The Canons of Dort affirm this in the Fifth Head of Doctrine, Article 10, saying that assurance is fostered not only by faith in God's promises and the witnessing testimony of the Holy Spirit, but also 'from a serious and holy desire to preserve a good conscience and to perform good works" (Beeke, "Perseverance and Assurance," 4).

According to Dort, assurance first and foremost comes from the Word, specifically the promises of God revealed in his Word, which he intentionally designed to comfort us. Notice, assurance is not found in some type of extra-biblical experience apart from God's Word but in the objective promises of God's Word. The reason for this is clear. Assurance "built on experiences will ultimately lead to confusion and doubt."[51] Instead, the Holy Spirit, utilizing the Word and working with the Word, testifies with our spirit that we are heirs of these promises. Here Dort is on a firm foundation, building off Romans 8:16. It is the Spirit who bears witness with our spirit that we belong to God and, as the apostle Paul goes on to say, it is the Spirit who helps us in our weakness, interceding for us with groanings too deep for words (Romans 8:26).

Nevertheless, Dort does not minimize or neglect the importance of other means of assurance, including "a serious and holy pursuit of a clear conscience and of good works."[52] While the objective promises of God's Word take on a fundamental role in the assurance of the believer, nevertheless, there is also a place for the subjective. The subjective in this case is the Christian's pursuit of a "clear conscience" as well as his persistence in good works.[53] These good works are not sought in order to somehow *earn* one's good standing before God (as the Roman Catholic Church maintains), but rather these good works are the *result* and *fruit* of justification. They are the substance of the believer's sanctification, for as James says, faith without works is dead (James 2:17,26). Therefore, good works, as the evidence of faith, are a healthy reminder to the believer that he is a steward and heir of the kingdom of God. Good works give the believer assurance that the faith he professed is real and alive rather than artificial and fake. Good works assure the believer that he is a follower and imitator of Christ rather than the devil. Many passages in Scripture emphasize Dort's double reference to a "clear conscience" and "good works." For exam-

---

51 Feenstra, *Unspeakable Comfort*, 169.

52 "Canons of Dort," 5.10, in *Creeds and Confessions of the Reformation Era*, 2:593. Feenstra observes how similar Dort's point is to Lord's Day 32 of the Heidelberg Catechism. See Feenstra, *Unspeakable Comfort*, 171.

53 Dort may be borrowing the language of a "clear conscience" from Acts 24:16.

ple, the author of Hebrews says, "and since we have a great priest over the house of God, let us draw near with a true heart in full assurance of faith, with our hearts sprinkled clean from an evil conscience and our bodies washed with pure water" (Hebrews 10:21–22).

Dort concludes article 10 by highlighting the significance of assurance: "And if God's chosen ones in this world did not have this well-founded comfort that the victory will be theirs and this reliable guarantee of eternal glory, they would be of all people most miserable."[54] Miserable indeed! The Christian who has no comfort that God will protect him and preserve him to the end has every right to be worried and miserable. His conscience cannot rest assured in the promises found in God's Word. His conscience is haunted with the possibility that he, though steadfast in the present, may neglect or abandon the faith at a later time, forfeiting his soul to eternal hell. What could be more miserable than this? As Joel Beeke comments, "Take away God's preservation, and every conscientious believer would despair; our failures would overwhelm whatever fruits we discover and destroy all assurance."[55] But this is not so for the Calvinist. He takes great comfort in God's electing purposes, for he recognizes God has chosen him and God will have the victory. He takes great comfort in knowing that God's promises to bring him into eternal paradise are reliable and guaranteed. As Beeke explains, "By speaking first of God's election and preservation, the canons show us that assurance is rooted in God's sovereign grace and promises—yes, in God Himself."[56]

Certainty of perseverance and Christian humility

Nevertheless, Dort recognizes that some Christians face "doubts of the flesh" and when under "severe temptation they do not always

---

54 "Canons of Dort," 5.10, in *Creeds and Confessions of the Reformation Era*, 2:593.

55 As Beeke observes, 5.10 draws the connection between assurance and sanctification. "Assurance further serves perseverance through sanctification. The Canons of Dort affirm this in Head V, Article 10, saying that assurance is fostered not only by faith in God's promises and the witnessing testimony of the Holy Spirit, but also 'from a serious and holy desire to preserve a good conscience and to perform good works'" [Joel R. Beeke, *Living for God's Glory: An Introduction to Calvinism* (Orlando: Reformation Trust, 2008), 120].

56 Beeke, *Living for God's Glory*, 120.

experience this full assurance of faith and certainty of perseverance."[57] However, Dort reminds the doubting soul of 1 Corinthians 10:13 that "God, the Father of all comfort, does not let them be tempted beyond what they can bear, but with the temptation he also provides a way out, and by the Holy Spirit revives in them the assurance of their perseverance."[58] Dort brings to the believer's mind God's sweet and Fatherly sovereignty in not allowing Christians to be tempted beyond what they can bear, but providing a way of escape and in due time, by the Holy Spirit, he "revives in them the assurance of their perseverance."[59] When the Christian does receive such assurance, humility, not pride, is to be the result. "This assurance of perseverance, however, so far from making true believers proud and carnally self-assured, is rather the true root of humility, of childlike respect, of genuine godliness, of endurance in every conflict, of fervent prayers, of steadfastness in crossbearing and in confessing the truth, and of well-founded joy in God."

Dort continues, "Reflecting on this benefit provides an incentive to a serious and continual practice of thanksgiving and good works, as is evident from the testimonies of Scripture and the examples of saints."[60] Dort's admonition is refreshing. The Calvinist, out of all people, is to be the prototype for Christian humility. As one who has the great assurance of perseverance he knows better than anyone that this is not his doing, as if he himself is to receive the glory, but it is the work of God. Therefore, with assurance should come "childlike respect." Moreover, such assurance is not the root of carnality and ungodliness, as the Arminian thinks, but is the very incentive for godliness, thanksgiving and good works, as the multitude of biblical characters in Scripture demonstrate. True, evangelical faith and assurance is not the root of pride but of thanksgiving, praise and gratitude toward God.[61] Dort's point is similar to the Heidelberg Catechism which states in

---

57 "Canons of Dort," 5.11, in *Creeds and Confessions of the Reformation Era*, 2:594.

58 "Canons of Dort," 5.11, in *Creeds and Confessions of the Reformation Era*, 2:594.

59 "Canons of Dort," 5.11, in *Creeds and Confessions of the Reformation Era*, 2:594.

60 "Canons of Dort," 5.12, in *Creeds and Confessions of the Reformation Era*, 2:594.

61 For a point-by-point explanation of each of these virtues (godliness, humility, etc.) in Dort, see Feenstra, *Unspeakable Comfort*, 174–176.

Lord's Day 24, "It is impossible that those grafted into Christ by true faith should not bring forth fruits of thankfulness."

Dort further explains how this Christian godliness takes form:

> Neither does the renewed confidence of perseverance produce immorality or lack of concern for godliness in those put back on their feet after a fall, but it produces a much greater concern to observe carefully the ways of the Lord which he prepared in advance.... They observe these ways in order that by walking in them they may maintain the assurance of their perseverance, lest, by their abuse of his fatherly goodness, the face of the gracious God (for the godly, looking upon his face is sweeter than life, but its withdrawal is more bitter than death) turn away from them again, with the result that they fall into greater anguish of spirit.[62]

So, humility, godliness, endurance, fervent prayer, steadfastness in persecution and suffering, unwavering profession of the truth and joy in God all result from the assurance that God provides through perseverance. Moreover, when the Christian reflects on all these benefits that flow from assurance he should be further moved to perpetual thanksgiving and good works. A redeemed assurance, however, does not lead to lax licentiousness or disinterest in godliness. Instead, it will foster a far deeper concern to guard oneself from again giving way to temptation. The motivation in observing the ways of the Lord is to gain a yet deeper assurance. The Christian, says Dort, must guard himself from taking God's grace for granted lest he once again abuse "his fatherly goodness" and grace. Dort reminds the Christian that looking upon the Father's face is "sweeter than life" (cf. Psalms 4:6; 67:1; 69:17; Isaiah 54:8) but withdrawing from it "is

---

62 "Canons of Dort," 5.13, in *Creeds and Confessions of the Reformation Era*, 2:594. Feenstra comments, "Confidence in the Lord does not make true believers proud or complacent. It does not make them careless or wicked either. Believers do not sin on purpose because they know the Lord will preserve the elect. They are ashamed of their sins, hate them and flee from them. Having felt the pain of sin and the wounds it leaves they pray all the more earnestly, 'Lead us not into temptation'" (Feenstra, *Unspeakable Comfort*, 175).

more bitter than death." If the Christian should withdraw again he may fall into yet a greater "anguish of spirit" than was experienced before. Therefore, God's discipline is never to be taken lightly, but it is severe and to be feared.

Exercises and means of godliness

Dort concludes canon 5 in the most practical manner. After reminding the Christian that it is God who is pleased to preserve him, Dort lists several ways perseverance is accomplished and joy in God is attained.

> And, just as it has pleased God to begin this work of grace in us by the proclamation of the gospel, so he preserves, continues, and completes his work by the hearing and reading of the gospel, by meditation on it, by its exhortations, threats, and promises, and also by the use of the sacraments.[63]

Hearing and reading the gospel, meditating on the gospel, listening to the gospel's exhortations, threats and promises, and taking the sacraments obediently are all *means* God uses to preserve his children, forming within them a greater joy and love for Christ. Notice Dort's emphasis on spiritual disciplines. The believer is strengthened in his faith through reading and meditating upon the Scriptures. It is by reading and meditating upon the Scriptures that he is reminded afresh of the gospel of Jesus Christ. Dort is once again following the Scriptures which remind us of the importance of Bible meditation. As Psalm 1:1–2 states, "Blessed is the man who walks not in the counsel of the wicked, nor stands in the way of sinners, nor sits in the seat of scoffers; but his delight is in the law of the LORD, and on his law he meditates day and night" (see also Psalms 19:14; 63:5–6; 119:48,97, 99)." It is no surprise then, as Feenstra observes, that seventeenth-century Dutch Calvinists read and meditated upon the Scriptures at breakfast, lunch, and supper![64]

---

63 "Canons of Dort," 5.14, in *Creeds and Confessions of the Reformation Era*, 2:594.
64 Feenstra, *Unspeakable Comfort*, 179.

However, Dort does not limit the means of grace God uses to preserve us in the faith to private spiritual disciplines. Dort also places
great emphasis on the means of grace received through the church,
namely, the preaching of the Word and participation in the sacraments
(baptism and the Lord's Supper). By the preaching of the Word we
hear the gospel which exhorts us, threatens us, warns us and makes
gracious promises to us. As 2 Timothy 3:16–17 states, "All Scripture is
breathed out by God and profitable for teaching, for reproof, for cor-
rection, and for training in righteousness, that the man of God may
be competent, equipped for every good work" (see also Revelation 1:3).
Likewise, the sacraments play a significant role. For example, the
Lord's Supper turns the believer from his sin and focuses his attention
upon the work of Christ on the cross. The sacraments remind the
believer of the gospel of salvation through Christ.

Dort's list of practical means for greater piety in the faith are not
arbitrary nor without cause. Dort is carefully demonstrating and arguing that God's sovereign preservation of the Christian and gift of assurance are actually the cause and root of the Christian's growth in
holiness and godliness.[65]

The Arminian Remonstrants did not view assurance the same way.
Dort rejects the Arminians who "teach that the teaching of the assurance of perseverance and of salvation is by its very nature and character an opiate of the flesh and is harmful to godliness, good morals,
prayer, and other holy exercises, but that, on the contrary, to have
doubt about this is praiseworthy."[66] Dort regrets how "these people

---

65 Dort concludes canon 5, "This teaching about the perseverance of true believers
and saints, and about their assurance of it—a teaching which God has very richly revealed
in his Word for the glory of his name and for the comfort of the godly and which he
impresses on the hearts of believers—is something which the flesh does not understand,
Satan hates, the world ridicules, the ignorant and the hypocrites abuse, and the spirits
of error attack. The bride of Christ, on the other hand, has always loved this teaching
very tenderly and defended it steadfastly as a priceless treasure; and God, against whom
no plan can avail and no strength can prevail, will ensure that she will continue to do
this. To this God alone, Father, Son, and Holy Spirit, be honor and glory forever. Amen"
("Canons of Dort," 5.15, in *Creeds and Confessions of the Reformation Era*, 2:594).

66 "Canons of Dort," Rejection of the Errors 5.6, in *Creeds and Confessions of the
Reformation Era*, 2:597.

.

show that they do not know the effective operation of God's grace and the work of the indwelling Holy Spirit."[67] Dort cites 1 John 3:2–3 where we read, "Dear friends, now we are children of God, but what we will be has not yet been made known. But we know that when he is made known, we shall be like him, for we shall see him as he is. Everyone who has this hope in him purifies himself, just as he is pure." John testifies to the effective operation of divine grace. We have a sure and certain promise that one day we will be like him and see him as he is. Dort denies that such an assurance leads to laxity in godliness for "the saints in both the Old and the New Testament, who though assured of their perseverance and salvation yet were constant in prayer and other exercises of godliness."[68]

Conclusion

For the Calvinist, Scripture is clear that perseverance and assurance of salvation are not a hindrance to but a supplement of "constant prayer and other exercises of godliness." Assurance that the God who sovereignly saves will also sovereignly preserve does not lead to a license to immorality nor a lax approach to godliness, but rather is a

---

67 "Canons of Dort," Rejection of the Errors 5.6, in *Creeds and Confessions of the Reformation Era*, 2:597.

68 "Canons of Dort," Rejection of the Errors 5.6, in *Creeds and Confessions of the Reformation Era*, 2:597. Dort also had in mind the Catholics, "[The synod rejects the errors of those] Who teach that apart from a special revelation no one can have the assurance of future perseverance in this life. For by this teaching the well-founded consolation of true believers in this life is taken away and the doubting of the Romanists is reintroduced into the church. Holy Scripture, however, in many places derives the assurance not from a special and extraordinary revelation but from the marks peculiar to God's children and from God's completely reliable promises. So especially the apostle Paul: "Nothing in all creation can separate us from the love of God that is in Christ Jesus our Lord" [Romans 8.39]; and John: "They who obey his commands remain in him and he in them. And this is how we know that he remains in us: by the Spirit he gave us" [1 John 3:24]" ("Canons of Dort," Rejection of the Errors 5.5, in *Creeds and Confessions of the Reformation Era*, 2:596–597). On Catholic responses to Dort and Dort's relevance for Catholic theology today see Cornelius Van Til, "The Significance of Dort for Today," in *Crisis in the Reformed Churches*, 181–196.

pure and true incentive to see God's grace effectively worked out through the indwelling fruit of the Holy Spirit.[69]

---

69 In the "Conclusion: Rejection of the Errors of False Accusations," Dort rejects those who would argue "that this teaching makes people carnally self-assured, since it persuades them that nothing endangers the salvation of the chosen, no matter how they live, so that they may commit the most outrageous crimes with self-assurance; and that on the other hand nothing is of use to the reprobate for salvation even if they have truly performed all the works of the saints" ("Canons of Dort," in *Creeds and Confessions of the Reformation Era*, 2:598).

Orthodox Calvinism achieved a complete triumph.... It [Dort] was undoubtedly an imposing assembly; and, for learning and piety, as respectable as any ever held since the days of the Apostles.—**PHILIP SCHAFF**

The Synod of Dort marked the triumph of Calvinist orthodoxy in the theology of the Dutch Reformed Church...its actions and conclusions expressed anew the vision of John Calvin, demonstrated the vitality of Reformed Christianity, and provided a rich source of wisdom from which the church's Calvinism drew strength and was renewed.—**W. ROBERT GODFREY**

7

Conclusion

"Your thoughts of God are too human," Martin Luther quipped at Erasmus in their debate over the bondage of the will.[1] For Luther, Erasmus gave far too much credit to man's ability and far too little credit to God's sovereignty. But there is far more meaning to Luther's words. As J.I. Packer explains, Luther can be interpreted as saying, "Your theology has too little worship in it."[2] Erasmus, by denying the bondage of the will, created a theology in which man is great and God is small. Such a theology does not result in doxology.

Packer's point is a simple one: to theologize is to worship, and

---

1   Martin Luther, *On the Bondage of the Will*, trans. O.R. Johnston and J.I . Packer (London: James Clarke, 1957), 87.

2   J.I. Packer, "An Introduction to Systematic Spirituality," *Crux* 26, no. 1 (1990), 7.

should we theologize wrong we will worship wrong as well. Therefore, theologizing is a dangerous task indeed. Packer demonstrates that we cannot separate or divorce theology from devotion. Doctrinal study is not muddied by devotional concerns but is the very impetus upon which our devotion to God is built. Therefore, we dare not drive a "wedge between theology and doxology, between orthodoxy and ortho-praxy, between knowing true notions about God and knowing the true God himself, between one's thinking and one's worshipping."[3] Should we divorce our theology from practical divinity, we will be left with a theology that "induces spiritual pride and produces spiritual sleep."[4]

Consequently, we come to God not merely to study him but to *know* him. He is a God not merely to be observed but worshipped. Packer explains the danger avoided in such a biblical approach,

> We shall be in less danger of forgetting the transcendent mystery of God's being and action, and of putting him in a box constructed out of our own concepts, which the detached intellect, longing to master that which it studies, is very prone to do. We shall be in less danger of the irreverence of treating God as if he were an impersonal object below us, frozen fast by us for the purposes of our study, and failing to remember that he is the great personal Subject, far above us, apart from whose ongoing life we should not exist at all. And we shall be shielded from the further irrever-ence of allowing ourselves to grade God's work in connection with the sovereign mysteries of predestination and evil, and to conclude that if we ourselves were God we could do a better job.[5]

Biblically sound doctrine, in other words, brings us low and lifts God up high where he belongs. Should we ignore Scripture's testimony as to who God is and how he saves, we inevitably will fashion a god after our own liking, one that can be tamed, one that can be humanized. Such a god, however, cannot be worshipped. As this book has sought to demonstrate, the Canons of Dort provide this biblical foundation

3   J.I. Packer, "An Introduction to Systematic Spirituality," *Crux* 26, no. 1 (1990), 6.
4   J.I. Packer, "An Introduction to Systematic Spirituality," *Crux* 26, no. 1 (1990), 6.
5   J.I. Packer, "An Introduction to Systematic Spirituality," *Crux* 26, no. 1 (1990), 7.

for understanding God's work of redemption in the world, a foundation that is inherently God-centred and God-glorifying.

German historian, Karl Holl, was observant to confess that "a good deal of the penetrating power of Calvinism depends upon its intellectualism. Calvinists know what they believe, and why they believe it."[6] No doubt, Holl is right. However, Holl's sentence is incomplete. Yes, Calvinism is an intellectual bulwark. Calvinists know the Bible. They know what they believe and why they believe it. But this intellectual acumen and biblical fidelity is only the foundation. Built upon the foundation of Reformed orthodoxy is a house of piety, a fortress of practical divinity. Without such a foundation, our comfort as believers is lost. Venema's insight is sobering,

> Here it needs to be observed that the Canons' God-centeredness does not diminish their comfort. For the believer's true comfort resides not in himself but in His God. When our salvation is made to depend, even in the slightest measure, on our own initiative and persistence in the course, it hangs not from the thinnest of threads but from nothing at all. Nothing could more certainly steal from the believer his hope and confidence, whether in this life or the life to come, than to rest on or place his trust in his own resources, pluck, or self-determination. The only solid comfort, by comparison, is to be found in God the Father's gracious election of His people, God the Son's perfect provision and atonement on their behalf, and God the Spirit's calling them into and preserving them in fellowship with Christ through the gospel.[7]

In summary, Dort is an excellent example of how Calvinism does not hinder but actually inspires sincere, genuine piety in the believer.[8]

---

6 Karl Holl, "Johannes Calvin," in *Gesammelte Aufsätze zur Kirchengeschichte III: Der Westen* (Tübingen: Siebeck, 1928), 267.

7 Cornelis P. Venema, *But for the Grace of God: An Exposition of the Canons of Dort* (Grandville: Reformed Fellowship, 2011), 120.

8 Many other Calvinists after Dort would do the same, as seen in the Second Reformation in the Netherlands. Such noteworthy Calvinists include: William Ames, Willem Teellinck, Gijsbertus Voetius, Herman Witsius, Jodocus van Lodensteyn, Wilhelmus à Brakel, Bernardus Smijtegeld, Theodorus van der Groe, etc. For example,

The doctrines of grace serve as the very bedrock to Christian assurance, humility, holiness, and delight in God. W. Robert Godfrey has described such a connection well when he states,

> The canons [of Dort] called Christians to humility before God as they realized their complete bondage to sin. The canons inspired gratitude for God's electing love and for the complete redemption accomplished in Christ and sovereignly applied by the Holy Spirit. The canons spoke comfort to Christian hearts, casting out fear and declaring God's love that would never let them go. The canons called people of God to be liberated from morbid self-concern and to serve God in the world with love and joy.[9]

Godfrey rightly concludes, "The theology of the canons did not bludgeon the Reformed community into inaction but rather armed the Reformed church with the whole counsel of God. Strengthened with a confidence in God taught in the canons, Reformed Christians became the most dynamic and effective witnesses to Christ in Europe."[10] Dort demonstrates not only that the doctrines of grace are faithful to

---

Cornelis Pronk says concerning Voetius, "To give you a sample of his writing, let me quote from his *Soliloquy*, in which we meet a child of God reflecting on his struggles as he comes to light. Seeing more and more how wicked he is, he almost despairs of mercy. Attacked by doubts as to his election, he asks himself: What if I am not elect? Is there any sense in praying? But when he takes this burden to the Lord, he is shown that election, far from being intended to produce fear, is meant to give comfort to a distressed soul, because now his salvation is entirely in God's hand, and not in man who is only vanity" [Cornelis Pronk, "The Dutch Puritans," *The Banner of Truth* 154–155 (1976): 5]. On Reformed piety in the Netherlands after Dort, see Fred A. van Lieburg, "From Pure Church to Pious Culture: The Further Reformation in the Seventeenth-Century Dutch Republic," in *Later Calvinism: International Perspectives*, ed. W. Fred Graham (Kirksville: Sixteenth Century Journal, 1994), 409–430; Joel R. Beeke, *Puritan Reformed Spirituality* (Grand Rapids: Reformation Heritage, 2004), 288–230; Joel R. Beeke, "The Dutch Second Reformation (*Nadere Reformatie*)," *Calvin Theological Journal* 28 (1993): 298–327.

9   W. Robert Godfrey, *Reformation Sketches: Insights in Luther, Calvin, and the Confessions* (Phillipsburg: P & R, 2003), 132.

10 Godfrey, *Reformation Sketches*, 132.

Scripture, but that sovereign grace itself is the very vehicle by which the Christian progresses in godliness and evangelical piety.

In closing, what we need today is a resurgence, renaissance, and rediscovery of the doctrines of grace, as articulated by the Canons of Dort. With such a recovery, our churches will flourish with believers who not only know who God is, but what God is doing to "lift up his countenance upon you and give you peace" (Numbers 6:26).

Appendix 1
The Synod of Dort and infralapsarianism

While it is not the main focus of this study, something must be said concerning the infralapsarian language in the Canons of Dort. Infralapsarianism or *infra lapsum* means below or subsequent to Adam's fall, which is in contrast to supralapsarianism or *supra lapsum* which means "above or prior to the fall." The debate revolves around the logical order of God's decree in the mind of God, or the *ordo rerum decretarum*.[1] The supralapsarian view argues that election and reproba-

---

1   I am following the definition provided by Richard A. Muller, *"supra lapsum,"* in *Dictionary of Latin and Greek Theological Terms: Drawn Principally from Protestant Scholastic Theology* (Grand Rapids: Baker, 1985), 292. For a discussion of the debate, especially in regards to Romans 9, see also Herman Bavinck, *The Doctrine of God*, trans. and ed. William Hendricksen (Edinburgh: Banner of Truth, 1951), 342–343.

tion of persons are prior, logically speaking, to God's decree to create and permit the fall. In other words, in God's mind the person elected or reprobated is creatable and fallible or *creabilis et labilis*. Richard Muller explains, "The prior purpose of God is the manifestation of his glory in the mercy of election and the justice of reprobation, while the creation itself and the decree to permit the fall are secondary purposes, or means to the end, of election and reprobation."[2] By contrast, the infralapsarian view, which many in the Reformed churches assumed even before Dort (see The Belgic Confession and Heidelberg Catechism), instead argues that God's will to create and his decree to permit the Fall are prior, logically speaking, to his decree to elect some to salvation. In other words, in God's mind the person elected or reprobated is created and fallen or *creatus et lapsus*. Muller again elaborates, "The prior purpose of God is the creation of human beings for fellowship with himself, and the decree to elect some to salvation appears as a means to the end of that fellowship."[3]

As already hinted at in the discussion of reprobation (see chapter 3), Dort's language is a clear adoption of the infralapsarian position. However, this position did not come without some resistance. On March 6, 1619, in session 103, the delegates first presented their judgment on predestination. When the Dutch professors (Polyander, Thysius, and especially Walaeus) delivered their article on predestination, Francis Gomarus, a supralapsarian, objected. As quoted already, Polyander, Thysius and Walaeus wrote that God had "chosen from the whole race, which had fallen through their own fault from their primitive state of rectitude into sin and destruction, a certain number of persons to redemption in Christ."[4] Here we see a clear affirmation of infralapsarianism (*homo creatus et lapsus*). The same can also be seen in their Leiden Synopsis.

God's eternal and immutable decree, by which from the entire human race that had fallen by its own fault from primaeval integrity into sin and destruction He elected a fixed multitude of

---

2 Muller, "*supra lapsum*," 292.
3 Muller, "*supra lapsum*," 292.
4 "Canons of Dort," 1.7, in *Creeds and Confessions of the Reformation Era*, 2:572.

individual men, neither better nor worthier than the rest, of His sole good pleasure, to salvation in Christ Jesus, and resolved to give them to His Son to redeem, and by a peculiar and effectual mode of operating to bring them to living faith in Himself and to a sure perseverance in the same living faith, and that for a proof of His gracious mercy and for the praise of His glorious grace.[5]

Gomarus, on the other hand, merely stated that when God elected he chose men out of the whole human race. No mention is made of mankind as sinful or fallen.[6]

Building on J.V. Fesko's study of the issue, three points should be made regarding the importance of Dort's infralapsarian view.

(1) *The infralapsarianism of Dort is Christological in its focus.* As Fesko observes, Dort did not like how the supralapsarians separated "predes-

---

5   The Leiden Synopsis, XXIV, 24, in Heinrich Heppe, *Reformed Dogmatics: Set Out and Illustrated from the Sources*, ed. Ernst Bizer, trans. G.T. Thomson (London: George Allen & Unwin, 1950), 163. See also J.V. Fesko, *Diversity Within the Reformed Tradition: Supra- and Infralapsarianism in Calvin, Dort, and Westminster* (Greenville: Reformed Academic Press, 2001), 192.

6   Fesko explains, "While the other Dutch professors defined the object of predestination as *homo creatus et lapsus*, Gomarus does not specify that man has indeed fallen; Gomarus simply uses the phrase, 'men out of the whole human race'.... He does not specify that mankind has fallen or has committed any sin. This reflects Gomarus' opinion that the object of predestination is *homo creabilis et labilis*." Fesko continues, "During the initial debate between Gomarus and the other Dutch professors, Gomarus made an appeal to the confessions of the Belgic, English and French churches. He argued that the object of predestination had not been determined by the church of those nations. The English delegation challenged this assertion." The English delegation actually showed that the Thirty-Nine Articles, especially article 17, did specify the object of predestination, namely as not just man but fallen man. While Gomarus had quoted the Thirty-Nine Articles to his favour, he had left out a crucial phrase which reads "*quosdam ex humano genere, in exitio et maledicto.*" Afterwards, Gomarus admitted he had misunderstood the confession (Fesko, *Diversity Within the Reformed Tradition*, 184, 185). See also John Hales, *The Golden Remains of the Ever Memorable Mr. John Hales of Eton College and Dr. Balcanquals Letters from the Synod of Dort to the R. Honourable Sir D. Carlton L. Embassador* (London: Printed for Tim Garthwait, 1659), 24–25. For the position of Gomarus, see Franciscus Gomarus, *Opera Theologica Omnia* (Amsterdam: Johannis Janssonii, 1664), 428.

tination from the means by which it was executed, namely salvation in Christ."[7] Such a point is exemplified in the Leiden Synopsis when they write that "God never elected anyone absolutely to salvation, if 'absolutely' excludes the means which God has ordained for securing salvation."[8] While for the supralapsarians election and reprobation are viewed apart from means, for the infralapsarians at Dort predestination and redemption through Christ are inseparably unified. Fesko contrasts the matter precisely, "In Gomarus' supralapsarianism, predestination is an expression of God's sovereignty, whereas in the Dutch professor's infralapsarianism predestination is an expression of God's saving mercy in Christ."[9]

(2) *The infralapsarians at Dort believed their view to be inferred in every biblical passage that addressed predestination.* Johannes Polyander, among others, makes this point certain.

For we are elect in Christ, so that we might be holy, Ephesians 1:4 and predestined to be adopted as sons, v. 5. Therefore we were outside of Christ previously, unrighteous, and unsuitable of the adoption of sons. We are elected unto salvation through the sanctification of the Spirit and through faith in the truth, 2 Thessalonians 2:12, therefore we were previously destitute of the sanctification of the Spirit and faith in the truth. Those whom he foreknew, he predestined to be conformed to the image of Christ, that image of God therefore, was not in them, Romans 8:30. The elect are vessels of mercy, just as the reprobate are vessels of wrath, Romans 9:22. God also exclusively pities the wretched, just as he only demonstrates his wrath toward sinners, Romans 1:18.[10]

---

7 Fesko, *Diversity Within the Reformed Tradition*, 193. Also consider Leiden Synopsis, XXIV, 18, in Heppe, *Reformed Dogmatics*, 171.

8 Leiden Synopsis, XXIV, 18, in Heppe, Reformed Dogmatics, 171–172.

9 Fesko, *Diversity Within the Reformed Tradition*, 193.

10 Johannes Polyander, et al., *Synopsis Purioris Theologiae*, ed. Herman Bavinck (Lugduni Batavorum: Didericum Donner, 1881), XXIV, 22: 226, as quoted in Fesko, *Diversity Within the Reformed Tradition*, 194, who also provides the Latin.

Fesko interprets Polyander as saying that "these passages of Scripture always speak of predestined man in need of salvation" and "they argue that for God to demonstrate mercy one must be in a miserable state; likewise, for God to demonstrate wrath one must be deserving wrath."[11]

(3) *Infralpsarianism avoids the charge that God is the author of sin.* As mentioned above, the Canons spoke of reprobation as God's act whereby he "passed by [man] in the eternal decree." However, man in this case is passed by *as a sinner who has fallen.* Dort, therefore, avoids the charge that God is made the author of sin. As Fesko explains, "They were very careful to place the blame for the fall and corrupt condition of man upon man himself.... Hence the Synod decided to specify in the Canons that the object of predestination was the infralapsarian *homo creates et lapsus.*"[12] It was difficult for the infralapsarians to see how God could be righteous if he predestines man to condemnation before he is guilty or fallen.[13]

In the end, infralapsarianism was the position assumed by the Synod of Dort for several reasons. For one, the infralapsarians held the majority and therefore wielded more influence at the synod.[14] More-

---

11 Fesko, *Diversity Within the Reformed Tradition*, 194.

12 Fesko, *Diversity Within the Reformed Tradition*, 199. See also G.C. Berkouwer, *Divine Election, Studies in Dogmatics*, trans. Hugo Bekker (Grand Rapids: Eerdmans, 1960), 264; Charles Hodge, *Systematic Theology* (Grand Rapids: Eerdmans, 1993), 2:317; Sinema, "Reprobation at the Synod of Dort (1618–19) in Light of the History of This Doctrine," 411, 431–432.

13 Fesko traces Dort's infralapsarianism back to Heinrich Bullinger who "was one of the original representatives of the infralapsarian position because he saw the fall of man as a rejection of God, and God was therefore justified in applying His judgment upon the rebellious creatures" (Fesko, *Diversity Within the Reformed Tradition*, 201). See also Berkouwer, *Divine Election*, 257.

14 Such a majority was reflective of Holland as a whole where infralapsarianism seems to have been the prominent view. Fesko notes that Bullinger's infralapsarianism had a tremendous influence in Holland. Fesko, *Diversity Within the Reformed Tradition*, 199, 208; William R. Godfrey, "Tensions Within International Calvinism: The Debate on the Atonement at the Synod of Dort, 1618–1619," (Ph.D. diss., Stanford University, 1974), 268; Hodge, *Systematic Theology*, 2:317; Philip Schaff, *The Creeds of Christendom*, vol. 1, *The History of Creeds* (reprint; Grand Rapids: Baker, 1983), 1:513.

over, the two major Reformed confessions that preceded Dort, the Belgic Confession (1561) and Heidelberg Catechism (1563), already assumed an infralapsarian position and, besides Dort's conviction that the infralapsarian view was in line with Scripture itself, Dort also knew it would be disadvantageous and problematic to contradict these Reformed confessions.[15] Also, while Gomarus stood up for his supralapsarian view, his fellow *supras* (Antonius Walaeus, Bishop Carlton, etc.) did not assist him.[16] However, we should not conclude that the supralapsarian view was considered heretical or unorthodox as was the Arminian view. While the supralapsarian view was considered by infralapsarians as missing the mark, nevertheless, it did not compromise God's sovereignty, as did the Arminian view. Furthermore, Dort, which consisted of both infra- and supralapsarians, desired a unified voice against the Remonstrants. As Fesko explains, "They did not want to show that there were any disagreements amongst themselves and that they were, supra- and infralapsarian alike, united in their opposition to anyone who would attempt to assign man too great a role in salvation."[17]

15 Fesko, *Diversity Within the Reformed Tradition*, 208–212.

16 Fesko, *Diversity Within the Reformed Tradition*, 199; Simon Kistemaker, "Leading Figures at the Synod of Dort," in *Crisis in the Reformed Churches*, 44, Bavinck, *Doctrine of God*, 364–365; Schaff, *Creeds*, 1:513.

17 "For this reason, when the synod was discussing the various verdicts upon the different heads of doctrine, they met in closed session so that if there was dissension or debate it would not be viewed by the public" (Fesko, *Diversity Within the Reformed Tradition*, 205). See also Hales, *Golden Remains*, 78; Sinnema, "Reprobation at the Synod of Dort," 160; Godfrey, "Tensions Within International Calvinism," 161–162.

Appendix 2
Delegates appointed to the Synod of Dort

Gelderland
Wilhelmus Stephani
Eilhardus van Mehen
Sebastianus Dammannus
Johannes Boulietus
Jacobus Verheyden
Henricus van Hel

South Holland
Balthazar Lydius
Henricus Arnoldi
Festus Hommius
Gisbertus Voetius

Arnoldus Muys van Holij
Johannes Latius

North Holland
Jacobus Rolandus
Jacobus Triglandius
Abrahamus van Doreslaer
Samuel Bartholdus
Theodorus Heyngius
Dominicus van Heemskerc

Zeeland
Hermannus Faukelius

Godefridus Udemans
Cornelius Regius
Lambertus de Rijcke
Josias Vosbergen
Adrianus Hofferus

Utrecht

Johannes Ibbetzius
Arnoldus Oortcampius
Lambertus Canterus
Isaacus Frederici
Samuel Naeranus
Stephanus van Helsdingen

Friesland

Johannes Bogermannus
Florentius Ioannis
Philippus Dannielis F. Eilshemius
Meinardus ab Idzerda
Kempo van Harinxma van Donia
Johannes vander Sande

Overijssel

Casparus Sibelius
Hermannus Wiferdingius
Hieronymus Vogelius
Johannes Langius
Guilielmus van Broeckhuyzen
Johannes van Lauwick

Groningen

Cornelius Hillenius
Georgius Placius
Wolfgangus Agricola
Johannes Lolingius
Egbertus Halbes
Johannes Ruffelaert

Drenthe

Themo van Asscheburge
Patroclus Rommelingius

Walloon churches

Daniel Colonius
Johannes de la Croix
Johannes Doucher
Jeremias de Pours
Everardus Becker
Petrus du Pont

Professors of Theology

Johannes Polyander
Francisus Gomarus
Anthonius Thysius
Antonius Walaeus

Great Britain

George Carleton
Josephus Hall
Johannes Davenantius
Samuel Wardus

Palatinate

Abrahamus Scultetus
Paulus Tossanus
Henricus Altingius

Hesse

Georgius Cruciger
Paulus Steinius
Daniel Angelocrator
Rudolphus Goclenus the Elder

Switzerland

Johannes Jacobus Breytingerus
Marcus Rutimeyerus
Sebastianus Beckius
Wolfgangus Meyerus
Johannes Conradus Kochius

Geneva

Johannes Deodatus
Theodorus Trochinus

Bremen

Matthias Martinius
Henricus Isselburgius
Ludovicus Crocius

Emden

Daniel Barnhardus Eilshemius
Ritzius Lucas Grimershemius

France[1]

Pierre DuMoulin
Andre Rivet
Jean Chauve
Daniel Chamier

Nassau-Wetteravia

Johannes Bisterveldius
Johannes Alstedius

Brandenburg[2]

Johannes Bergius
Christoph Storch

---

1   The Synod received notice on October 2, 1618, that the King of France refused to grant permission for these French delegates to leave the country. Seats remained empty at the Synod in their honour.

2   Although Johannes Bergius and Christoph Storch were delegated from the Reformed churches of Brandenburg by Margrave Georg Wilhelm, they were prohibited from attending the Synod due to Lutheran opposition.

Appendix 3
Remonstrants to appear at the Synod of Dort

Gelderland
Henricus Leonem
Bernerus Vezekius
Henricus Hollingerus

South Holland
Simon Episcopius
Johannes Arnoldi Corvinus
Bernardus Dwinglo
Eduardus Poppius
Nicolas Grevinckhoven*
Theophilus Rijckewaert

North Holland
Johannes Geesteranus*
Dominicus Sapma

Overijssel
Thomas Goswinus
Assuerus Matthysius

Walloon churches
Carolus Niellius
Simon Goulart

---

* Grevinckhoven and Geesteranus were deposed from the ministry and were not called to the synod but Philippus Pijnacker of Alkmaar replaced them.

Appendix 4
The Remonstrance of 1610

In order that your Worships may know what the Remonstrants believe
and teach concerning these same matters, we declare that our opinion
on this is as follows:

1. that God by an eternal and immutable decree has in Jesus Christ
   his Son determined before the foundation of the world to save
   out of the fallen sinful human race those in Christ, for Christ's
   sake, and through Christ who by the grace of the Holy Spirit
   shall believe in this his Son Jesus Christ and persevere in this
   faith and obedience of faith to the end; and on the other hand
   to leave the incorrigible and unbelieving in sin and under wrath
   and condemn (them) as alienated from Christ—according to
   the word of the holy gospel in John 3:36, "He that believeth on

the Son hath eternal life, and whosoever is disobedient to the Son shall not see life, but the wrath of God abideth on him." And also other passages of the Scriptures.

2. that in agreement with this Jesus Christ the Saviour of the world died for all men and for every man, so that he merited reconciliation and forgiveness of sins for all through the death of the cross; yet so that no one actually enjoys this forgiveness of sins except the believer—also according to the word of the gospel of John 3:16, "God so loved the world that he gave his only-begotten Son that whosoever believeth in him shall not perish but have eternal life." And in the First Epistle of John 2:2, "He is the propitiation for our sins; and not only for ours, but also for the sins of the whole world."

3. that man does not have saving faith of himself nor by the power of his own free will, since he, in the state of apostasy and sin, cannot of and through himself think, will or do any good which is truly good (such as is especially saving faith); but that it is necessary that he be regenerated by God, in Christ, through his Holy Spirit, and renewed in understanding, affections or will, and all powers, in order that he may rightly understand, mediate upon, will, and perform that which is truly good according to the word of Christ, John 13:5, "Without me ye can do nothing."

4. that this grace of God is the commencement, progression and completion of all good, also insofar that regenerate man cannot, apart from this prevenient or assisting, awakening, consequent and cooperating grace, think, will or do good or resist any temptations to evil; so that all good works or activities which can be conceived must be ascribed to the grace of God in Christ. But with respect to the mode of this grace, it is not irresistible, since it is written concerning many that they resisted the Holy Spirit. Acts 7 and elsewhere in many places.

5. that those who are incorporated into Jesus Christ and thereby become partakers of his life-giving Spirit have abundant strength to strive against Satan, sin, the world and their own flesh and to obtain the victory; it being well understood (that this is) through the assistance of the grace of the Holy Spirit, and that Jesus Christ assists them through his Spirit in all temptations, extends the hand, and—if only they are prepared for warfare and desire his help and are not negligent—keeps them standing, so that by no cunning or power of Satan can they be led astray or plucked out of Christ's hands, according to the word of Christ, John 10:28, "No one shall pluck them out of my hand." But whether they can through negligence fall away from the first principle of their life in Christ, again embrace the present world, depart from the pure doctrine once given to them, lose the good conscience, and neglect grace, must first be more carefully determined from the Holy Scriptures before we shall be able to teach this with the full persuasion of our heart.

These articles here set forth and taught the Remonstrants hold to be conformable to God's Word, edifying, and with respect to this matter sufficient unto salvation, so that it is neither necessary nor edifying to rise higher or to descend more deeply.

Appendix 5
The Counter Remonstrance of 1611

With respect to the points of doctrine, when they present certain teachings which they claim are carried to extremes by us, we cannot find therein that they have dealt honestly and in good faith, since they begin with the profound point of predestination concerning which we endeavor to speak with restraint and caution, solely for the sake of demonstrating God's undeserved grace and removing all human merits and worth. They ascribe to us such things to which we have never thought to consent, much less to teach. The articles wherein they claim that their opinion is set forth are stated in an ambiguous and dubious manner of speaking; in part they conflict with God's Word. In our churches the preaching is as follows:

1. As in Adam the whole human race, created in the image of God, has with Adam fallen into sin and thus become so corrupt that all men are conceived and born in sin and thus are by nature children of wrath, lying dead in their trespasses so that there is within them no more power to convert themselves truly unto God and to believe in Christ than a corpse has power to raise itself from the dead; so God draws out of his condemnation and delivers a certain number of men who in his eternal and immutable counsel He has chosen out of mere grace, according to the good pleasure of his will, unto salvation in Christ, passing by the others in his just judgment and leaving them in their sins.

2. that not only adults who believe in Christ and accordingly walk worthy of the gospel are to be reckoned as God's elect children, but also the children of the covenant so long as they do not in their conduct manifest the contrary; and that therefore believing parents, when their children die in infancy, have no reason to doubt the salvation of these their children.

3. that God in his election has not looked to the faith or conversion of his elect, nor to the right use of his gifts, as the grounds of election; but that on the contrary He in his eternal and immutable counsel has purposed and decreed to bestow faith and perseverance in godliness and thus to save those whom He according to his good pleasure has chosen to salvation.

4. that to this end He has first of all presented and given to them his only-begotten Son Jesus Christ, whom He delivered up to the death of the cross in order to save his elect, so that, although the suffering of Christ as that of the only-begotten and unique Son of God is sufficient unto the atonement of the sins of all men, nevertheless the same, according to the counsel and decree of God, has its efficacy unto reconciliation and forgiveness of sins only in the elect and true believer.

5. that furthermore to the same end God the Lord has his holy gospel preached, and that the Holy Spirit externally through

the preaching of that same gospel and internally through a special grace works so powerfully in the hearts of God's elect, that He illumines their minds, transforms and renews their wills, removing the heart of stone and giving them a heart of flesh, in such a manner that by these means they not only receive power to convert themselves and believe but also actually and willingly do repent and believe.

6. that those whom God has decreed to save are not only once so enlightened, regenerated and renewed in order to believe in Christ and convert themselves to God, but that they by the same power of the Holy Spirit by which they were converted to God without any contribution of themselves are in like manner continually supported and preserved; so that, although many weaknesses of the flesh cleave to them as long as they are in this life and are engaged in a continual struggle between flesh and Spirit and also sometimes fall into grievous sins, nevertheless this same Spirit prevails in this struggle, not permitting that God's elect by the corruption of the flesh should so resist the Spirit of sanctification that this would at any time be extinguished in them, and that in consequence they could completely or finally lose the true faith which was once bestowed on them and the Spirit of adoption as God's children which they had once received.

7. that nevertheless the true believers find no excuse in this teaching to pursue carelessly the lusts of the flesh, since it is impossible that those who by a true faith are ingrafted into Christ should not produce the fruits of thankfulness; but, on the contrary, the more they assure themselves and feel that God works in them both to will and to do according to his good pleasure, the more they persist in working their own salvation with fear and trembling, since they know that this is the only means by which it pleases God to keep them standing and to bring them to salvation. For this reason He also employs in his Word all manner of warnings and threatenings, not in order to cause them to despair or doubt their salvation but rather to

awaken in them a childlike fear by observing the weakness of their flesh in which they would surely perish, unless the Lord keep them standing in his undeserved grace, which is the sole cause and ground of their perseverance; so that, although He warns them in his Word to watch and pray, they nevertheless do not have this of themselves that they desire God's help and lack nothing, but only from the same Spirit who by a special grace prepares them for this and thus also powerfully keeps them standing.

Appendix 6
The Opinions of the Remonstrants (1618)

I. The Opinion of the Remonstrants regarding the first article, dealing with the decree of Predestination.

1. God has not decided to elect anyone to eternal life, or to reject anyone from the same, prior to the decree to create him, without any consideration of preceding obedience or disobedience, according to His good pleasure, for the demonstration of the glory of His mercy and justice, or of His absolute power and dominion.

2. Since the decree of God concerning both the salvation and perdition of each man is not a decree of the end absolutely intended, it follows that neither are such means subordinated

to that same decree by which the elect and the reprobate are efficaciously and inevitably led to their final destination.

3. Therefore God has not with this plan created in the one Adam all men in a state of rectitude, has not ordained the Fall and the permission of it, has not withdrawn from Adam the grace which was necessary and sufficient, has not brought it about that the Gospel is preached and that men are externally called, does not confer on them any gifts of the Holy Spirit by means of which he leads some of them to life, but deprives others of the benefit of life. Christ, the Mediator, is not solely the executor of election, but also the foundation of that same decree of election: the reason why some are efficaciously called, justified, persevere in faith and are glorified is not that they have been absolutely elected to eternal life. That others are left in the Fall, that Christ is not given to them, that they are either not called at all or not efficaciously called—these are not the reasons why they are absolutely rejected from eternal salvation.

4. God has not decreed to leave the greatest part of men in the Fall, excluded from every hope of salvation, apart from intervening actual sins.

5. God has ordained that Christ should be a propitiation for the sins of the whole world, and by virtue of that decree He has determined to justify and to save those who believe in Him, and to provide for men means necessary and sufficient for faith in such a way as He knows to be in harmony with His wisdom and justice. But He has by no means determined, by virtue of an absolute decree, to give Christ the Mediator solely to the elect, and through an efficacious calling to bestow faith upon, justify, preserve in the faith and glorify them alone.

6. No one is rejected from life eternal, nor from the means sufficient for it, by an absolute antecedent decree, so that the merit of Christ, calling and all the gifts of the Spirit can be profitable to salvation for all, and truly are, unless they themselves by the

abuse of these gifts pervert them to their own perdition; but to unbelief, to impiety and to sins, as means and causes of damnation, no one is predestined.

7. The election of particular persons is decisive, out of consideration of faith in Jesus Christ and of perseverance; not, however, apart from a consideration of faith and perseverance in the true faith, as a condition prerequisite for electing.

8. Rejection from eternal life is made on the basis of a consideration of antecedent unbelief and perseverance in unbelief; not, however, apart from a consideration of antecedent unbelief and perseverance in unbelief.

9. All the children of believers are sanctified in Christ, so that no one of them who leaves this life before the use of reason will perish. By no means, however, are to be considered among the number of the reprobate certain children of believers who leave this life in infancy before they have committed any actual sin in their own persons, so that neither the holy bath of baptism nor the prayers of the church for them can in any way be profitable for their salvation.

10. No children of believers who have been baptized in the name of the Father, the Son and the Holy Spirit, living in the state of infancy, are reckoned among the reprobate by an absolute decree.

II. The Opinion of the Remonstrants regarding the second article, which deals with the universality of the merit of the death of Christ.

1. The price of the redemption which Christ offered to God the Father is not only in itself and by itself sufficient for the redemption of the whole human race but has also been paid for all men and for every man, according to the decree, will and grace of God the Father; therefore no one is absolutely excluded from participation in the fruits of Christ's death by an absolute and antecedent decree of God.

2. Christ has, by the merit of his death, so reconciled God the Father to the whole human race that the Father, on account of that merit, without giving up His righteousness and truth, has been able and has willed to make and confirm a new covenant of grace with sinners and men liable to damnation.

3. Though Christ has merited reconciliation with God and remission of sins for all men and for every man, yet no one, according to the pact of the new and gracious covenant, becomes a true partaker of the benefits obtained by the death of Christ in any other way than by faith; nor are sins forgiven to sinning men before they actually and truly believe in Christ.

4. Only those for whom Christ has died are obliged to believe that Christ died for them. The reprobates, however, as they are called, for whom Christ has not died, are not obligated to such faith, nor can they be justly condemned on account of the contrary refusal to believe this. In fact, if there should be such reprobates, they would be obligated to believe that Christ has not died for them.

III–IV. The Opinion of the Remonstrants regarding the third and fourth articles, concerning the grace of God and the conversion of man.

1. Man does not have saving faith of himself, nor out of the powers of his free will, since in the state of sin he is able of himself and by himself neither to think, will, or do any good (which would indeed be saving good, the most prominent of which is saving faith). It is necessary therefore that by God in Christ through His Holy Spirit he be regenerated and renewed in intellect, affections, will and in all his powers, so that he might be able to understand, reflect upon, will and carry out the good things which pertain to salvation.

2. We hold, however, that the grace of God is not only the beginning but also the progression and the completion of every good, so much so that even the regenerate himself is unable to think,

will, or do the good, or to resist any temptations to evil, apart from that preceding or prevenient, awakening, following and cooperating grace. Hence all good works and actions which anyone by cogitation is able to comprehend are to be ascribed to the grace of God.

3. Yet we do not believe that all zeal, care and diligence applied to the obtaining of salvation before faith itself and the Spirit of renewal are vain and ineffectual—indeed, rather harmful to man than useful and fruitful. On the contrary, we hold that to hear the Word of God, to be sorry for sins committed, to desire saving grace and the Spirit of renewal (none of which things man is able to do without grace) are not only not harmful and useless, but rather most useful and most necessary for the obtaining of faith and of the Spirit of renewal.

4. The will in the fallen state, before calling, does not have the power and the freedom to will any saving good. And therefore we deny that the freedom to will saving good as well as evil, is present to the will in every state.

5. The efficacious grace by which anyone is converted is not irresistible; and though God so influences the will by the Word and the internal operation of His Spirit that He both confers the strength to believe or supernatural powers, and actually causes man to believe—yet man is able of himself to despise that grace and not to believe, and therefore to perish through his own fault.

6. Although according to the most free will of God the disparity of divine grace is very great, nevertheless the Holy Spirit confers, or is ready to confer, as much grace to all men and to each man to whom the Word of God is preached as is sufficient for promoting the conversion of men in its steps. Therefore sufficient grace for faith and conversion falls to the lot not only of those whom God is said to will to save according to the decree of absolute election, but also of those who are not actually converted.

7. Man is able through the grace of the Holy Spirit to do more good than he actually does, and to avoid more evil than he actually avoids; and we do not believe that God simply does not will that man should do more good than he does and avoid more evil than he does avoid, and that God has decreed precisely from eternity that both should so happen.

8. Whomever God calls to salvation, he calls seriously, that is, with a sincere and completely unhypocritical intention and will to save; nor do we assent to the opinion of those who hold that God calls certain ones externally whom He does not will to call internally, that is, as truly converted, even before the grace of calling has been rejected.

9. There is not in God a secret will which so contradicts the will of the same revealed in the Word that according to it (that is, the secret will) He does not will the conversion and salvation of the greatest part of those whom He seriously calls and invites by the Word of the Gospel and by His revealed will; and we do not here, as some say, acknowledge in God a holy simulation, or a double person.

10. Nor do we believe that God calls the reprobate, as they are called, to these ends: that He should the more harden them, or take away excuse, or punish them the more severely, or display their inability; nor, however, that they should be converted, should believe, and should be saved.

11. It is not true that all things, not only good but also bad, necessarily occur, from the power and efficacy of the secret will or decree of God, and that indeed those who sin, out of consideration of the decree of God, are not able to sin; that God wills to determine and to bring about the sins of men, their insane, foolish and cruel works, and the sacrilegious blasphemy of His name—in fact, to move the tongues of men to blasphemy, and so on.

12. To us the following is false and horrible: that God impels men to sins which He openly prohibits; that those who sin do not act contrary to the will of God properly named; that what is unrighteous (that is, what is contrary to His precept) is in agreement with the will of God; indeed, that it is truly a capital crime to do the will of God.

V. The Opinion of the Remonstrants with respect to the fifth article, which concerns Perseverance.

1. The perseverance of believers in the faith is not an effect of that absolute decree by which God is said to have chosen singular persons defined by no condition of obedience.

2. God provides true believers with as much grace and supernatural powers as He judges, according to His infinite wisdom, to be sufficient for persevering and for overcoming the temptations of the devil, the flesh and the world; it is never to be charged to God's account that they do not persevere.

3. True believers can fall from true faith and can fall into such sins as cannot be consistent with true and justifying faith; not only is it possible for this to happen, but it even happens frequently.

4. True believers are able to fall through their own fault into shameful and atrocious deeds, to persevere and to die in them; and therefore finally to fall and to perish.

5. Nevertheless we do not believe that true believers, though they may sometimes fall into grave sins which are vexing to their consciences, immediately fall out of every hope of repentance; but we acknowledge that it can happen that God, according to the multitude of His mercies, may recall them through His grace to repentance; in fact, we believe that this happens not infrequently, although we cannot be persuaded that this will certainly and indubitably happen.

6. The following dogmas, therefore, which by public writings are being scattered among the people, we reject with our whole mind and heart as harmful to piety and good morals: namely, (1) True believers are not able to sin deliberately, but only out of ignorance and weakness. (2) True believers through no sins can fall out of the grace of God. (3) A thousand sins, even all the sins of the whole world, are not able to render election invalid.... (4) To believers and to the elect no sins, however great and grave they can be, are imputed; but all present and future sins have already been remitted. (5) True believers, having fallen into destructive heresies, into grave and most atrocious sins, like adultery and homicide, on account of which the church, after the justification of Christ, is compelled to testify that it is not able to tolerate them in its external communion and that they will have no part in the kingdom of Christ unless they are converted, nevertheless are not able to fall from faith totally and finally.

7. A true believer, as for the present time he can be certain about his faith and integrity of his conscience, and thus also concerning his salvation and the saving benevolence of God toward him, for that time can be and ought to be certain; and on this point we reject the pontifical opinion.

8. A true believer can and ought indeed to be certain for the future that he is able, by diligent watchfulness, through prayers and through other holy exercises, to persevere in true faith, and he ought also to be certain that divine grace for persevering will never be lacking; but we do not see how he can be certain that he will never afterwards be remiss in his duty but that he will persevere in faith and in those works of piety and love which are fitting for a believer in this school of Christian warfare; neither do we deem it necessary that concerning this thing a believer should be certain.

Appendix 7
The Canons of Dort (1619)

THE FIRST MAIN POINT OF DOCTRINE
Divine election and reprobation

The judgment concerning divine predestination which the Synod declares to be in agreement with the Word of God and accepted till now in the Reformed churches, set forth in several articles[1]

ARTICLE 1 · God's right to condemn all people
Since all people have sinned in Adam and have come under the sentence of the curse and eternal death, God would have done no one an

---

1   All quotations from Scripture are translations of the original Latin manuscript.

injustice if it had been his will to leave the entire human race in sin and under the curse, and to condemn them on account of their sin. As the apostle says: "The whole world is liable to the condemnation of God" (Romans 3:19), "All have sinned and are deprived of the glory of God" (Romans 3:23), and "The wages of sin is death" (Romans 6:23).

ARTICLE 2 · The manifestation of God's love
But this is how God showed his love: "He sent his only begotten Son into the world, so that whoever believes in him should not perish but have eternal life." [John 3:16]

ARTICLE 3 · The preaching of the gospel
In order that people may be brought to faith, God mercifully sends proclaimers of this very joyful message to the people he wishes and at the time he wishes. By this ministry people are called to repentance and faith in Christ crucified. "For how shall they believe in him of whom they have not heard? And how shall they hear without someone preaching? And how shall they preach unless they have been sent?" (Romans 10:14–15).

ARTICLE 4 · A twofold response to the gospel
God's anger remains on those who do not believe this gospel. But those who do accept it and embrace Jesus the Saviour with a true and living faith are delivered through him from God's anger and from destruction, and receive the gift of eternal life.

ARTICLE 5 · The sources of unbelief and of faith
The cause or blame for this unbelief, as well as for all other sins, is not at all in God, but in man. Faith in Jesus Christ, however, and salvation through him is a free gift of God. As Scripture says, "It is by grace you have been saved, through faith, and this not from yourselves; it is a gift of God" (Ephesians 2:8). Likewise: "It has been freely given to you to believe in Christ" (Philippians 1:29).

ARTICLE 6 · God's eternal decision
The fact that some receive from God the gift of faith within time, and that others do not, stems from his eternal decision. For all his works

are known to God from eternity (Acts 15:18; Ephesians 1:11). In accordance with this decision he graciously softens the hearts, however hard, of his chosen ones and inclines them to believe, but by his just judgment he leaves in their wickedness and hardness of heart those who have not been chosen. And in this especially is disclosed to us his act—unfathomable, and as merciful as it is just—of distinguishing between people equally lost. This is the well-known decision of election and reprobation revealed in God's Word. This decision the wicked, impure and unstable distort to their own ruin, but it provides holy and godly souls with comfort beyond words.

ARTICLE 7 · Election

Election [or choosing] is God's unchangeable purpose by which he did the following: Before the foundation of the world, by sheer grace, according to the free good pleasure of his will, he chose in Christ to salvation a definite number of particular people out of the entire human race, which had fallen by its own fault from its original innocence into sin and ruin. Those chosen were neither better nor more deserving than the others, but lay with them in the common misery. He did this in Christ, whom he also appointed from eternity to be the mediator, the head of all those chosen, and the foundation of their salvation. And so he decided to give the chosen ones to Christ to be saved, and to call and draw them effectively into Christ's fellowship through his Word and Spirit. In other words, he decided to grant them true faith in Christ, to justify them, to sanctify them, and finally, after powerfully preserving them in the fellowship of his Son, to glorify them. God did all this in order to demonstrate his mercy, to the praise of the riches of his glorious grace. As Scripture says, "God chose us in Christ, before the foundation of the world, so that we should be holy and blameless before him with love; he predestined us whom he adopted as his children through Jesus Christ, in himself, according to the good pleasure of his will, to the praise of his glorious grace, by which he freely made us pleasing to himself in his beloved" (Ephesians 1:4–6). And elsewhere, "Those whom he predestined, he also called; and those whom he called, he also justified; and those whom he justified, he also glorified" (Romans 8:30).

ARTICLE 8 · A single decision of election

This election is not of many kinds; it is one and the same election for all who were to be saved in the Old and the New Testament. For Scripture declares that there is a single good pleasure, purpose and plan of God's will, by which he chose us from eternity both to grace and to glory, both to salvation and to the way of salvation, which he prepared in advance for us to walk in.

ARTICLE 9 · Election not based on foreseen faith

This same election took place, not on the basis of foreseen faith, of the obedience of faith, of holiness, or of any other good quality and disposition, as though it were based on a prerequisite cause or condition in the person to be chosen, but rather for the purpose of faith, of the obedience of faith, of holiness, and so on. Accordingly, election is the source of each of the benefits of salvation. Faith, holiness, and the other saving gifts, and at last eternal life itself, flow forth from election as its fruits and effects. As the apostle says, "He chose us (not because we were, but) so that we should be holy and blameless before him in love" (Ephesians 1:4).

ARTICLE 10 · Election based on God's good pleasure

But the cause of this undeserved election is exclusively the good pleasure of God. This does not involve his choosing certain human qualities or actions from among all those possible as a condition of salvation, but rather involves his adopting certain particular persons from among the common mass of sinners as his own possession. As Scripture says, "When the children were not yet born, and had done nothing either good or bad…, she (Rebecca) was told, 'The older will serve the younger.' As it is written, 'Jacob I loved, but Esau I hated'" (Romans 9:11–13). Also, "All who were appointed for eternal life believed" (Acts 13:48).

ARTICLE 11 · Election unchangeable

Just as God himself is most wise, unchangeable, all-knowing, and almighty, so the election made by him can neither be suspended nor altered, revoked or annulled; neither can his chosen ones be cast off, nor their number reduced.

ARTICLE 12 · The assurance of election
Assurance of this their eternal and unchangeable election to salvation is given to the chosen in due time, though by various stages and in differing measure. Such assurance comes not by inquisitive searching into the hidden and deep things of God, but by noticing within themselves, with spiritual joy and holy delight, the unmistakable fruits of election pointed out in God's Word—such as a true faith in Christ, a childlike fear of God, a godly sorrow for their sins, a hunger and thirst for righteousness, and so on.

ARTICLE 13 · The fruit of this assurance
In their awareness and assurance of this election, God's children daily find greater cause to humble themselves before God, to adore the fathomless depth of his mercies, to cleanse themselves, and to give fervent love in return to him who first so greatly loved them. This is far from saying that this teaching concerning election, and reflection upon it, make God's children lax in observing his commandments or carnally self-assured. By God's just judgment this does usually happen to those who casually take for granted the grace of election or engage in idle and brazen talk about it but are unwilling to walk in the ways of the chosen.

ARTICLE 14 · Teaching election properly
Just as, by God's wise plan, this teaching concerning divine election has been proclaimed through the prophets, Christ himself, and the apostles, in Old and New Testament times, and has subsequently been committed to writing in the Holy Scriptures, so also today in God's church, for which it was specifically intended, this teaching must be set forth—with a spirit of discretion, in a godly and holy manner, at the appropriate time and place, without inquisitive searching into the ways of the Most High. This must be done for the glory of God's most holy name, and for the lively comfort of his people.

ARTICLE 15 · Reprobation
Moreover, Holy Scripture most especially highlights this eternal and undeserved grace of our election and brings it out more clearly for us, in that it further bears witness that not all people have been chosen

but that some have not been chosen or have been passed by in God's eternal election—those, that is, concerning whom God, on the basis of his entirely free, most just, irreproachable and unchangeable good pleasure, made the following decision: to leave them in the common misery into which, by their own fault, they have plunged themselves; not to grant them saving faith and the grace of conversion; but finally to condemn and eternally punish them (having been left in their own ways and under his just judgment), not only for their unbelief but also for all their other sins, in order to display his justice. And this is the decision of reprobation, which does not at all make God the author of sin (a blasphemous thought!) but rather its fearful, irreproachable, just judge and avenger.

ARTICLE 16 · Responses to the teaching of reprobation

Those who do not yet actively experience within themselves a living faith in Christ or an assured confidence of heart, peace of conscience, a zeal for childlike obedience and a glorying in God through Christ, but who nevertheless use the means by which God has promised to work these things in us—such people ought not to be alarmed at the mention of reprobation, nor to count themselves among the reprobate; rather they ought to continue diligently in the use of the means, to desire fervently a time of more abundant grace, and to wait for it in reverence and humility. On the other hand, those who seriously desire to turn to God, to be pleasing to him alone and to be delivered from the body of death, but are not yet able to make such progress along the way of godliness and faith as they would like—such people ought much less to stand in fear of the teaching concerning reprobation, since our merciful God has promised that he will not snuff out a smoldering wick and that he will not break a bruised reed. However, those who have forgotten God and their Saviour Jesus Christ and have abandoned themselves wholly to the cares of the world and the pleasures of the flesh—such people have every reason to stand in fear of this teaching, as long as they do not seriously turn to God.

ARTICLE 17 · The salvation of the infants of believers

Since we must make judgments about God's will from his Word, which testifies that the children of believers are holy, not by nature but by virtue of the gracious covenant in which they together with their parents are included, godly parents ought not to doubt the election and salvation of their children whom God calls out of this life in infancy.

ARTICLE 18 · The proper attitude toward election and reprobation

To those who complain about this grace of an undeserved election and about the severity of a just reprobation, we reply with the words of the apostle, "Who are you, O man, to talk back to God?" (Romans 9:20), and with the words of our Saviour, "Have I no right to do what I want with my own?" (Matthew 20:15). We, however, with reverent adoration of these secret things, cry out with the apostle: "Oh, the depths of the riches both of the wisdom and the knowledge of God! How unsearchable are his judgments, and his ways beyond tracing out! For who has known the mind of the Lord? Or who has been his counselor? Or who has first given to God, that God should repay him? For from him and through him and to him are all things. To him be the glory forever! Amen" (Romans 11:33–36).

Rejection of the errors
by which the Dutch churches have for some time been disturbed

Having set forth the orthodox teaching concerning election and reprobation, the Synod rejects the errors of those

1. *Who teach that the will of God to save those who would believe and persevere in faith and in the obedience of faith is the whole and entire decision of election to salvation, and that nothing else concerning this decision has been revealed in God's Word.*

   For they deceive the simple and plainly contradict Holy Scripture in its testimony that God does not only wish to save those who would believe, but that he has also from eternity chosen certain particular people to whom, rather than to others, he would within time grant faith in Christ and perseverance. As Scripture says, "I have revealed your name to those whom you gave me"

(John 17:6). Likewise, "All who were appointed for eternal life believed" (Acts 13:48), and "He chose us before the foundation of the world so that we should be holy." (Ephesians 1:4).

2. *Who teach that God's election to eternal life is of many kinds: one general and indefinite, the other particular and definite; and the latter in turn either incomplete, revocable, nonperemptory (or conditional), or else complete, irrevocable and peremptory (or absolute). Likewise, who teach that there is one election to faith and another to salvation, so that there can be an election to justifying faith apart from a peremptory election to salvation.*

    For this is an invention of the human brain, devised apart from the Scriptures, which distorts the teaching concerning election and breaks up this golden chain of salvation: "Those whom he predestined, he also called; and those whom he called, he also justified; and those whom he justified, he also glorified" (Romans 8:30).

3. *Who teach that God's good pleasure and purpose, which Scripture mentions in its teaching of election, does not involve God's choosing certain particular people rather than others, but involves God's choosing, out of all possible conditions (including the works of the law) or out of the whole order of things, the intrinsically unworthy act of faith, as well as the imperfect obedience of faith, to be a condition of salvation; and it involves his graciously wishing to count this as perfect obedience and to look upon it as worthy of the reward of eternal life.*

    For by this pernicious error, the good pleasure of God and the merit of Christ are robbed of their effectiveness and people are drawn away, by unprofitable inquiries, from the truth of undeserved justification and from the simplicity of the Scriptures. It also gives the lie to these words of the apostle: "God called us with a holy calling, not in virtue of works, but in virtue of his own purpose and the grace which was given to us in Christ Jesus before the beginning of time" (2 Timothy 1:9).

4. *Who teach that in election to faith a prerequisite condition is that man should rightly use the light of nature, be upright, unassuming, humble and disposed to eternal life, as though election depended to some extent on these factors.*

For this smacks of Pelagius, and it clearly calls into question the words of the apostle: "We lived at one time in the passions of our flesh, following the will of our flesh and thoughts, and we were by nature children of wrath, like everyone else. But God, who is rich in mercy, out of the great love with which he loved us, even when we were dead in transgressions, made us alive with Christ, by whose grace you have been saved. And God raised us up with him and seated us with him in heaven in Christ Jesus, in order that in the coming ages we might show the surpassing riches of his grace, according to his kindness toward us in Christ Jesus. For it is by grace you have been saved, through faith (and this not from yourselves; it is the gift of God) not by works, so that no one can boast" (Ephesians 2:3–9).

5. *Who teach that the incomplete and nonperemptory election of particular persons to salvation occurred on the basis of a foreseen faith, repentance, holiness and godliness, which has just begun or continued for some time; but that complete and peremptory election occurred on the basis of a foreseen perseverance to the end in faith, repentance, holiness, and godliness. And that this is the gracious and evangelical worthiness, on account of which the one who is chosen is more worthy than the one who is not chosen. And therefore that faith, the obedience of faith, holiness, godliness and perseverance are not fruits or effects of an unchangeable election to glory, but indispensable conditions and causes, which are prerequisite in those who are to be chosen in the complete election, and which are foreseen as achieved in them.*

This runs counter to the entire Scripture, which throughout impresses upon our ears and hearts these sayings among others: Election is "not by works, but by him who calls" (Romans 9:11–12); "All who were appointed for eternal life believed" (Acts 13:48); "He chose us in himself so that we should be holy" (Ephesians 1:4); "You did not choose me, but I chose you"

(John 15:16); "If by grace, not by works" (Romans 11:6); "In this is love, not that we loved God, but that he loved us and sent his Son" (1 John 4:10).

6. *Who teach that not every election to salvation is unchangeable, but that some of the chosen can perish and do in fact perish eternally, with no decision of God to prevent it.*

   By this gross error they make God changeable, destroy the comfort of the godly concerning the steadfastness of their election and contradict the Holy Scriptures, which teach that the elect cannot be led astray (Matthew 24:24), that Christ does not lose those given to him by the Father (John 6:39) and that those whom God predestined, called and justified, he also glorifies (Romans 8:30).

7. *Who teach that in this life there is no fruit, no awareness, and no assurance of one's unchangeable election to glory, except as conditional upon something changeable and contingent.*

   For not only is it absurd to speak of an uncertain assurance, but these things also militate against the experience of the saints, who with the apostle rejoice from an awareness of their election and sing the praises of this gift of God; who, as Christ urged, rejoice with his disciples that their names have been written in heaven (Luke 10:20); and finally who hold up against the flaming arrows of the devil's temptations the awareness of their election, with the question, "Who will bring any charge against those whom God has chosen?" (Romans 8:33).

8. *Who teach that it was not on the basis of his just will alone that God decided to leave anyone in the Fall of Adam and in the common state of sin and condemnation or to pass anyone by in the imparting of grace necessary for faith and conversion.*

   For these words stand fast: "He has mercy on whom he wishes, and he hardens whom he wishes" (Romans 9:18). And also: "To you it has been given to know the secrets of the kingdom of heaven, but to them it has not been given" (Matthew 13:11). Likewise: "I give glory to you, Father, Lord of heaven and earth, that you have hidden these things from the wise and under-standing, and have revealed them to little children; yes, Father, because that was your pleasure" (Matthew 11:25–26).

9. *Who teach that the cause for God's sending the gospel to one people rather than to another is not merely and solely God's good pleasure, but rather that one people is better and worthier than the other to whom the gospel is not communicated.*

   For Moses contradicts this when he addresses the people of Israel as follows: "Behold, to Jehovah your God belong the heavens and the highest heavens, the earth and whatever is in it. But Jehovah was inclined in his affection to love your ances-tors alone, and chose out their descendants after them, you above all peoples, as at this day" (Deuteronomy 10:14–15). And also Christ: "Woe to you, Korazin! Woe to you, Bethsaida! for if those mighty works done in you had been done in Tyre and Sidon, they would have repented long ago in sackcloth and ashes" (Matthew 11:21).

THE SECOND MAIN POINT OF DOCTRINE
Christ's death and human redemption through it

ARTICLE 1 · The punishment which God's justice requires
God is not only supremely merciful, but also supremely just. His jus-tice requires (as he has revealed himself in the Word) that the sins we have committed against his infinite majesty be punished with both temporal and eternal punishments, of soul as well as body. We cannot escape these punishments unless satisfaction is given to God's justice.

ARTICLE 2 · The satisfaction made by Christ
Since, however, we ourselves cannot give this satisfaction or deliver ourselves from God's anger, God in his boundless mercy has given us as a guarantee his only begotten Son, who was made to be sin and a curse for us, in our place, on the cross, in order that he might give satisfaction for us.

ARTICLE 3 · The infinite value of Christ's death

This death of God's Son is the only and entirely complete sacrifice and satisfaction for sins; it is of infinite value and worth, more than sufficient to atone for the sins of the whole world.

ARTICLE 4 · Reasons for this infinite value

This death is of such great value and worth for the reason that the person who suffered it is—as was necessary to be our Saviour—not only a true and perfectly holy man, but also the only begotten Son of God, of the same eternal and infinite essence with the Father and the Holy Spirit. Another reason is that this death was accompanied by the experience of God's anger and curse, which we by our sins had fully deserved.

ARTICLE 5 · The mandate to proclaim the gospel to all

Moreover, it is the promise of the gospel that whoever believes in Christ crucified shall not perish but have eternal life. This promise, together with the command to repent and believe, ought to be announced and declared without differentiation or discrimination to all nations and people, to whom God in his good pleasure sends the gospel.

ARTICLE 6 · Unbelief—man's responsibility

However, that many who have been called through the gospel do not repent or believe in Christ but perish in unbelief is not because the sacrifice of Christ offered on the cross is deficient or insufficient, but because they themselves are at fault.

ARTICLE 7 · Faith—God's gift

But all who genuinely believe and are delivered and saved by Christ's death from their sins and from destruction receive this favour solely from God's grace—which he owes to no one—given to them in Christ from eternity.

ARTICLE 8 · The saving effectiveness of Christ's death

For it was the entirely free plan and very gracious will and intention of God the Father that the enlivening and saving effectiveness of his Son's costly death should work itself out in all his chosen ones, in order that he might grant justifying faith to them only and thereby lead them without fail to salvation. In other words, it was God's will that Christ through the blood of the cross (by which he confirmed the new covenant) should effectively redeem from every people, tribe, nation and language all those and only those who were chosen from eternity to salvation and given to him by the Father; that he should grant them faith (which, like the Holy Spirit's other saving gifts, he acquired for them by his death); that he should cleanse them by his blood from all their sins, both original and actual, whether committed before or after their coming to faith; that he should faithfully preserve them to the very end; and that he should finally present them to himself, a glorious people, without spot or wrinkle.

ARTICLE 9 · The fulfillment of God's plan
This plan, arising out of God's eternal love for his chosen ones, from the beginning of the world to the present time has been powerfully carried out and will also be carried out in the future, the gates of hell seeking vainly to prevail against it. As a result, the chosen are gathered into one, all in their own time, and there is always a church of believers founded on Christ's blood, a church which steadfastly loves, persistently worships, and—here and in all eternity—praises him as her Saviour who laid down his life for her on the cross, as a bridegroom for his bride.

Rejection of the errors

Having set forth the orthodox teaching, the Synod rejects the errors of those

1. *Who teach that God the Father appointed his Son to death on the cross without a fixed and definite plan to save anyone by name, so that the necessity, usefulness and worth of what Christ's death obtained could have stood intact and altogether perfect, complete and whole, even if the redemption that was obtained had never in actual fact been applied to any individual.*
   For this assertion is an insult to the wisdom of God the Father

and to the merit of Jesus Christ, and it is contrary to Scripture. For the Saviour speaks as follows: "I lay down my life for the sheep, and I know them" (John 10:15,27). And Isaiah the prophet says concerning the Saviour: "When he shall make himself an offering for sin, he shall see his offspring, he shall prolong his days, and the will of Jehovah shall prosper in his hand" (Isaiah 53:10). Finally, this undermines the article of the creed in which we confess what we believe concerning the church.

2. *Who teach that the purpose of Christ's death was not to establish in actual fact a new covenant of grace by his blood, but only to acquire for the Father the mere right to enter once more into a covenant with men, whether of grace or of works.*
For this conflicts with Scripture, which teaches that Christ has become the guarantee and mediator of a better—that is, a new covenant (Hebrews 7:22; 9:15), and that a will is in force only when someone has died (Hebrews 9:17).

3. *Who teach that Christ, by the satisfaction which he gave, did not certainly merit for anyone salvation itself and the faith by which this satisfaction of Christ is effectively applied to salvation, but only acquired for the Father the authority or plenary will to relate in a new way with men and to impose such new conditions as he chose, and that the satisfying of these conditions depends on the free choice of man; consequently, that it was possible that either all or none would fulfill them.*
For they have too low an opinion of the death of Christ, do not at all acknowledge the foremost fruit or benefit which it brings forth and summon back from hell the Pelagian error.

4. *Who teach that what is involved in the new covenant of grace which God the Father made with men through the intervening of Christ's death is not that we are justified before God and saved through faith, insofar as it accepts Christ's merit, but rather that God, having withdrawn his demand for perfect obedience to the law, counts faith itself, and the imperfect obedience of faith, as*

perfect obedience to the law, and graciously looks upon this as worthy of the reward of eternal life.

For they contradict Scripture: "They are justified freely by his grace through the redemption that came by Jesus Christ, whom God presented as a sacrifice of atonement, through faith in his blood" (Romans 3:24–25). And along with the ungodly Socinus, they introduce a new and foreign justification of man before God, against the consensus of the whole church.

5. *Who teach that all people have been received into the state of reconciliation and into the grace of the covenant, so that no one on account of original sin is liable to condemnation, or is to be condemned, but that all are free from the guilt of this sin.*

   For this opinion conflicts with Scripture which asserts that we are by nature children of wrath.

6. *Who make use of the distinction between obtaining and applying in order to instill in the unwary and inexperienced the opinion that God, as far as he is concerned, wished to bestow equally upon all people the benefits which are gained by Christ's death; but that the distinction by which some rather than others come to share in the forgiveness of sins and eternal life depends on their own free choice (which applies itself to the grace offered indiscriminately) but does not depend on the unique gift of mercy which effectively works in them, so that they, rather than others, apply that grace to themselves.*

   For, while pretending to set forth this distinction in an acceptable sense, they attempt to give the people the deadly poison of Pelagianism.

7. *Who teach that Christ neither could die, nor had to die, nor did die for those whom God so dearly loved and chose to eternal life, since such people do not need the death of Christ.*

   For they contradict the apostle, who says: "Christ loved me and gave himself up for me" (Galatians 2:20), and likewise: "Who will bring any charge against those whom God has chosen? It is God who justifies. Who is he that condemns? It

is Christ who died, that is, for them" (Romans 8:33–34). They
also contradict the Saviour, who asserts: "I lay down my life
for the sheep" (John 10:15) and "My command is this: 'Love
one another as I have loved you. Greater love has no one
than this, that one lay down his life for his friends'" (John
15:12–13).

THE THIRD AND FOURTH MAIN POINTS OF DOCTRINE
Human corruption, conversion to God
and the way it occurs

ARTICLE 1 · The effect of the Fall on human nature
Man was originally created in the image of God and was furnished in
his mind with a true and salutary knowledge of his Creator and things
spiritual, in his will and heart with righteousness, and in all his emotions with purity; indeed, the whole man was holy. However, rebelling
against God at the devil's instigation and by his own free will, he
deprived himself of these outstanding gifts. Rather, in their place he
brought upon himself blindness, terrible darkness, futility and distortion of judgment in his mind; perversity, defiance and hardness in his
heart and will; and finally impurity in all his emotions.

ARTICLE 2 · The spread of corruption
Man brought forth children of the same nature as himself after the
Fall. That is to say, being corrupt he brought forth corrupt children.
The corruption spread, by God's just judgment, from Adam to all his
descendants—except for Christ alone—not by way of imitation (as in
former times the Pelagians would have it) but by way of the propagation of his perverted nature.

ARTICLE 3 · Total inability
Therefore, all people are conceived in sin and are born children of
wrath, unfit for any saving good, inclined to evil, dead in their sins and
slaves to sin; without the grace of the regenerating Holy Spirit they
are neither willing nor able to return to God, to reform their distorted
nature, or even to dispose themselves to such reform.

ARTICLE 4 · The inadequacy of the light of nature

There is, to be sure, a certain light of nature remaining in man after the Fall, by virtue of which he retains some notions about God, natural things, and the difference between what is moral and immoral, and demonstrates a certain eagerness for virtue and for good outward behavior. But this light of nature is far from enabling man to come to a saving knowledge of God and conversion to him—so far, in fact, that man does not use it rightly even in matters of nature and society. Instead, in various ways he completely distorts this light, whatever its precise character, and suppresses it in unrighteousness. In doing so, he renders himself without excuse before God.

ARTICLE 5 · The inadequacy of the law

In this respect, what is true of the light of nature is true also of the Ten Commandments given by God through Moses specifically to the Jews. For man cannot obtain saving grace through the Decalogue, because, although it does expose the magnitude of his sin and increasingly convict him of his guilt, yet it does not offer a remedy or enable him to escape from his misery, and, indeed, weakened as it is by the flesh, leaves the offender under the curse.

ARTICLE 6 · The saving power of the gospel

What, therefore, neither the light of nature nor the law can do, God accomplishes by the power of the Holy Spirit, through the Word or the ministry of reconciliation. This is the gospel about the Messiah, through which it has pleased God to save believers, in both the Old and the New Testament.

ARTICLE 7 · God's freedom in revealing the gospel

In the Old Testament, God revealed this secret of his will to a small number; in the New Testament (now without any distinction between peoples) he discloses it to a large number. The reason for this difference must not be ascribed to the greater worth of one nation over another, or to a better use of the light of nature, but to the free good pleasure and undeserved love of God. Therefore, those who receive so much grace, beyond and in spite of all they deserve, ought to acknowledge it with humble and thankful hearts; on the other hand, with the apostle they ought to adore (but certainly not inquisitively search into) the severity and justice of God's judgments on the others, who do not receive this grace.

ARTICLE 8 · The serious call of the gospel
Nevertheless, all who are called through the gospel are called seriously. For seriously and most genuinely God makes known in his Word what is pleasing to him: that those who are called should come to him. Seriously he also promises rest for their souls and eternal life to all who come to him and believe.

ARTICLE 9 · Human responsibility for rejecting the gospel
The fact that many who are called through the ministry of the gospel do not come and are not brought to conversion must not be blamed on the gospel, nor on Christ, who is offered through the gospel, nor on God, who calls them through the gospel and even bestows various gifts on them, but on the people themselves who are called. Some in self-assurance do not even entertain the Word of life; others do entertain it but do not take it to heart, and for that reason, after the fleeting joy of a temporary faith, they relapse; others choke the seed of the Word with the thorns of life's cares and with the pleasures of the world and bring forth no fruits. This our Saviour teaches in the parable of the sower (Matthew 13).

ARTICLE 10 · Conversion as the work of God
The fact that others who are called through the ministry of the gospel do come and are brought to conversion must not be credited to man, as though one distinguishes himself by free choice from others who are furnished with equal or sufficient grace for faith and conversion (as the proud heresy of Pelagius maintains). No, it must be credited to God: just as from eternity he chose his own in Christ, so within time he effectively calls them, grants them faith and repentance, and, having rescued them from the dominion of darkness, brings them into the kingdom of his Son, in order that they may declare the wonderful deeds of him who called them out of darkness into this marvelous light, and may boast not in themselves, but in the Lord, as apostolic words frequently testify in Scripture.

ARTICLE 11 · The Holy Spirit's work in conversion

Moreover, when God carries out this good pleasure in his chosen ones, or works true conversion in them, he not only sees to it that the gospel is proclaimed to them outwardly, and enlightens their minds powerfully by the Holy Spirit so that they may rightly understand and discern the things of the Spirit of God, but, by the effective operation of the same regenerating Spirit, he also penetrates into the inmost being of man, opens the closed heart, softens the hard heart and circumcises the heart that is uncircumcised. He infuses new qualities into the will, making the dead will alive, the evil one good, the unwilling one willing and the stubborn one compliant; he activates and strengthens the will so that, like a good tree, it may be enabled to produce the fruits of good deeds.

ARTICLE 12 · Regeneration a supernatural work

And this is the regeneration, the new creation, the raising from the dead, and the making alive so clearly proclaimed in the Scriptures, which God works in us without our help. But this certainly does not happen only by outward teaching, by moral persuasion, or by such a way of working that, after God has done his work, it remains in man's power whether or not to be reborn or converted. Rather, it is an entirely supernatural work, one that is at the same time most powerful and most pleasing, a marvelous, hidden and inexpressible work, which is not lesser than or inferior in power to that of creation or of raising the dead, as Scripture (inspired by the author of this work) teaches. As a result, all those in whose hearts God works in this marvelous way are certainly, unfailingly and effectively reborn and do actually believe. And then the will, now renewed, is not only activated and motivated by God but in being activated by God is also itself active. For this reason, man himself, by that grace which he has received, is also rightly said to believe and to repent.

ARTICLE 13 · The incomprehensible way of regeneration

In this life believers cannot fully understand the way this work occurs; meanwhile, they rest content with knowing and experiencing that by this grace of God they do believe with the heart and love their Saviour.

ARTICLE 14 · The way God gives faith

In this way, therefore, faith is a gift of God, not in the sense that it is offered by God for man to choose, but that it is in actual fact bestowed on man, breathed and infused into him. Nor is it a gift in the sense that God bestows only the potential to believe, but then awaits assent—the act of believing—from man's choice; rather, it is a gift in the sense that he who works both willing and acting and, indeed, works all things in all people produces in man both the will to believe and the belief itself.

ARTICLE 15 · Responses to God's grace

God does not owe this grace to anyone. For what could God owe to one who has nothing to give that can be paid back? Indeed, what could God owe to one who has nothing of his own to give but sin and falsehood? Therefore the person who receives this grace owes and gives eternal thanks to God alone; the person who does not receive it either does not care at all about these spiritual things and is satisfied with himself in his condition, or else in self-assurance foolishly boasts about having something which he lacks. Furthermore, following the example of the apostles, we are to think and to speak in the most favorable way about those who outwardly profess their faith and better their lives, for the inner chambers of the heart are unknown to us. But for others who have not yet been called, we are to pray to the God who calls things that do not exist as though they did. In no way, however, are we to pride ourselves as better than they, as though we had distinguished ourselves from them.

ARTICLE 16 · Regeneration's effect

However, just as by the Fall man did not cease to be man, endowed with intellect and will, and just as sin, which has spread through the whole human race, did not abolish the nature of the human race but distorted and spiritually killed it, so also this divine grace of regeneration does not act in people as if they were blocks and stones; nor does it abolish the will and its properties or coerce a reluctant will by force, but spiritually revives, heals, reforms, and—in a manner at once pleasing and powerful—bends it back. As a result, a ready and sincere obedience of the Spirit now begins to prevail where before the rebellion and resistance of the flesh were completely dominant. It is in this that the true and spiritual restoration and freedom of our will consists. Thus, if the marvelous Maker of every good thing were not dealing with us, man would have no hope of getting up from his fall by his free choice, by which he plunged himself into ruin when still standing upright.

ARTICLE 17· God's use of means in regeneration

Just as the almighty work of God by which he brings forth and sustains our natural life does not rule out but requires the use of means, by which God, according to his infinite wisdom and goodness, has wished to exercise his power, so also the aforementioned supernatural work of God by which he regenerates us in no way rules out or cancels the use of the gospel, which God in his great wisdom has appointed to be the seed of regeneration and the food of the soul. For this reason, the apostles and the teachers who followed them taught the people in a godly manner about this grace of God, to give him the glory and to humble all pride, and yet did not neglect meanwhile to keep the people, by means of the holy admonitions of the gospel, under the administration of the Word, the sacraments and discipline. So even today it is out of the question that the teachers or those taught in the church should presume to test God by separating what he in his good pleasure has wished to be closely joined together. For grace is bestowed through admonitions, and the more readily we perform our duty, the more lustrous the benefit of God working in us usually is and the better his work advances. To him alone, both for the means and for their saving fruit and effectiveness, all glory is owed forever. Amen.

Rejection of the errors

Having set forth the orthodox teaching, the Synod rejects the errors of those

1. *Who teach that, properly speaking, it cannot be said that original sin in itself is enough to condemn the whole human race or to warrant temporal and eternal punishments.*
   For they contradict the apostle when he says: "Sin entered the world through one man, and death through sin, and in this way death passed on to all men because all sinned" (Romans

5:12); also: "The guilt followed one sin and brought condemnation" (Romans 5:16); likewise: "The wages of sin is death"
(Romans 6:23).

2. *Who teach that the spiritual gifts or the good dispositions and
virtues such as goodness, holiness and righteousness could not
have resided in man's will when he was first created, and therefore
could not have been separated from the will at the Fall.*
For this conflicts with the apostle's description of the image
of God in Ephesians 4:24, where he portrays the image in
terms of righteousness and holiness, which definitely reside
in the will.

3. *Who teach that in spiritual death the spiritual gifts have not been
separated from man's will, since the will in itself has never been
corrupted but only hindered by the darkness of the mind and the
unruliness of the emotions, and since the will is able to exercise its
innate free capacity once these hindrances are removed, which is
to say, it is able of itself to will or choose whatever good is set before
it—or else not to will or choose it.*
This is a novel idea and an error and has the effect of elevating
the power of free choice, contrary to the words of Jeremiah the
prophet: "The heart itself is deceitful above all things and
wicked" (Jeremiah 17:9); and of the words of the apostle: "All
of us also lived among them (the sons of disobedience) at one
time in the passions of our flesh, following the will of our flesh
and thoughts" (Ephesians 2:3).

4. *Who teach that unregenerate man is not strictly or totally dead in
his sins or deprived of all capacity for spiritual good but is able to
hunger and thirst for righteousness or life and to offer the sacrifice
of a broken and contrite spirit which is pleasing to God.*
For these views are opposed to the plain testimonies of Scripture: "You were dead in your transgressions and sins" (Ephesians 2:1,5); "The imagination of the thoughts of man's heart
is only evil all the time" (Genesis 6:5; 8:21). Besides, to
hunger and thirst for deliverance from misery and for life,

and to offer God the sacrifice of a broken spirit is characteristic only of the regenerate and of those called blessed (Psalm
51:17; Matthew 5:6).

5. *Who teach that corrupt and natural man can make such good use
    of common grace (by which they mean the light of nature) or of
    the gifts remaining after the Fall that he is able thereby gradually
    to obtain a greater grace—evangelical or saving grace—as well as
    salvation itself; and that in this way God, for his part, shows him-
    self ready to reveal Christ to all people, since he provides to all, to
    a sufficient extent and in an effective manner, the means necessary
    for the revealing of Christ, for faith and for repentance.*
    For Scripture, not to mention the experience of all ages, testi-
    fies that this is false: "He makes known his words to Jacob, his
    statutes and his laws to Israel; he has done this for no other
    nation, and they do not know his laws" (Psalm 147:19–20); "In
    the past God let all nations go their own way" (Acts 14:16);
    "They (Paul and his companions) were kept by the Holy Spirit
    from speaking God's word in Asia" and "When they had come
    to Mysia, they tried to go to Bithynia, but the Spirit would not
    allow them to" (Acts 16:6–7).

6. *Who teach that in the true conversion of man new qualities, disposi-
    tions, or gifts cannot be infused or poured into his will by God, and
    indeed that the faith [or believing] by which we first come to conver-
    sion and from which we receive the name "believers" is not a quality
    or gift infused by God, but only an act of man, and that it cannot be
    called a gift except in respect to the power of attaining faith.*
    For these views contradict the Holy Scriptures, which testify
    that God does infuse or pour into our hearts the new qualities
    of faith, obedience and the experiencing of his love: "I will put
    my law in their minds, and write it on their hearts" (Jeremiah
    31:33); "I will pour water on the thirsty land, and streams on
    the dry ground; I will pour out my Spirit on your offspring"
    (Isaiah 44:3); "The love of God has been poured out in our
    hearts by the Holy Spirit, who has been given to us" (Romans
    5:5). They also conflict with the continuous practice of the

church, which prays with the prophet: "Convert me, Lord, and I shall be converted" (Jeremiah 31:18).

7. *Who teach that the grace by which we are converted to God is nothing but a gentle persuasion, or (as others explain it) that the way of God's acting in man's conversion that is most noble and suited to human nature is that which happens by persuasion, and that nothing prevents this grace of moral suasion even by itself from making natural men spiritual; indeed, that God does not produce the assent of the will except in this manner of moral suasion, and that the effectiveness of God's work by which it surpasses the work of Satan consists in the fact that God promises eternal benefits while Satan promises temporal ones.*

For this teaching is entirely Pelagian and contrary to the whole of Scripture, which recognizes besides this persuasion also another, far more effective and divine way in which the Holy Spirit acts in man's conversion. As Ezekiel 36:26 puts it: "I will give you a new heart and put a new spirit in you; and I will remove your heart of stone and give you a heart of flesh."

8. *Who teach that God in regenerating man does not bring to bear that power of his omnipotence whereby he may powerfully and unfailingly bend man's will to faith and conversion, but that even when God has accomplished all the works of grace which he uses for man's conversion, man nevertheless can, and in actual fact often does, so resist God and the Spirit in their intent and will to regenerate him, that man completely thwarts his own rebirth; and, indeed, that it remains in his own power whether or not to be reborn.*

For this does away with all effective functioning of God's grace in our conversion and subjects the activity of Almighty God to the will of man; it is contrary to the apostles, who teach that we believe by virtue of "the effective working of God's mighty strength" (Ephesians 1:19), and that God fulfills the undeserved good will of his kindness and the work of faith in us with power (2 Thessalonians 1:11), and likewise that "his divine power has given us everything we need for life and godliness" (2 Peter 1:3).

9. *Who teach that grace and free choice are concurrent partial causes which cooperate to initiate conversion, and that grace does not precede—in the order of causality—the effective influence of the will; that is to say, that God does not effectively help man's will to come to conversion before man's will itself motivates and determines itself.*

For the early church already condemned this doctrine long ago in the Pelagians, on the basis of the words of the apostle: "It does not depend on man's willing or running but on God's mercy" (Romans 9:16); also: "Who makes you different from anyone else? and What do you have that you did not receive? (1 Corinthians 4:7); likewise: "It is God who works in you to will and act according to his good pleasure" (Philippians 2:13).

THE FIFTH MAIN POINT OF DOCTRINE
The perseverance of the saints

ARTICLE 1 · The regenerate not entirely free from sin
Those people whom God according to his purpose calls into fellowship with his Son Jesus Christ our Lord and regenerates by the Holy Spirit, he also sets free from the reign and slavery of sin, though in this life not entirely from the flesh and from the body of sin.

ARTICLE 2 · The believer's reaction to sins of weakness
Hence daily sins of weakness arise, and blemishes cling to even the best works of God's people, giving them continual cause to humble themselves before God, to flee for refuge to Christ crucified, to put the flesh to death more and more by the Spirit of supplication and by holy exercises of godliness, and to strain toward the goal of perfection, until they are freed from this body of death and reign with the Lamb of God in heaven.

ARTICLE 3 · God's preservation of the converted
Because of these remnants of sin dwelling in them and also because of the temptations of the world and Satan, those who have been converted could not remain standing in this grace if left to their own resources.

But God is faithful, mercifully strengthening them in the grace once conferred on them and powerfully preserving them in it to the end.

ARTICLE 4 · The danger of true believers falling into serious sins

Although that power of God strengthening and preserving true believers in grace is more than a match for the flesh, yet those converted are not always so activated and motivated by God that in certain specific actions they cannot by their own fault depart from the leading of grace, be led astray by the desires of the flesh, and give in to them. For this reason they must constantly watch and pray that they may not be led into temptations. When they fail to do this, not only can they be carried away by the flesh, the world, and Satan into sins, even serious and outrageous ones, but also by God's just permission they sometimes are so carried away—witness the sad cases, described in Scripture, of David, Peter and other saints falling into sins.

ARTICLE 5 · The effects of such serious sins

By such monstrous sins, however, they greatly offend God, deserve the sentence of death, grieve the Holy Spirit, suspend the exercise of faith, severely wound the conscience and sometimes lose the awareness of grace for a time—until, after they have returned to the way by genuine repentance, God's fatherly face again shines upon them.

ARTICLE 6· God's saving intervention

For God, who is rich in mercy, according to his unchangeable purpose of election does not take his Holy Spirit from his own completely, even when they fall grievously. Neither does he let them fall down so far that they forfeit the grace of adoption and the state of justification, or commit the sin which leads to death (the sin against the Holy Spirit), and plunge themselves, entirely forsaken by him, into eternal ruin.

ARTICLE 7 · Renewal to repentance

For, in the first place, God preserves in those saints when they fall his imperishable seed from which they have been born again, lest it perish or be dislodged. Secondly, by his Word and Spirit he certainly and effectively renews them to repentance so that they have a heartfelt and godly sorrow for the sins they have committed; seek and obtain, through faith and with a contrite heart, forgiveness in the blood of the Mediator; experience again the grace of a reconciled God; through faith adore his mercies; and from then on more eagerly work out their own salvation with fear and trembling.

ARTICLE 8 · The certainty of this preservation
So it is not by their own merits or strength but by God's undeserved mercy that they neither forfeit faith and grace totally nor remain in their downfalls to the end and are lost. With respect to themselves this not only easily could happen, but also undoubtedly would happen; but with respect to God it cannot possibly happen, since his plan cannot be changed, his promise cannot fail, the calling according to his purpose cannot be revoked, the merit of Christ as well as his interceding and preserving cannot be nullified and the sealing of the Holy Spirit can neither be invalidated nor wiped out.

ARTICLE 9 · The assurance of this preservation
Concerning this preservation of those chosen to salvation and concerning the perseverance of true believers in faith, believers themselves can and do become assured in accordance with the measure of their faith, by which they firmly believe that they are and always will remain true and living members of the church, and that they have the forgiveness of sins and eternal life.

ARTICLE 10 · The ground of this assurance
Accordingly, this assurance does not derive from some private revelation beyond or outside the Word, but from faith in the promises of God which he has very plentifully revealed in his Word for our comfort, from the testimony of the Holy Spirit testifying with our spirit that we are God's children and heirs (Romans 8:16–17), and finally from a serious and holy pursuit of a clear conscience and of good works. And if God's chosen ones in this world did not have this well-founded comfort that the victory will be theirs and this reliable guarantee of eternal glory, they would be of all people most miserable.

ARTICLE 11 · Doubts concerning this assurance

Meanwhile, Scripture testifies that believers have to contend in this life with various doubts of the flesh and that under severe temptation they do not always experience this full assurance of faith and certainty of perseverance. But God, the Father of all comfort, does not let them be tempted beyond what they can bear, but with the temptation he also provides a way out (1 Corinthians 10:13), and by the Holy Spirit revives in them the assurance of their perseverance.

ARTICLE 12 · This assurance as an incentive to godliness

This assurance of perseverance, however, so far from making true believers proud and carnally self-assured, is rather the true root of humility, of childlike respect, of genuine godliness, of endurance in every conflict, of fervent prayers, of steadfastness in crossbearing and in confessing the truth and of well-founded joy in God. Reflecting on this benefit provides an incentive to a serious and continual practice of thanksgiving and good works, as is evident from the testimonies of Scripture and the examples of the saints.

ARTICLE 13 · Assurance no inducement to carelessness

Neither does the renewed confidence of perseverance produce immorality or lack of concern for godliness in those put back on their feet after a fall, but it produces a much greater concern to observe carefully the ways of the Lord which he prepared in advance. They observe these ways in order that by walking in them they may maintain the assurance of their perseverance, lest, by their abuse of his fatherly goodness, the face of the gracious God (for the godly, looking upon his face is sweeter than life, but its withdrawal is more bitter than death) turn away from them again, with the result that they fall into greater anguish of spirit.

ARTICLE 14 · God's use of means in perseverance

And, just as it has pleased God to begin this work of grace in us by the proclamation of the gospel, so he preserves, continues and completes his work by the hearing and reading of the gospel, by meditation on it, by its exhortations, threats and promises, and also by the use of the sacraments.

ARTICLE 15 · Contrasting reactions to the teaching of perseverance

This teaching about the perseverance of true believers and saints, and about their assurance of it—a teaching which God has very richly revealed in his Word for the glory of his name and for the comfort of the godly and which he impresses on the hearts of believers—is something which the flesh does not understand, Satan hates, the world ridicules, the ignorant and the hypocrites abuse and the spirits of error attack. The bride of Christ, on the other hand, has always loved this teaching very tenderly and defended it steadfastly as a priceless treasure; and God, against whom no plan can avail and no strength can prevail, will ensure that she will continue to do this. To this God alone, Father, Son, and Holy Spirit, be honour and glory forever. Amen.

Rejection of the errors

Having set forth the orthodox teaching, the Synod rejects the errors of those

1. *Who teach that the perseverance of true believers is not an effect of election or a gift of God produced by Christ's death, but a condition of the new covenant which man, before what they call his "peremptory" election and justification, must fulfill by his free will.*
   For Holy Scripture testifies that perseverance follows from election and is granted to the chosen by virtue of Christ's death, resurrection, and intercession: The chosen obtained it; the others were hardened (Romans 11:7); likewise, "He who did not spare his own Son, but gave him up for us all—how will he not, along with him, grant us all things? Who will bring any charge against those whom God has chosen? It is God who justifies. Who is he that condemns? It is Christ Jesus who died—more than that, who was raised—who also sits at the right hand of God, and is also interceding for us. Who shall separate us from the love of Christ?" (Romans 8:32–35).

2. *Who teach that God does provide the believer with sufficient strength to persevere and is ready to preserve this strength in him if he performs his duty, but that even with all those things in place which are necessary to persevere in faith and which God is pleased to use to preserve faith, it still always depends on the choice of man's will whether or not he perseveres.*

For this view is obviously Pelagian; and though it intends to make men free it makes them sacrilegious. It is against the enduring consensus of evangelical teaching which takes from man all cause for boasting and ascribes the praise for this benefit only to God's grace. It is also against the testimony of the apostle: "It is God who keeps us strong to the end, so that we will be blameless on the day of our Lord Jesus Christ" (1 Corinthians 1:8).

3. *Who teach that those who truly believe and have been born again not only can forfeit justifying faith as well as grace and salvation totally and to the end, but also in actual fact do often forfeit them and are lost forever.*

For this opinion nullifies the very grace of justification and regeneration as well as the continual preservation by Christ, contrary to the plain words of the apostle Paul: "If Christ died for us while we were still sinners, we will therefore much more be saved from God's wrath through him, since we have now been justified by his blood" (Romans 5:8–9); and contrary to the apostle John: "No one who is born of God is intent on sin, because God's seed remains in him, nor can he sin, because he has been born of God" (1 John 3:9); also contrary to the words of Jesus Christ: "I give eternal life to my sheep, and they shall never perish; no one can snatch them out of my hand. My Father, who has given them to me, is greater than all; no one can snatch them out of my Father's hand" (John 10:28–29).

4. *Who teach that those who truly believe and have been born again can commit the sin that leads to death (the sin against the Holy Spirit).*

For the same apostle John, after making mention of those who commit the sin that leads to death and forbidding prayer for

them (1 John 5:16–17), immediately adds: "We know that anyone born of God does not commit sin (that is, that kind of sin),
but the one who was born of God keeps himself safe, and the
evil one does not touch him" (v.18).

5. *Who teach that apart from a special revelation no one can have
the assurance of future perseverance in this life.*
For by this teaching the well-founded consolation of true
believers in this life is taken away and the doubting of the
Romanists is reintroduced into the church. Holy Scripture,
however, in many places derives the assurance not from a special and extraordinary revelation but from the marks peculiar
to God's children and from God's completely reliable promises.
So especially the apostle Paul: "Nothing in all creation can
separate us from the love of God that is in Christ Jesus our Lord"
(Romans 8:39); and John: "They who obey his commands
remain in him and he in them. And this is how we know that
he remains in us: by the Spirit he gave us" (1 John 3:24).

6. *Who teach that the teaching of the assurance of perseverance and
of salvation is by its very nature and character an opiate of the
flesh and is harmful to godliness, good morals, prayer and other
holy exercises, but that, on the contrary, to have doubt about this
is praiseworthy.*
For these people show that they do not know the effective
operation of God's grace and the work of the indwelling Holy
Spirit, and they contradict the apostle John, who asserts the
opposite in plain words: "Dear friends, now we are children of
God, but what we will be has not yet been made known. But
we know that when he is made known, we shall be like him, for
we shall see him as he is. Everyone who has this hope in him
purifies himself, just as he is pure" (1 John 3:2–3). Moreover,
they are refuted by the examples of the saints in both the Old
and the New Testament, who though assured of their perseverance and salvation yet were constant in prayer and other exercises of godliness.

7. *Who teach that the faith of those who believe only temporarily does not differ from justifying and saving faith except in duration alone.*
For Christ himself in Matthew 13:20ff. and Luke 8:13ff. clearly defines these further differences between temporary and true believers: he says that the former receive the seed on rocky ground, and the latter receive it in good ground, or a good heart; the former have no root, and the latter are firmly rooted; the former have no fruit, and the latter produce fruit in varying measure, with steadfastness, or perseverance.

8. *Who teach that it is not absurd that a person, after losing his former regeneration, should once again, indeed quite often, be reborn.*
For by this teaching they deny the imperishable nature of God's seed by which we are born again, contrary to the testimony of the apostle Peter: "Born again, not of perishable seed, but of imperishable" (1 Peter 1:23).

9. *Who teach that Christ nowhere prayed for an unfailing perseverance of believers in faith.*
For they contradict Christ himself when he says: "I have prayed for you, Peter, that your faith may not fail" (Luke 22:32); and John the gospel writer when he testifies in John 17 that it was not only for the apostles, but also for all those who were to believe by their message that Christ prayed: "Holy Father, preserve them in your name" (v.11); and "My prayer is not that you take them out of the world, but that you preserve them from the evil one" (v.15).

CONCLUSION
Rejection of false accusations

And so this is the clear, simple and straightforward explanation of the orthodox teaching on the five articles in dispute in the Netherlands, as well as the rejection of the errors by which the Dutch churches have for some time been disturbed. This explanation and rejection the Synod declares to be derived from God's Word and in agreement with the confessions of the Reformed churches. Hence it clearly appears that those of whom one could hardly expect it have shown no truth, equity and charity at all in wishing to make the public believe:

- that the teaching of the Reformed churches on predestination and on the points associated with it by its very nature and tendency draws the minds of people away from all godliness and religion, is an opiate of the flesh and the devil, and is a stronghold of Satan where he lies in wait for all people, wounds most of them and fatally pierces many of them with the arrows of both despair and self-assurance;

- that this teaching makes God the author of sin, unjust, a tyrant and a hypocrite; and is nothing but a refurbished Stoicism, Manicheism, Libertinism and Mohammedanism;

- that this teaching makes people carnally self-assured, since it persuades them that nothing endangers the salvation of the chosen, no matter how they live, so that they may commit the most outrageous crimes with self-assurance; and that on the other hand nothing is of use to the reprobate for salvation even if they have truly performed all the works of the saints;

- that this teaching means that God predestined and created, by the bare and unqualified choice of his will, without the least regard or consideration of any sin, the greatest part of the world to eternal condemnation; that in the same manner in which election is the source and cause of faith and good works, reprobation is the cause of unbelief and ungodliness; that many infant children of believers are snatched in their innocence from their mothers' breasts and cruelly cast into hell so that neither the blood of Christ nor their baptism nor the prayers of the church at their baptism can be of any use to them; and very many other slanderous accusations of this kind which the Reformed churches not only disavow but even denounce with their whole heart.

Therefore this Synod of Dort in the name of the Lord pleads with all who devoutly call on the name of our Saviour Jesus Christ to form their judgment about the faith of the Reformed churches, not on the basis of false accusations gathered from here or there, or even on the basis of the personal statements of a number of ancient and modern authorities—statements which are also often either quoted out of context or misquoted and twisted to convey a different meaning—but on the basis of the churches' own official confessions and of the present explanation of the orthodox teaching which has been endorsed by the unanimous consent of the members of the whole Synod, one and all.

Moreover, the Synod earnestly warns the false accusers themselves to consider how heavy a judgment of God awaits those who give false testimony against so many churches and their confessions, trouble the consciences of the weak and seek to prejudice the minds of many against the fellowship of true believers.

Finally, this Synod urges all fellow ministers in the gospel of Christ to deal with this teaching in a godly and reverent manner, in the academic institutions as well as in the churches; to do so, both in their speaking and writing, with a view to the glory of God's name, holiness of life and the comfort of anxious souls; to think and also speak with Scripture according to the analogy of faith; and, finally, to refrain from all those ways of speaking which go beyond the bounds set for us by the genuine sense of the Holy Scriptures and which could give impertinent sophists a just occasion to scoff at the teaching of the Reformed churches or even to bring false accusations against it.

May God's Son Jesus Christ, who sits at the right hand of God and gives gifts to men, sanctify us in the truth, lead to the truth those who err, silence the mouths of those who lay false accusations against sound teaching and equip faithful ministers of his Word with a spirit of wisdom and discretion, that all they say may be to the glory of God and the building up of their hearers. Amen.

Bibliography
Resources for further study

Augustijn, Cornelius. "Synod of Dordrecht." In *The Oxford Encyclopedia of the Reformation*. Edited by Hans J. Hillerbrand. Oxford: Oxford University Press, 1996.

Bangs, Carl. *Arminius: A Study in the Dutch Reformation*. Grand Rapids: Zondervan, 1985.

Bangs, Carl. "Arminius as a Reformed Theologian." In *The Heritage of John Calvin*, ed. John H. Bratt, 209–222. Grand Rapids: Eerdmans, 1973.

Barrett, Matthew. *Salvation by Grace: The Case for Effectual Calling and Regeneration*. Phillipsburg: P & R, 2013.

Barrett, Matthew and Thomas J. Nettles, eds. *Whomever He Wills: A Surprising Display of Sovereign Grace*. Cape Coral: Founders, 2012.

Bavinck, Herman. *Saved by Grace: The Holy Spirit's Work in Calling and Regeneration*. Edited by Mark Beach. Translated by Nelson D. Kloosterman. Grand Rapids: Reformation Heritage, 2008.

Beeke, Joel R. *Living for God's Glory: An Introduction to Calvinism*. Orlando: Reformation Trust, 2008.

Beeke, Joel R. "The Belgic Confession of Faith and The Canons of Dort." *Reformation and Revival* 10, no. 2 (Spring 2001): 91–96.

Beeke, Joel R., ed. *Three Forms of Unity.* Vestavia Hills: Solid Ground Christian Books, n.d.

Beeke, Joel R. and Sinclair Ferguson. *Reformed Confessions Harmonized.* Grand Rapids: Baker, 1999.

Benedict, Philip. *Christ's Churches Purely Reformed: A Social History of Calvinism.* New Haven and London: Yale University Press, 2002.

Boettner, Loraine. *The Reformed Doctrine of Predestination.* Phillipsburg: P & R, 1963.

Brandt, C. *The Life of James Arminius, D.D.* Translated by John Cuthrie. London: n.p., 1854.

Brandt, Gerard. *Arminianism.* London: Duckworth, 1937.

Brandt, Gerard. *The History of the Reformation and Other Ecclesiastical Transactions in and about the Low Countries, from the Beginning of the Eighth Century, down to the Famous Synod of Dort.* 4 vols. Translated by John Chamberlayne. London: n.p., 1720–1723. Reprint, New York: AMS, 1979.

Bratt, John H., ed. *The Rise and Development of Calvinism.* Grand Rapids: Eerdmans, 1959.

Clarke, F. Stuart. "Arminius's Understanding of Calvin." *Evangelical Quarterly* 54 (1982): 25–35.

Clarke, F. Stuart. *The Ground of Election: Jacobus Arminius' Doctrine of the Work and Person of Christ.* Milton Keynes: Paternoster, 2006.

Clarke, F. Stuart. "Theology of Arminius." *London Quarterly and Holborn Review* 185 (1960): 248–253.

Collinson, Patrick. "England and International Calvinism, 1558-1640." In *International Calvinism, 1541-1715,* ed. Menna Prestwich, 197–224. Oxford: Clarendon, 1985.

Cunningham, William. *The Reformers & the Theology of the Reformation.* Edinburgh: Banner of Truth, 2000.

Cunningham, William. *Historical Theology.* vol. 2. Edinburgh: Banner of Truth, 1994.

Daniel, Curt. *The History and Theology of Calvinism.* Dallas: Scholarly Reprints, 1993.

De Jong, Peter Y., ed. *Crisis in the Reformed Churches: Essays in Commemoration of the Great Synod of Dort, 1618–1619.* Grand Rapids: Reformed Fellowship, 1968.

De Reuver, Arie. *Sweet Communion: Trajectories of Spirituality from the Middle Ages through the Further Reformation.* Edited by Richard A. Muller. Translated by James A. De Jong. Texts & Studies in Reformation & Post-Reformation Thought. Grand Rapids: Baker, 2004.

de Witt, John R. "The Arminian Conflict." In *Puritan Papers,* vol. 5, ed. J.I. Packer, 3–24. Phillipsburg: P & R, 2000.

Den Boer, William. *God's Twofold Love: The Theology of Jacob Arminius (1559–1609).* Translated by Albert Gootjes. *Reformed Historical Theology,* vol. 14. Edited by Herman S. Selderhuis. Göttingen: Vandenhoeck & Ruprecht, 2010.

Dickens, A.G. *The English Reformation.* 2nd ed. University Park: Pennsylvania State University Press, 1989.

Ellis, Mark A. "Simon Episcopius and the Doctrine of Original Sin." Ph.D. diss., Dallas Theological Seminary, 2002.

Faber, J., H. J. Meijerink, C. Trimp and G. Zomer. *To the Praise of His Glory: Outlines on the Canons of Dort.* Tasmania: The Free Reformed Church of Launceston, 1986.

Feenstra, Peter G. *Unspeakable Comfort: A Commentary on the Canons of Dort.* Winnipeg: Premier, 1997.

Fesko, J.V. *Diversity Within the Reformed Tradition: Supra- and Infralapsarianism in Calvin, Dort, and Westminster.* Greenville: Reformed Academic, 2001.

Foster, Herbert Darling. "Liberal Calvinism: the Remonstrants at the Synod of Dort in 1618." *Harvard Theological Review* 16 (1973): 1-37.

Girod, Gordon. *The Deeper Faith, Reformed Publications, 1619.* Grand Rapids: Reformed, 1958.

Goudriaan, Aza and Fred van Lieburg, eds. *Revisiting the Synod of Dort (1618–1619).* Brill's Series in Church History 49. Leiden: Brill, 2011.

Godfrey, W. Robert. "Calvin and Calvinism in the Netherlands." In *John Calvin, His Influence in the Western World*, ed. W. Standford Reid and Paul Woolley, 95–122. Grand Rapids: Zondervan, 1982.

Godfrey, W. Robert. *Reformation Sketches: Insights into Luther, Calvin, and the Confessions.* Phillipsburg: P & R, 2003.

Godfrey, W. Robert. "Reformed Thought on the Extent of the Atonement to 1618," *Westminster Theological Journal* 37, no. 2 (Winter 1975):133–171.

Godfrey, W. Robert. "Tensions Within International Calvinism: The Debate on the Atonement at the Synod of Dort, 1618–1619." Ph.D. diss., Stanford University, 1974.

Godfrey, W. Robert. "Who Was Arminius?" *Modern Reformation* 1, no. 3 (1992): 5–24.

Goudriaan, Aza and Fred van Lieburg. *Revisiting the Synod of Dordt (1618–1619).* Brill's Series in Church History 49. Leiden: Brill, 2011.

Graham, W. Fred, ed. *Later Calvinism: International Perspectives.* Kirksville: Sixteenth Century Journal, 1994.

Gunter, W. Stephen. *Arminius and His Declaration of Sentiments: An Annotated Translation with Introduction and Theological Commentary.* Waco: Baylor University Press, 2012.

Hargrave, O.T. "The Freewillers in the English Reformation." *Church History* 37 (1968): 271–280.

Harrison, A.W. *Arminianism.* London: Duckworth, 1937.

Harrison, A.W. *The Beginnings of Arminianism to the Synod of Dort.* London: University of London Press, 1926.

Heppe, Heinrich. *Reformed Dogmatics.* Edited by Ernst Bizer. Translated by G.T. Thomson. Eugene: Wipf & Stock, 1950.

Hoekema, Anthony A. "A New Translation of the Canons of Dort." *Calvin Theological Journal* 3, no. 2 (1968): 133–161.

Hoekema, Anthony A. "The Missionary Focus of the Canons of Dort." *Calvin Theological Journal* 7, no. 2 (1972): 209–220.

Hoeksema, Homer C. *The Voice of Our Fathers.* Grand Rapids: Reformed Free, 1980.

Hoenderdaal, Gerrit Jan. "The Debate about Arminius Outside the Netherlands." In *Leiden University in the Seventeenth Century*, ed. Th. H. Lunsingh Scheurleer and G.H.M. Posthumus Meyjes, 1–20. Leiden: E.J. Brill, 1975.

Horton, Michael. *For Calvinism*. Grand Rapids: Zondervan, 2011.

Israel, Jonathan. *The Dutch Republic: Its Rise, Greatness, and Fall 1477–1806*. Oxford: Clarendon, 1995.

Letham, Robert. "Saving Faith and Assurance in Reformed Theology: Zwinglie to the Synod of Dort." 2 vols. Ph.D. thesis, University of Aberdeen, 1979.

McComish, William A. *The Epigones: A Study of the Theology of the Genevan Academy at the Time of the Synod of Dort, with Special Reference to Giovanni Diodati*. Allison Park: Pickwick, 1989.

McCulloh, Gerald O., ed. *Man's Faith and Freedom*. Eugene: Wipf & Stock, 2007.

McGonigle, Herbert Boyd. *Sufficient Saving Grace: John Wesley's Evangelical Arminianism*. Milton Keynes: Paternoster, 2001.

McNeil, John T. *The History and Character of Calvinism*. New York: Oxford University Press, 1973.

Miller, Samuel. *The Articles of the Synod of Dort*. Philadelphia: Presbyterian Board of Publication, 1856.

Milton, Anthony, ed. *The British Delegation and the Synod of Dort (1618–1619)*. Woodbridge: The Boydell, 2005.

Muller, Richard. "Arminius and Arminianism." In *The Dictionary of Historical Theology*. Edited by Trevor A. Hart. Grand Rapids: Eerdmans, 2000.

Muller, Richard. "Arminius and the Reformed Tradition." *Westminster Journal of Theology* 70 (2008): 19–48.

Muller, Richard. "Arminius and the Scholastic Tadition." *Calvin Theological Journal* 24, no. 2 (1989): 263–277

Muller, Richard. *God, Creation, and Providence in the Thought of Jacob Arminius: Sources and Directions of Scholastic Protestantism in the Era of Early Orthodoxy*. Grand Rapids: Baker, 1991.

Muller, Richard. "Grace, Election, and Contingent Choice: Arminius's Gambit and the Reformed Response." *The Grace of God, the Bondage of the Will*, vol. 2, eds. Thomas R. Schreiner and Bruce A. Ware, 251–278. Grand Rapids: Baker, 1995.

Muller, Richard. "Predestination and Christology in Sixteenth Century Reformed Theology." Ph.D. diss., Duke University, 1976.

Mulsow, Martin and Jan Rohls, eds. *Socinianism and Arminianism: Antitrinitarians, Calvinists and Cultural Exchange in Seventeenth-Century Europe*. Leiden: Brill, 2005.

Olson, Roger E. *Arminian Theology: Myths and Realities*. Downers Grove: InterVarsity, 2006.

Olson, Roger E. *The Story of Christian Theology: Twenty Centuries of Tradition and Reform*. Downers Grove: InterVarsity, 1999.

Palmer, Edwin H. *The Five Points of Calvinism*. Grand Rapids: Baker, 1980.

Pelikan, Jaroslav and Valerie Hotchkiss, eds. *Creeds and Confessions of the Reformation Era*. *Creeds and Confessions of Faith in the Christian Tradition*, vol. 2. New Haven and

London: Yale University Press, 2003.

Pelikan, Jaroslav. *Reformation of Church and Dogma (1300–1700). The Christian Tradition: A History of Development of Doctrine*, vol. 4. Chicago: University of Chicago Press, 1984.

Petersen, Henry. *The Canons of Dort*. Grand Rapids: Baker, 1968.

Peterson, Robert A. and Michael D. Williams, *Why I Am Not An Arminian*. Downers Grove: InterVarsity, 2004.

Pettegree, Andrew, Alastair Duke and Gillian Lewis, eds. *Calvinism in Europe, 1540–1620*. Cambridge: Cambridge University Press, 1994.

Porter, H.C. *Reformation and Reaction in Tudor Cambridge*. Cambridge: Cambridge University Press, 1958.

Prestwich, Menna, ed. *International Calvinism, 1541–1715*. Oxford: Clarendon, 1985.

Pronk, Cornelis (Neil). *Expository Sermons on the Canons of Dort*. St. Thomas, ON: Free Reformed, 1999.

Rohls, Jan. *Reformed Confessions: Theology from Zurich to Barmen*. Translated by John Hoffmeyer, Columbia Series in Reformed Theology. Louisville: Westminster John Knox, 1997.

Schaff, Philip, ed. *The History of Creeds. The Creeds of Christendom*, vol. 1. Grand Rapids: Baker, 1983.

Schaff, Philip, ed. *The Evangelical Protestant Creeds. The Creeds of Christendom*, vol. 3. Grand Rapids: Baker, 1983.

Schreiner, Thomas R. and Bruce A. Ware, eds. *Still Sovereign: Contemporary Perspectives on Election, Foreknowledge, and Grace*. Grand Rapids: Baker, 2000.

Sell, Alan P.F. *The Great Debate: Calvinism, Arminianism, and Salvation*. Grand Rapids: Baker, 1982.

Shaw, Mark R. "William Perkins and the New Pelagians: Another Look at the Cambridge Predestination Controversy of the 1590's." *Westminster Theological Journal* 58 (1996): 267–301.

Sinnema, Donald. "The Issue of Reprobation at the Synod of Dort (1618–19) in Light of the History of this Doctrine." Ph.D. diss. University of St. Michael's College, 1985.

Sinnema, Donald. "The Origin of the Form of Subscription in the Dutch Reformed Tradition." *Calvin Theological Journal* 42 (2007): 256–282.

Slatte, Howard A. *The Arminian Arm of Theology: The Theologies of John Fletcher, First Methodist Theologian, and His Precursor, James Arminius*. Washington: University Press of America, 1979.

Steele, David N., Curtis C. Thomas and S. Lance Quinn. *The Five Points of Calvinism: Defined, Defended, and Documented*. Phillipsburg: P & R, 2004.

Stanglin, Keith D. *Arminius on the Assurance of Salvation: The Context, Roots, and Shape of the Leiden Debate, 1603–1609*. Brill's Series in Church History 27. Leiden: Brill, 2007.

Stanglin, Keith D. "Arminius Avant la Lettre: Peter Baro, Jacob Arminius, and the Bond of Predestinarian Polemic." *Westminster Theological Journal* 67 (2005): 51–74.

Stanglin, Keith D. and Thomas H. McCall. *Jacob Arminius: Theologian of Grace*. Oxford: Oxford University Press, 2012.

Stewart, Kenneth J. *Ten Myths About Calvinism: Recovering the Breadth of the Reformed Tradition.* Downers Grove: InterVarsity, 2011.

Strehle, Stephen. "The Extent of the Atonement and the Synod of Dort." *Westminster Theological Journal* 51, no. 1 (Spring 1989): 1–23.

Strehle, Stephen. "Universal Grace and Amyraldianism." *Westminster Theological Journal* 51 no 2 (Fall 1989): 345–357.

Thuesen, Peter J. *Predestination: The American Career of a Contentious Doctrine.* Oxford and New York: Oxford University Press, 2009.

Toon, Peter. *Puritans and Calvinism.* Swengel: Reiner, 1973.

Tyacke, Nicholas. *Anti-Calvinists: The Rise of English Arminianism, c. 1590–1640.* Oxford: Oxford University Press, 1987.

van Leeuwen, Marius, Keith D. Stanglin and Marijke Tolsma, eds. *Arminius, Arminianism, and Europe: Jacobus Arminius (1559/60–1609).* Brill's Series in Church History 39. Leiden: Brill, 2009.

Venema, Cornelis P. *But for the Grace of God: An Exposition of the Canons of Dort.* Wyoming: Reformed Fellowship, 1994.

Venema, Cornelis P. "The Election and Salvation of the Children of Believers Who Die in Infancy: A Study of Article I/17 of the Canons of Dort." *Mid-America Journal of Theology* 17 (2006): 57–100.

Wagenaar, L.H. *Van Strijd en Overwinning: De Groote Synode van 1618 op'19 en Wat aan Haar Voorafging.* Utrecht: G.J.A. Ruys, 1909.

Wallace, Jr., Dewey D. "Arminianism." In *Puritans and Puritanism in Europe and America: A Comprehensive Encyclopedia*, ed. Francis J. Bremer and Tom Webster, 2:312–313. Santa Barbara: ABC-CLIO, 2006.

Wallace, Jr., Dewey D. *Puritans and Predestination: Grace in English Protestant Theology 1525–1695.* Chapel Hill: The University of North Carolina Press, 1982.

White, Peter. *Predestination, Policy and Polemic: Conflict and Consensus in the English Church from the Reformation to the Civil War.* Cambridge: Cambridge University Press, 1992.

Witt, William Gene. "Creation, Redemption and Grace in the Theology of Jacob Arminius." 2 vols. Ph.D. diss., University of Notre Dame, 1993.

Other titles available from Joshua Press...

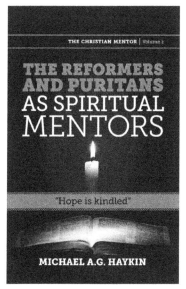

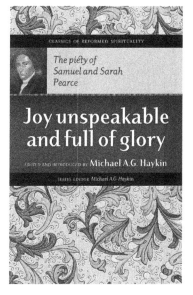

*The Christian Mentor	Volume 2*	*Classics of Reformed spirituality*

The Reformers and Puritans as spiritual mentors
"Hope is kindled"

By Michael A. G. Haykin

REFORMERS SUCH as Tyndale, Cranmer and Calvin, and Puritans Richard Greenham, John Owen, etc. are examined to see how their display of the light of the gospel provides us with models of Christian conviction and living.

ISBN 978–1-894400-39–8

Joy unspeakable and full of glory
The piety of
Samuel and Sarah Pearce

By Michael A. G. Haykin

SAMUEL PEARCE played a key role in the formation and early days of the Baptist Missionary Society in eighteenth-century England. Through Samuel and Sarah's letters we are given a window into their rich spiritual life and living piety.

ISBN 978–1-894400-48–0

Other titles available from Joshua Press...

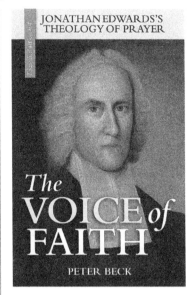

Great themes in Puritan preaching	The voice of faith

Great themes in Puritan preaching

Compiled and edited
By Mariano Di Gangi

DRAWING FROM a gold mine of Puritan writings, this book provides a taste of the riches of Puritan theology and its application to life. This title will whet your appetite and stir your faith to greater views of Christ, his Person and his work.

ISBN 978–1-894400-26–8 (HC)

ISBN 978-1-894400-24–4 (PB)

The voice of faith

Jonathan Edwards's theology of prayer

By Peter Beck

EXPLORING THE sermons and writings of Jonathan Edwards, Dr. Beck draws a comprehensive picture of his theology of prayer and why Edwards believed God would hear the prayers of his people. Interspersed are three external biographies that set the historical and theological scene.

ISBN 978–1-894400-33–6 (HC)

ISBN 978-1-894400-32–9 (PB)

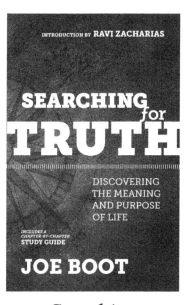

Friendship

By Hugh Black

HUGH BLACK addresses the challenges and responsibilities of friendship, including the consequences of wrecked friendships. In true friendship, accountability and love inspire us to live with more honour, integrity and grace. Ultimately, we see that in Jesus Christ we can have that "higher friendship" which revolutionizes the way we live and think and what we value.

ISBN 978-1-894400-28-2 (HC)

ISBN 978-1-894400-27-5 (PB)

Searching for truth

Discovering the meaning and purpose of life

By Joe Boot

BEGINNING WITH a basic understanding of the world, Joe Boot explains the biblical worldview, giving special attention to the life and claims of Jesus Christ. He wrestles with questions about suffering, truth, morality and guilt.

ISBN 978-1-894400-40-4

Deo Optimo et Maximo Gloria
To God, best and greatest, be glory

www.joshuapress.com

CPSIA information can be obtained
at www.ICGtesting.com
Printed in the USA
BVOW08s1840110117
473260BV00001B/12/P